Better Regulation Practices across the European Union 2022

This document, as well as any data and map included herein, are without prejudice to the status of or sovereignty over any territory, to the delimitation of international frontiers and boundaries and to the name of any territory, city or area.

The statistical data for Israel are supplied by and under the responsibility of the relevant Israeli authorities. The use of such data by the OECD is without prejudice to the status of the Golan Heights, East Jerusalem and Israeli settlements in the West Bank under the terms of international law.

Note by Turkey
The information in this document with reference to "Cyprus" relates to the southern part of the Island. There is no single authority representing both Turkish and Greek Cypriot people on the Island. Turkey recognises the Turkish Republic of Northern Cyprus (TRNC). Until a lasting and equitable solution is found within the context of the United Nations, Turkey shall preserve its position concerning the "Cyprus issue".

Note by all the European Union Member States of the OECD and the European Union
The Republic of Cyprus is recognised by all members of the United Nations with the exception of Turkey. The information in this document relates to the area under the effective control of the Government of the Republic of Cyprus.

Please cite this publication as:
OECD (2022), *Better Regulation Practices across the European Union 2022*, OECD Publishing, Paris, https://doi.org/10.1787/6e4b095d-en.

ISBN 978-92-64-45242-8 (print)
ISBN 978-92-64-60853-5 (pdf)
ISBN 978-92-64-93739-0 (HTML)
ISBN 978-92-64-65775-5 (epub)

Preface

Starting in 2008, the OECD and the European Commission have worked together to assess the capacities for effective regulatory management within the EU and across Member States. Since then, challenges have escalated, making trusted, evidence-based, internationally co-ordinated, and well-implemented and administered regulation all the more urgent.

Against the backdrop of a global health and economic crisis, the *2022 Better Regulation Practices across the European Union* report underscores the crucial role of regulation in enabling resilience and recovery. With the right regulatory settings, governments can achieve their policy goals, strengthening people's trust in public institutions and the capacity of governments to address a growing number of concerns, such as improving the well-being of citizens, increasing inclusion, and driving a greener recovery.

Together, the European Institutions and the Member States, are ultimately responsible for the regulations that govern nearly 500 million people. It reinforces the importance of the EU's commitment to a clear and stable Better Regulation framework.

Using the OECD Indicators of Regulatory Policy and Governance, the report tracks progress in better regulation across EU Member States since the first edition in 2019. This latest edition shows EU Member States' commitment to the effective use of regulatory management tools such as impact assessment, stakeholder engagement and *ex post* evaluation. Nevertheless, scope for improvement remains, especially in ensuring that regulations keep pace with change.

A focus on proportionality is crucial for making sure that policy makers consider the most relevant alternatives before regulating and fully understand the expected impacts of rules, including those that may be felt across borders. Engaging with those directly affected by regulations is key to improving policies, boosting trust in government action. Ultimately, better regulation helps ensure that policies deliver the promised benefits to citizens.

The EU already stands out for its uptake and commitment to better regulation. Ensuring integrated approaches to the design, delivery, and review of regulations will support the seamless functioning of the single market. By monitoring and sharing country practices, it is hoped that the report will encourage further progress towards international best practices throughout the EU. We trust that this report will serve as a timely reminder of the benefits of working together on quality regulations, whilst improving opportunities and outcomes for all EU citizens.

Mathias Cormann
Secretary-General, OECD

Maroš Šefčovič
Vice-President, European Commission

Foreword

The *2022 Better Regulation Practices across the European Union* report, the second in the series, analyses current and developing practices for improving the quality of laws and regulations across all 27 EU Member States and the European Union. The report systematically assesses the use of evidence-based tools and stakeholder participation to improve the design and review of both domestic and EU laws and regulations, and identifies current and future trends in regulatory policy. It is based on empirical evidence, research and data, including the OECD 2021 Indicators of Regulatory Policy and Governance and complemented by information collected during a series of interviews with four EU Member States – namely Denmark, Estonia, Germany, and Cyprus. Reflecting practical experiences, discussions and lessons learned from EU Member States and OECD countries, the report offers many examples of how to benefit from sound regulatory policy and effect positive change. It also presents good regulatory practices and highlights areas that should receive further attention and investment.

Chapter 1 explores the EU Member States' general content of regulatory policies, their institutional settings, their engagement in multiple mechanisms of international regulatory co-operation, and the allocation of regulatory oversight functions within government. Based on the results of the 2021 Indicators of Regulatory Policy and Governance, subsequent chapters provide an overview of the trends in the use of regulatory management tools in all 27 EU Member States and in the European Union, for domestic and EU laws and regulations. Chapter 2 assesses the timing and content of stakeholder engagement practices at various stages of policy development as well as how governments use input received from interested parties. Chapter 3 analyses the European Union and the Member States' requirements and use of RIA with a focus on the proportionality principle. Chapter 4 discusses the types of *ex post* evaluations commonly conducted in EU Member States and the general approaches taken to regulatory stock management and to stakeholder engagement when undertaking evaluations. Chapters 2, 3, and 4 also discuss respectively the use of stakeholder engagement, RIA, and *ex post* evaluation when EU Member States negotiate or adopt regulatory proposals of the European Commission. Chapter 5 provides the country profiles for each EU Member State and the European Union including an overview of regulatory practices, key achievements and areas for improvement.

This report was approved by the OECD Regulatory Policy Committee on 11 April 2022 and prepared for publication by the OECD Secretariat.

Acknowledgements

The *Better Regulation Practices across the European Union 2022* report was prepared by the OECD Public Governance Directorate under the leadership of Elsa Pilichowski. The project was led by Christiane Arndt-Bascle and Paul Davidson under the direction of Nick Malyshev, Head of the Regulatory Policy Division.

The main report authors include Paul Davidson, Marie-Gabrielle de Liedekerke, Christiane Arndt-Bascle, and Renny Reyes. Guillermo Hernández drafted the section on regulatory oversight. Jan Hildebrandt and Marianna Karttunen drafted the section on international regulatory co-operation. Significant inputs were provided by Daniel Trnka, Deputy Head of the Regulatory Policy Division, and Camila Saffirio, Advisor, Public Governance Directorate, and research assistance was provided by Franz Karg, Estera Szakadatova and Ernesto Truqui. Composite indicators and country profiles for OECD member countries are based on those published in the *OECD Regulatory Policy Outlook 2021*. Composite indicators and country profiles for the five EU Member States that are not members of the OECD (Bulgaria, Croatia, Romania, Cyprus, and Malta) benefited from significant inputs from Christiane Arndt-Bascle, Marie-Gabrielle de Liedekerke, Franz Karg, Renny Reyes, Yola Thuerer, and Supriya Trivedi.

We thank the members of the OECD Regulatory Policy Committee, BIAC, Gregor Virant, Bagrat Tunyan, Tatyana Teplova, Anna Piccinni, and government representatives of Bulgaria, Croatia, Romania, Cyprus, and Malta for their comments. The OECD Secretariat extends special thanks to government representatives from Denmark, Germany, Estonia, and Cyprus who provided supplementary information during a series of interviews as part of the project. The survey and indicators methodology was developed in close co-operation with the Steering Group on Measuring Regulatory Performance through a series of meetings and consultations.

This report was prepared for publication by Jennifer Stein. It benefitted from editorial assistance from Andrea Uhrhammer. Communication advice was provided by Vanessa Berry-Chatelain and Justin Kavanagh. Statistical advice was provided by Alessandro Lupi.

The OECD thanks the European Union for its financial contribution to this project.

The work on regulatory policy is conducted under the supervision of the OECD Regulatory Policy Committee, whose mandate is to assist both members and non-members in building and strengthening capacity for regulatory quality and regulatory reform. The Regulatory Policy Committee is supported by the Regulatory Policy Division of the Public Governance Directorate. The Directorate's mission is to help governments at all levels design and implement strategic, evidence-based and innovative policies to strengthen public governance, respond effectively to diverse and disruptive economic, social and environmental challenges and deliver on government's commitments to citizens.

Table of contents

FIGURES

TABLES

Abbreviations and acronyms

ACAAs	Agreements on Conformity Assessment and Acceptance of Industrial Products
ASA	Belgian Agency for Administrative Simplification
ATR	Dutch Advisory Board on Regulatory Burden
BMKOES	Austrian Federal Ministry for Arts, Culture, Civil Service and Sport
BRO	Greece Better Regulation Office
BRU	Better Regulation Unit
CAS	Polish Center for Strategic Analysis
CETA	EU-Canada Comprehensive Economic and Trade Agreement
COVID	Coronavirus disease
COVID-19	Coronavirus disease of 2019
CRPD	United Nations Convention on the Rights of Persons with Disabilities
DAGL	Italian Department for Legal and Legislative Affairs
DBA	Danish Business Authority
DBRF	Danish Business Regulation Forum
DCMS	United Kingdom Department for Digital, Culture, Media and Sport
DCPP	Romanian Department for Coordinating Policies and Priorities
DPA	Danish Protection Agency
EC	European Commission
EPRS	European Parliamentary Research Service
EU	European Union
FCRIA	Finnish Council of Regulatory Impact Analysis
FPMO	Austrian Federal Performance Management Office
GDPR	General Data Protection Regulation
GEIEAN	Romanian Group for Assessing the Economic Impact of Normative Acts on SMEs
GGO	German Joint Rules of Procedures of the Federal Ministries
GLO	Croatian Government Legislation Office
GoL	Slovenian Government Office of Legislation
GRPs	Good regulatory practices
IAC	Belgian Impact Assessment Committee
IAK	Dutch Integraal Afwegingskader (*Dutch Integral Assessment Framework*)

IoT	Internet of Things
IRC	International regulatory co-operation
iREG	Indicators of Regulatory Policy and Governance survey
LRV	Czech Government Legislative Council
MoU	Memoranda of understanding
MPA	Slovenian Ministry of Public Administration
MRAs	Mutual Recognition Agreements
MSD	Maltese Ministry within the Office of the Prime Minister
NKR	German National Regulatory Control Council
REFIT	European Commission Regulatory Fitness and Performance Programme
RIA	Regulatory impact assessment
ROBs	Regulatory oversight bodies
RSB	Regulatory Scrutiny Board
SBA	Maltese Small Business Act
SCM	Standard Cost Model
SGG	French Secrétariat Général du Gouvernement
UTAIL	Portuguese Technical Unit for Legislative Impact Assessment
WTO	World Trade Organization

Executive summary

Main findings and recommendations

EU Member States could better pursue regulatory co-operation beyond the borders of the European Union. The second edition of the *Better Regulation Practices across the European Union* report highlights that the European Union is the world's most integrated form of international regulatory co-operation (IRC). Outside of EU integration, however, nearly 90% of Member States have only partial IRC policies in place. The European institutions – the European Commission, the European Parliament and the Council of the European Union –all need to work together and with Member States to tackle current and future challenges. Co-operative rule making and policy coherence are becoming an increasingly important part of the global regulatory system.

Member States have a critical role to play in ensuring that EU policies deliver for their citizens; they are uniquely placed to hear the voices of those affected by EU policies. Around 70% of Member States alert domestic stakeholders to consultations organised by the European Commission. However, only around one-third systematically use the Commission's analysis as input to their negotiating position. Furthermore, few Member States currently complement the Commission's analysis by using their own regulatory management tools on proposed EU regulations. The negotiation phase represents the final opportunity to modify these proposals; Member States would therefore benefit from additional evidence at this stage.

Member States can build on their current use of regulatory management tools when transposing EU directives to ensure all impacts are assessed. All Member States have formal requirements to use some regulatory management tools when transposing EU directives; these requirements, when followed, can help to determine the best implementation path. However, only one-fifth of Member States require the systematic assessment of additional impacts of domestic provisions beyond those in the directive. If EU rules are to improve community well-being, the complete set of their potential impacts should be understood before they are implemented.

The appraisal of costs and benefits should be balanced and could better account for community impacts. Although systematic requirements to identify the benefits of proposed rules exist in 70% of Member States, policy makers remain focussed on costs – more than 90 percent of Member States have systematic requirements to assess costs, especially costs for government and business. While these costs are important to consider, costs to individuals and NGOs are not assessed to the same extent. The fact that some costs are less systematically considered means decision makers are presented with an inaccurate picture that may result in regulation that is not in the best interests of the community. Furthermore, the unequal consideration of costs and benefits may lead to a focus on cost minimisation rather than the maximisation of community net benefits. The clear identification of benefits is crucial for subsequent monitoring and evaluation of whether rules have delivered the anticipated gains to citizens.

The application of the proportionality principle is often unclear and varies widely across Member States. A focus on proportionality is crucial for making sure that policy makers consider alternatives before regulating and fully understand the expected impacts of rules, including those that may be felt across borders. Two-thirds of Member States both formally recognise proportionality as a guiding principle and are required to consider a range of potential impacts when making rules. However, in practice, analysis differs substantially in both scale and scope. In some Member States, policy makers determine the depth of analysis and their decision is not subject to scrutiny from regulatory oversight. While the discretion afforded provides flexibility to policy makers, it is important to ensure that all relevant impacts are adequately assessed.

Governments have yet to fully explore non-regulatory options for meeting citizen and business needs. Regulation is just one lever of government. Only around half of Member States require alternatives to regulation, especially non-regulatory ones, to be considered. There is a need to move from "regulate first" to "first, reflect" and consider all feasible options before making a decision about the solution that will best deliver for citizens and business.

Policy makers can and should use all available information before rules are made to ensure they work as intended. This starts with discussions involving those affected by proposed rules – citizens, businesses, NGOs, and others. These stakeholders have direct experience regarding the actual impacts of rules. They can also help policy makers avoid repeating past mistakes. In EU Member States, stakeholders are engaged to varying degrees on draft rules – although around 85% of Member States provide some opportunity, less than half do so systematically, and scope remains to improve consultation at the problem identification stage to discuss different policy options. Moreover, fostering trust among stakeholders helps to achieve regulatory goals – compliance is improved where stakeholders feel heard and have had opportunities to suggest solutions. Providing feedback to stakeholders about how their input has or has not helped shape rules is critical, yet only 40% of Member States do so systematically.

Making better use of evaluations could help Member States understand if rules work in practice for citizens. One-quarter of Member States do not have systems to manage regulatory stocks to ensure that existing rules deliver benefits to the community. Incentives for improvement are also weak: less than one-fifth of Member States have a body in charge of checking the quality of reviews of existing regulation, suggesting that the quality of evaluations is likely to be highly variable. Technological advancements have made monitoring outcomes easier and less costly in many more areas of economic activity than was previously possible. Yet, governments are not making the most of the information age. Governments can better deliver on their promises when they are informed by all available evidence. Better informed decision makers make better policies and, ultimately, improve lives for citizens.

Reader's guide

The data presented in this report, including the composite indicators, are the results of the 2014, 2017 and 2021 Indicators of Regulatory Policy and Governance (iREG) surveys, and their extension to the five EU Member States that are not OECD member countries: Bulgaria, Croatia, Cyprus, Malta, and Romania. This Reader's guide aims to help readers understand the scope of the data collected through these surveys and some of the limitations related to the use of indicators. Please note that this Report also features results of new survey questions that were designed in conjunction with the Measuring Regulatory Performance (MRP) Steering Group on *ex post* evaluation, reflecting the developed normative thinking from the published *Best Practice Principles* (OECD, 2020[1]). The Secretariat updated the *ex post* evaluation composite indicator prior to the launch of the survey in 2020. In order to maintain an accurate time series, a limited number of answers from 2014 and 2017 relating to new questions needed to be completed that formed part of the composite indicator for *ex post* evaluation. The Secretariat reviewed the questions regarding the EU legislation making process, and extended the survey to cover *ex post* evaluations.

The iREG surveys gathered information at three points in time: as of 31 December 2014, 31 December 2017, and 1 January 2021. Data for 2014 are from 34 OECD member countries (which includes 20 EU Member States) and the European Union, which formed the basis of the *2015 Regulatory Policy Outlook* (OECD, 2015[2]). Data from the 2017 survey are from the 36 OECD member and two accession countries (at the time of data collection) as well as the European Union. This formed the basis of the *2018 Regulatory Policy Outlook* (OECD, 2018[3]). The 2021 survey collects data from the 38 OECD member countries and the European Union, which formed the basis of the *2021 Regulatory Policy Outlook* (OECD, 2021[4]). This report extends the coverage to include the five EU Member States that are not OECD member countries. The surveys focus on countries' regulatory policy practices as described in the *2012 OECD Recommendation of the Council on Regulatory Policy and Governance* (OECD, 2012[5]). Please note that reforms undertaken in EU Member States after 1 January 2021 are not reflected in the report.

The surveys investigate in detail three principles of the 2012 Recommendation: stakeholder engagement, regulatory impact assessment (RIA) and *ex post* evaluation. The composite indicators are presented in the respective chapters that follow. For each of these areas, the surveys have collected information on formal requirements and have gathered evidence on their implementation. This information forms the basis for the recommendations in the individual country profiles in Chapter 5.

While stakeholder engagement, RIA, and *ex post* evaluation are all very important elements of regulatory policy, they do not constitute the whole better regulation framework. For instance, other principles from the *2012 Recommendation* are currently not assessed, and it is also recognised that countries may have quite disparate approaches to achieving better regulation. Some EU countries for example have dedicated policies for administrative burden reduction and administrative simplification in place that are not fully covered in this report (OECD, 2010[6]).

Scope of the Regulatory Indicators survey data and its use in the report

The survey focuses on the processes of developing laws (both primary and subordinate) that are carried out by the executive branch of the national government and that apply to all policy areas. However, questions regarding *ex post* evaluation cover all national regulations regardless of whether they were initiated by parliament or the executive. Based on available information, most national regulations are covered by survey answers, with some variation across countries. Most countries in the sample have parliamentary systems. The majority of their national primary laws therefore largely originate from initiatives of the executive. This is not the case, however, for Bulgaria, the Czech Republic and Portugal where the share of primary laws initiated by the executive is low compared to OECD member countries. Results for the European Union apply to all acts (regulations, directives and implementing and delegated acts) initiated by the European Commission, who is the executive of the European Union. It proposes new legislative acts, which are adopted by the European Parliament and the Council of the EU, usually through the ordinary legislative procedure. Throughout this procedure, the Council, comprised of representatives from EU Member States, and the European Parliament can suggest amendments to the European Commission's proposals. While the Council and the European Parliament can invite the European Commission to submit a legislative proposal, the European Commission is the sole initiator of legislation in the EU system. Further information on the EU's regulatory system and the legislative process are provided in the country profile of the EU in Chapter 5. The different types of EU legislative acts and subordinate regulations of the EU's legal framework are discussed in Chapter 1.

Survey results are used throughout the Report in multiple ways. First, results of individual questions are displayed to show trends in the number of countries picking up particular practices. Second, qualitative information and examples provided through the survey are used to enrich the analysis. Third, composite indicators for stakeholder engagement, RIA and *ex post* evaluation were constructed to provide an overview of country practices.

Each composite indicator is composed of four equally weighted categories: 1) Systematic adoption which records formal requirements and how often these requirements are conducted in practice; 2) Methodology which gathers information on the methods used in each area, e.g. the type of impacts assessed or how frequently different forms of consultation are used; 3) Oversight and quality control records the role of oversight bodies and publically available evaluations; and 4) Transparency which records information from the questions that relate to the principles of open government, e.g. whether government decisions are made publically available.

Limitations of the Regulatory Indicators survey and composite indicators

In interpreting the survey results, it is important to bear in mind the methodological limitations of composite indicators, particularly those that, as in the current survey, are based on categorical variables.

Composite indicators are useful in their ability to integrate large amounts of information into an easily understood format (Freudenberg, 2003[7]). However, by their very nature, cross-country comparable indicators cannot be context specific and cannot fully capture the complex realities of the quality, use and impact of regulatory policy. While the current survey, compared to previous editions, puts a stronger focus on evidence and examples to support country responses, it does not constitute an in-depth assessment of the quality of country practices. For example, while countries needed to provide examples of assessments of some specific elements required in RIA to validate their answers, the OECD Secretariat did not evaluate the quality of these assessments nor discussed with stakeholders the actual impact of the RIAs on the quality of regulations.

In-depth country reviews are therefore required to complement the indicators. Reviews provide readers with a more detailed analysis of the content, strengths and shortcomings of countries' regulatory policies, as well as detailed and context-specific recommendations for improvement. OECD member countries have a wide range of governance structures, administrative cultures and institutional and constitutional settings that are important to take into consideration to fully assess regulatory practices and policies. While these are taken into account in OECD member country peer reviews, it is not possible to reflect all these country specific factors in a cross-country comparison of regulatory practices.

It is also important to bear in mind that the indicators should not be interpreted as a measurement of the quality of regulation itself. While the implementation of the measures assessed by the indicators aim to deliver regulations that meet public policy objectives and will have a positive impact on the economy and society, the indicators themselves do not assess the achievement of these objectives.

The results of composite indicators are always sensitive to methodological choices, unless country answers are homogeneous across all practices. It is therefore not advisable to make statements about the relative performance of countries with similar scores. Instead composite indicators should be seen as a means of initiating discussion and stimulating public interest (OECD/European Union/EC-JRC, 2008[8]). To ensure full transparency, the methodology for constructing the composite indicators and underlying data as well as the results of the sensitivity analysis to different methodological choices, including the weighting system, has been made available publicly on the OECD website.

References

Freudenberg, M. (2003), "Composite Indicators of Country Performance: A Critical Assessment", *OECD Science, Technology and Industry Working Papers*, No. 2003/16, OECD Publishing, Paris, https://dx.doi.org/10.1787/405566708255. [7]

OECD (2021), *OECD Regulatory Policy Outlook 2021*, OECD Publishing, Paris, https://dx.doi.org/10.1787/38b0fdb1-en. [4]

OECD (2020), *Reviewing the Stock of Regulation, OECD Best Practice Principles for Regulatory Policy*, OECD Publishing, Paris, https://doi.org/10.1787/1a8f33bc-en. [1]

OECD (2018), *OECD Regulatory Policy Outlook 2018*, OECD Publishing, Paris, https://dx.doi.org/10.1787/9789264303072-en. [3]

OECD (2015), *OECD Regulatory Policy Outlook 2015*, OECD Publishing, Paris, https://dx.doi.org/10.1787/9789264238770-en. [2]

OECD (2012), *Recommendation of the Council on Regulatory Policy and Governance*, OECD Publishing, Paris, https://dx.doi.org/10.1787/9789264209022-en. [5]

OECD (2010), *Why Is Administrative Simplification So Complicated?: Looking beyond 2010*, Cutting Red Tape, OECD Publishing, Paris, https://dx.doi.org/10.1787/9789264089754-en. [6]

OECD/European Union/EC-JRC (2008), *Handbook on Constructing Composite Indicators: Methodology and User Guide*, OECD Publishing, Paris, https://dx.doi.org/10.1787/9789264043466-en. [8]

1 General trends and institutional settings

The European Commission has invested heavily in improving its better regulation agenda and has steadily refined its approach to regulatory policy. This chapter summarises the European Union's legislative procedure and explores some of the general trends of regulatory policy across the EU and its Member States. It also presents an overview of the use of key regulatory management tools by EU Member States in the development and transposition of EU legislation. This chapter discusses the EU Member States' engagement in multiple layers of international regulatory co-operation and, finally, reviews the institutional settings of regulatory oversight across EU Member States.

Key messages

- Political commitment and transparent adoption of the established principles for regulatory reform are crucial to the success of regulatory quality management systems. This is universally recognised by EU Member States as all have several explicit and published regulatory policy documents that promote whole-of-government regulatory policy and almost all have a high-level official or minister responsible for advancing the regulatory agenda.

- EU Member States have the possibility to undertake stakeholder engagement and regulatory impact assessment to inform both the negotiation and transposition of EU legislation. They can also rely on the results of the European Commission's use of regulatory management tools. EU Member States require the use of regulatory management tools more systematically when transposing directives than to inform the negotiation stage of the EU legislative procedure. This is a particular concern when EU Member States engage with EU regulations that are directly applicable, as the negotiation stage is the final opportunity for Member States to use evidence on domestic impacts to influence policy proposals.

- The regulatory management tools used by the European Commission appear to be relied on by EU Member States more during the negotiation phase than the transposition phase. The exception is the use of the European Commission's *ex post* evaluations, which generally do not appear to be utilised by EU Member States much at all neither to evaluate existing laws nor as input for preparation of new proposals. EU Member States may benefit from further using the information resulting from the European Commission's use of regulatory management tools to inform their negotiation and transposition of EU adopted acts.

- The Council of the European Union needs to implement the Interinstitutional Agreement on Better Law Making signed in 2016, in particular in the analysis of impacts of its significant amendments. All three European institutions involved in the legislative process should systematically implement good regulatory practices to fully embed better regulation across all parts of the EU's decision-making procedures.

- International regulatory co-operation (IRC) occurs in multiple layers: "intra-EU IRC" covers co-operation between EU Member States within the EU; "external EU IRC" where EU Member States engage in IRC outside of the EU (i.e. common EU action by the European Commission vis-à-vis third countries or international organisations); and "residual EU Member State IRC" covers individual engagement of those states in IRC outside the EU framework. Overall, EU Member States have extensive experience and institutional frameworks to conduct "intra-EU IRC" and "external EU IRC". Despite this rich EU experience, Member States' better regulation frameworks rarely reflect "residual IRC".

- EU Member States' policies/ strategies on IRC, even though most frequently targeted to intra-EU IRC, are an evident avenue to clarify roles, responsibilities and strategic objectives on IRC within their domestic administration. EU Member States have opportunity to build on these policies/strategies, and more broadly on their ongoing intra-EU IRC experience to make strategic and evidence-based use of the global normative landscape at large to achieve both EU-wide as well as their specific domestic policy objectives.

- Regulatory oversight bodies (ROBs) have a major role to play in promoting the systematic and consistent use of regulatory management tools, as well as in fostering strong institutional co-ordination. All EU Member States have at least one dedicated body in charge of promoting and monitoring regulatory reform and quality. While this arguably reflects their awareness of regulatory oversight's importance for Better Regulation, the coverage of core regulatory oversight functions in EU Member States remains patchy. Oversight continues to focus primarily on RIA. Relatively few Member States have an oversight body in charge of systematically reviewing the quality of either stakeholder engagement or *ex post* evaluations processes.

- ROBs can enhance governments' ability to reap the benefits from regulatory reform and target limited public resources by improving how the performance of regulatory management tools, and regulatory policy more broadly, is assessed and communicated upon. Performance assessment in this area is, however, neither fully transparent nor systematic in most EU Member States. Opportunities remain to enhance the systematic monitoring and evaluation of ROBs' contribution to regulatory improvement.

Introduction

Regulation is a core government activity that affects all areas of businesses and citizens' lives. It is a crucial determinant of any society's welfare and, when done well, regulation can improve societal wellbeing, improve business competition, and enhance environmental outcomes. When done poorly, however, regulation may unnecessarily increase burden on both business and regulators and can adversely affect citizens' lives. Regulatory policy is thus centrally important to ensure governments make laws that improve welfare.

A number of synergies exist between this report – which focuses exclusively on the European Union Member States and the European Union – and the recently published *OECD Regulatory Policy Outlook* (2021[1]), albeit with a more limited scope. The principal similarity is that both reports assess requirements and practices regarding the same regulatory management tools – namely stakeholder engagement,[1] regulatory impact assessment[2] (RIA), and *ex post* evaluation[3] – on a consistent basis, thereby allowing for the comparison of results between OECD member countries and EU Member States. This report also builds on the previous edition of *Better Regulation Practices across the European Union* (OECD, 2019[2]), which examined the use of impact assessment and stakeholder participation in the design and review of domestic laws and in the development and transposition of EU legislation.

The OECD and the European Union have both long-recognised the potential of regulatory policy. The OECD *Recommendation of the Council on Regulatory Policy and Governance* (2012[3]) is the product of decades of research at the OECD and sets the normative framework to measure regulatory performance in member countries. Regulatory policy in the European Union was advanced under the Better Regulation Agenda, which played a crucial role in shaping the European Commission's regulatory processes. The OECD *Recommendation* (2012[3]) and the EU Better Regulation Agenda share the same objectives, approaches and key principles. Both have a particularly strong focus on stakeholder engagement, regulatory impact assessment (RIA), and *ex post* evaluation, regulatory oversight, and international regulatory co-operation as critical pillars of regulatory quality.

The analysis in this report is based on the OECD Indicators of Regulatory Policy and Governance (iREG) survey. The iREG survey results in the construction of composite indicators relating to the three assessed areas of stakeholder engagement, RIA, and *ex post* evaluation. As for the previous edition, this report also extends the iREG survey to include all EU Member States, including countries that are not members of the OECD[4] – namely Bulgaria, Croatia, Cyprus, Malta and Romania. While stakeholder engagement, RIA, and *ex post* evaluation are all very important elements of regulatory policy, they do not constitute the whole better regulation framework. For instance, other principles from the OECD *Recommendation* (2012[3]) are currently not assessed, and it is also recognised that countries may have quite disparate approaches to achieving better regulation. While this report and the survey put a strong focus on evidence and examples, it does not constitute an in-depth assessment of the quality of country practices. In-depth country reviews are therefore required to complement the indicators presented in this report. Reviews provide readers with a more detailed analysis of the content, strengths and shortcomings of countries' regulatory policies, as well as detailed and context-specific recommendations for improvement.

This chapter explores some of the general trends of regulatory policy across EU Member States. The section below reviews the existence and features of policy documents that frame EU Member States' Better Regulation agendas as well as high-level political responsibility and standard procedures to develop regulations. The second section summarises the European Union's legislative procedure. The third section provides an overview on the use of key regulatory management tools by EU Member States in the development and transposition of EU legislation (which are then assessed in more detail in Chapters 2, 3, and 4). The fourth section explores the EU Member States' engagement with multiple layers of international regulatory co-operation (IRC). The final part of this chapter discusses the institutional setting of regulatory oversight across EU Member States, including the allocation of oversight functions within the administration.

Regulatory policy in the EU Member States

The OECD *Recommendation of the Council on Regulatory Policy and Governance* (2012[3]) is a framework for regulatory policy. The *Recommendation* (2012[3]) seeks to help OECD member and non-member countries deliver ongoing improvements to regulatory quality. This framework elaborates a system of institutions, processes and tools that, when functioning properly, help support better regulatory decision making. The content of the *Recommendation* is listed in Box 1.1. Whilst the *Recommendation* (2012[3]) is officially recognised by OECD members, it also provides useful measures for non-member countries when supporting the implementation and advancement of systemic regulatory reform.

Principle 1 of the *Recommendation* (2012[3]) calls for effective regulatory policy to be adopted at the highest political level and for the importance of regulatory quality to be adequately communicated to lower levels of the administration. The endorsement of a clear political commitment to the established principles for regulatory reform is a key component for a successful system of regulatory quality management (OECD, 2012[3]). Such commitment should be transparently adopted and available to all officials across the entire national administration. The "whole-of-government" perspective is essential in order to capture the interrelations which allow a proper functioning of central government and determine the quality of regulation (OECD, 2012[3]).

Box 1.1. OECD Recommendation of the Council on Regulatory Policy and Governance

The *Recommendation* (2012[3]) sets out the measures that Governments can and should take to support the implementation and advancement of systemic regulatory reform to deliver regulations that meet public policy objectives and will have a positive impact on the economy and society. These measures are integrated in a comprehensive policy cycle in which regulations are designed, assessed and evaluated *ex ante* and *ex post*, revised and enforced at all levels of government, supported by appropriate institutions.

1. Commit at the highest political level to an explicit whole-of-government policy for regulatory quality. The policy should have clear objectives and frameworks for implementation to ensure that, if regulation is used, the economic, social and environmental benefits justify the costs, the distributional effects are considered and the net benefits are maximised.

---

2. Adhere to principles of open government, including transparency and participation in the regulatory process to ensure that regulation serves the public interest and is informed by the legitimate needs of those interested in and affected by regulation. This includes providing meaningful opportunities (including on-line) for the public to contribute to the process of preparing draft regulatory proposals and to the quality of the supporting analysis. Governments should ensure that regulations are comprehensible and clear and that parties can easily understand their rights and obligations.

3. Establish mechanisms and institutions to actively provide oversight of regulatory policy procedures and goals, support and implement regulatory policy, and thereby foster regulatory quality.

4. Integrate Regulatory Impact Assessment (RIA) into the early stages of the policy process for the formulation of new regulatory proposals. Clearly identify policy goals, and evaluate if regulation is necessary and how it can be most effective and efficient in achieving those goals. Consider means other than regulation and identify the trade-offs of the different approaches analysed to identify the best approach.

5. Conduct systematic programme reviews of the stock of significant regulation against clearly defined policy goals, including consideration of costs and benefits, to ensure that regulations remain up to date, cost justified, cost effective and consistent, and deliver the intended policy objectives.

6. Regularly publish reports on the performance of regulatory policy and reform programmes and the public authorities applying the regulations. Such reports should also include information on how regulatory tools such as Regulatory Impact Assessment (RIA), public consultation practices and reviews of existing regulations are functioning in practice.

7. Develop a consistent policy covering the role and functions of regulatory agencies in order to provide greater confidence that regulatory decisions are made on an objective, impartial and consistent basis, without conflict of interest, bias or improper influence.

8. Ensure the effectiveness of systems for the review of the legality and procedural fairness of regulations and of decisions made by bodies empowered to issue regulatory sanctions. Ensure that citizens and businesses have access to these systems of review at reasonable cost and receive decisions in a timely manner.

9. As appropriate apply risk assessment, risk management, and risk communication strategies to the design and implementation of regulations to ensure that regulation is targeted and effective. Regulators should assess how regulations will be given effect and should design responsive implementation and enforcement strategies.

10. Where appropriate promote regulatory coherence through co-ordination mechanisms between the supranational, the national and sub-national levels of government. Identify cross-cutting regulatory issues at all levels of government, to promote coherence between regulatory approaches and avoid duplication or conflict of regulations.

11. Foster the development of regulatory management capacity and performance at sub-national levels of government.

12. In developing regulatory measures, give consideration to all relevant international standards and frameworks for co-operation in the same field and, where appropriate, their likely effects on parties outside the jurisdiction.

Source: OECD (2012[3]), Recommendation of the Council on Regulatory Policy and Governance, OECD Publishing, Paris, http://dx.doi.org/10.1787/9789264209022-en.

All twenty-seven EU Member States show some commitment to Principle 1 of the *Recommendation* (2012[3]). All indeed have an explicit and published regulatory policy documents that promote government-wide regulatory reform. There is however no blueprint to embed these documents into practice as there is strong divergence across EU Member States. Data show that regulatory policy is rarely expressed in a single high-level document. Instead, a majority of EU Member States have four documents or more that embed requirements and that can take the form of laws, manuals or guidelines, and government strategies and programmes. These policies cover various areas of regulatory governance (Figure 1.1). Universally across all EU Member States, regulatory policy covers *ex ante* RIAs and government transparency and consultation, whilst it covers *ex post* evaluation of regulations in 24 EU Member States.

Figure 1.1. *Ex ante* impact assessment, transparency and consultation, as well as administrative simplification or burden reduction are the most commonly covered areas of regulatory governance in EU Member States

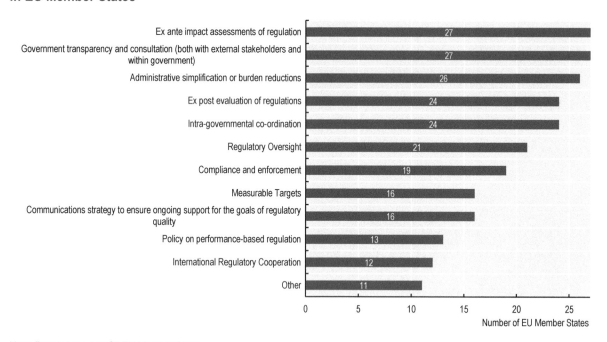

Note: Data is based on 27 EU Member States.
Source: Indicators of Regulatory Policy and Governance (iREG) Survey 2021.

Almost all EU Member States also have a high-level official or minister responsible for promoting government-wide progress on regulatory reform. In 21 EU Member States, the person responsible is a minister whose portfolio includes responsibility for implementing the better regulation agenda. In four EU Member States – **Belgium**, **Hungary**, **Latvia**, and **Malta** – it is a high-level appointment whilst in **Lithuania** it is the head of the Government Office who is responsible for regulatory policy. **Ireland** is the only EU Member State that reported having no person responsible for the development of the better regulation agenda and of regulatory reform.

EU legislative process and regulatory policy in the European Union

The three main institutions within the European Union are the European Commission, the Council of the European Union (henceforth referred to as "the Council"), and the European Parliament. The right of initiative for EU legislation lies, as a rule, with the European Commission, except for some specific political areas, whether either the European Parliament, the Council or a number of Member States have the right to initiate legislation. While some special legislative procedures in the EU treaties provide that the Council adopts the EU legislative proposal, most EU legislative acts are adopted under the so-called "ordinary legislative procedure", where it is for the Council and the European Parliament to negotiate, amend, adopt and/or reject the proposals tabled by the European Commission. The European Parliament and the Council are often referred to as "co-legislators" as they are on par with each other under the ordinary legislative procedure. The two main types of legislative and regulatory tools available to the European Union are further described in Box 1.2.

Box 1.2. The main types of EU legislative acts and subordinate regulations

The two main types of EU legislative acts are regulations and directives. Both the nature of and processes for these types of EU legislative acts have important differences. The differences are relevant to the regulatory management tools that individual Member States employ when implementing these acts.

EU regulations have general application and are directly applicable in all EU Member States and binding in their entirety. Regulations are used most commonly where it is important to achieve a uniform implementation of a policy intervention, such as in the internal market or the governance of mergers. They leave individual Member States limited scope to determine how they implement these laws. EU directives on the other hand, afford Member States considerable latitude to choose the method and form of implementation. They are binding on the Member States to which they are addressed in respect of the result to be achieved but the specific form and methods are left to national authorities to decide.

The main types of EU subordinate regulations are delegated acts and implementing acts. In the legislative acts they adopt, the European Parliament and the Council can empower the Commission to adopt acts to supplement or amend non-essential parts of EU legislative acts (in case of delegated acts) or where uniform conditions for implementing legally binding acts are needed (in case of implementing acts). Both delegated and implementing acts may take the form of either regulations, directives or decisions.

The European Commission's regulatory process for preparing proposals for legislative acts and delegated and implementing acts involves both stakeholder consultation and impact assessment (see Chapters 2 and 3). Once the Commission has adopted a proposal for a legislative act under the ordinary legislative procedure, the proposed regulation or directive (as the case may be) is subject to the legislative process in the Parliament and the Council, where proposals can be refused or amendments are negotiated before the EU legislative act is finally adopted. Delegated and implementing acts are not subject to a legislative process per se. However, delegated acts only enter into force if the European Parliament and the Council of the European Union have no objections. Additionally, delegated and implementing acts are usually prepared in consultation with an expert group (the former) or a committee (the latter) comprised of representatives from EU countries.

EU regulations take effect in individual Member States once they have been published in the Official Journal of the EU or later if the regulation so provides. EU directives are subject to an additional transposition procedure, as the individual Member States need to incorporate them into national law. The European Commission monitors whether legislation has been correctly transposed into the individual Member States' legal orders and has the power to launch infringement proceedings before the European Court of Justice against individual Member States, if the transposition is deemed insufficient or unduly delayed.

Source: Indicators of Regulatory Policy and Governance (iREG) Survey 2021; OECD (2019[2]), Better Regulation Practices across the European Union, OECD Publishing, Paris, https://dx.doi.org/10.1787/9789264311732-en.

The better regulation agenda was introduced in the EU policy procedure in the early 2000s, in response to some of the EU Member States' efforts to embed good regulatory practices within their domestic legislative procedures (Goldberg, 2018[4]). In the early stages, the European Commission's better regulation agenda was strongly underpinned by the rationale to simplify and improve the quality of EU legislation (European Commission, 2002[5]), to strengthen the competitiveness of the European economies, and to ensure that the analysis addressed economic, environmental and social regulatory impacts (European Commission, 2005[6]). The EU's approach to regulatory policy has been refined over the years as subsequent Commissions (e.g. the Barroso Commissions, 2005-2015; the Juncker Commission, 2015-2020) attempted to improve the existing framework by refining the various tools included in the better regulation agenda. Most recently, the von der Leyen Commission (2020-present) published a new Communication on better regulation in April 2021 (European Commission, 2021[7]) as well as new *Guidelines on Better Regulation* and an updated *Better Regulation Toolbox* in November 2021 (European Commission, 2021[8]; European Commission, 2021[9]).

The European Commission has the general right of legislative initiative, but it does not control the end-product that is adopted as the Council and the European Parliament, under the ordinary legislative procedure, need to jointly agree on the final legislative act. Even though the European Commission follows rigorous regulatory procedures, the negotiations and amendments tabled by the co-legislators could introduce elements of poor regulation in EU legislative acts (Goldberg, 2018[4]). In light of this, the Interinstitutional Agreement on Better Law Making was established in 2003 and revised in 2016 to support evidence-based decision-making across all three institutions and to ensure that the adopted EU legislation remains in line with better regulation principles. Amongst other things, the Council and the European Parliament agreed in 2016 to consider the European Commission's impact assessments when debating the legislative proposal and to carry out impact assessments in relation to any of their substantial amendments to a proposal, when appropriate and necessary for the legislative process (European Union, 2016[10]). There is, however, no agreed definition of what constitutes a "substantial" amendment (European Court of Auditors, 2020[11]).

The use of regulatory management tools, and particularly RIAs, remains a difficult issue in the application of the better regulation agenda across the European Institutions. In light of the 2016 Interinstitutional agreement, the European Parliament has created a Directorate for Impact Assessment and European Added Value, as part of the European Parliamentary Research Service, that offers parliamentary committees a range of support in relation to *ex ante* impact assessment and *ex post* evaluation, including the development of impact assessments on parliamentary amendments (European Parliamentary Research Service, 2021[12]). Since 2016, the relevant units within the European Parliament have in some instances undertaken impact assessments of the amendments introduced by European Members of Parliament (European Parliamentary Research Service, 2020[13]). The Council of the European Union however does not engage with RIA at all (Simonelli and Iacob, 2021[14]). As argued by Goldberg (2018[4]), the European Commission's legislative proposal is by nature a draft as it is likely to be amended by the Council and by the European Parliament during the legislative process. Furthermore, stakeholders continue to raise concerns about the lack of transparency during the "trilogues" (i.e. the negotiation between the European Commission, the European Parliament, and the Council of the European Union) as these continue to operate behind closed doors without the possibility for stakeholders to follow or contribute to the debates (Business Europe, 2018[15]). As a result, the European Commission's assessment may only identify and assess some of the costs and benefits that European citizens and businesses will experience when the final legislation is implemented. There thus continues to be thousands of amendments introduced yearly in the Council and/or Parliament whose impacts are not understood and that have not been consulted with affected parties. This is a significant weakness for EU law-making and demonstrates that, until all three European institutions involved in the legislative process systematically implement good regulatory practices, it is unlikely that better regulation can be considered as successfully embedded into the EU's decision-making procedures. The European Commission calls for the European Parliament and the Council to assess the anticipated impacts of their amendments and to relaunch a common political dialogue in its recent *Communication on Better Regulation* (European Commission, 2021[7]).

Overview of the use of regulatory management tools in EU Member States in the development and transposition of EU legislation

In its Communication on Better Regulation, the European Commission highlighted the role of EU Member States in improving transparency of evidence-based policy and to reduce the burden of EU legislation (European Commission, 2021[7]). Legislation and regulatory policy emanating from the EU naturally affects EU Member States, so the regulatory management systems of the EU institutions and of the EU Member State need to be mutually reinforcing in order to operate effectively and efficiently (OECD, 2019[2]).

The results from the iREG survey demonstrate that there has been little change since the previous edition of this report (2019[2]) and less than half of the EU Member States require either stakeholder engagement or RIA to be conducted during the negotiation stage. In fact, only 10 EU Member States require both regulatory management tools to be used to assist the negotiation of proposed EU directives and regulations, namely **Bulgaria**, **Denmark**, **Estonia**, **Finland**, **France**, **Hungary**, **Italy**, **Poland**, the **Slovak Republic**, and **Slovenia**. The negotiation phase of the EU legislative process is a major opportunity for EU Member States to directly amend the European Commission's legislative proposal. Using regulatory management tools at the negotiation stage helps to identify specific domestic issues and sensitivities to the European Commission's regulatory proposals, which can then be utilised to inform the negotiation debate. This is particularly relevant for EU regulations as these are directly applicable and binding in their entirety, meaning that Member States have no discretion to amend any element or to determine how to implement such laws once they are adopted by the EU (see Box 1.2). The negotiation is thus the last stage in the EU legislative procedure where Member States can use evidence on domestic impacts to influence a proposed EU regulation. The efficient use of evidence in the negotiation of proposed EU regulations will become increasingly significant as the European Union appears to move towards adopting more of them. The short timing between the publication of the European Commission's legislative proposal and the beginning of the negotiation can however impede the development of suitable regulatory management tools to inform the domestic negotiation position, particularly RIA as discussed in Chapter 3.

In contrast, the requirement to use regulatory management tools when transposing directives continues to be more common across EU Member States. All EU Member States require either stakeholder engagement or RIA to be conducted when transposing EU directives. Given that transposing EU directives involves amending existing or developing new domestic regulations (see Box 1.2), it is unsurprising that the RIA requirements for laws originating at the EU level are identical to those originating domestically. In addition, all Member States require both regulatory management tools, with the exception of four countries. **Ireland**, **the Netherlands**, and **Portugal** require RIA but not stakeholder engagement to be undertaken during transposition, whilst **Romania** requires the opposite. Generally, the requirements governing stakeholder engagement and RIA for the transposition of EU directives are identical to the requirements on regulations originating domestically. Few EU Member States however generally report assessing the impacts resulting from additional provisions added to EU directives.

The results from the iREG survey also indicate that a majority EU Member States report facilitating the engagement of domestic stakeholders in the European Commission's public consultation process, which is open for 12 weeks. EU Member States also report using the results from the European Commission's consultation processes and its impact assessment more systematically as input to inform the negotiating position for proposed directives and regulations rather than when transposing directives. In contrast, there appears to be less interface between the European Commission and the EU Member States regarding the use of *ex post* evaluation than the use of the other two regulatory management tools. Indeed, few EU Member States reported using the results of the European Commission's *ex post* evaluation at any stages in the negotiation or transposition of EU legislation.

The requirements and practices of EU Member States regarding stakeholder engagement, RIA, and *ex post* evaluation on EU legislative proposals are discussed and assessed in more details in Chapters 2, 3 and 4, respectively.

EU Member States inherently engage in international regulatory co-operation within the EU and can deploy their experience beyond the EU framework

EU Member States are pioneers of international regulatory co-operation (IRC) by virtue of being part of the European Union. In practice, IRC takes place in multiple layers within the EU, ranging from "intra-EU IRC" including co-operation between EU Member States facilitated by the EU framework, and "external EU IRC" where EU Member States commonly engage in IRC beyond the EU framework, to "specific EU Member State IRC" including individual engagement in IRC. Each layer of IRC is explained below. Overall, while EU Member States have an extensive experience and institutional framework to conduct "intra-EU IRC", specific EU Member States' better regulation frameworks often fail to reflect the experience gained from regulating within the EU context. This section illustrates EU Member States' manifold engagement in IRC while identifying opportunities for leveraging on this experience.

What is IRC?

IRC has become a critical building block of Better Regulation, recognised as a principle enshrined in the *2012 OECD Recommendation on Regulatory Policy and Governance* (OECD, 2012[3]). On this basis, the OECD has studied a variety of approaches to IRC and mapped the benefits and challenges in using it to support its members in applying an international lens in the regulatory process. The body of knowledge gathered by the OECD in this area since 2012 is compiled in the *OECD Best Practice Principles on IRC* (2021[16]). Understood in very broad terms, IRC extends "any agreement or organisational arrangement, formal or informal, between countries to promote some form of co-operation in the design, monitoring, enforcement, or ex-post management of regulation" (OECD, 2013, p. 153[17]).

Three layers of IRC of EU Member States

As mentioned above, EU Member States can be considered to have three "layers" of IRC, resulting in different levels of integration between regulatory frameworks.

First, the most integrated "layer" of IRC is among the EU Member States themselves, or "intra-EU IRC". To this effect, EU Member States have developed an ambitious set of legal and institutional settings that can be equated to a complex IRC framework seeking regional economic integration and, more broadly, promoting economic and social progress for citizens, taking into account the principle of sustainable development. As such, the EU can be considered not only as a highly developed product of IRC created by an international treaty, but also as an ongoing platform for IRC to take place in many forms. Based on treaties between the EU Member States, certain national regulatory competences leave way to supranational law making and institutions. In other words, EU Member States have pooled their sovereignty in joint institutions (including the European Commission, the Council of the EU, the European Parliament and the European Court of Justice) and empowered them to adopt and interpret legislation (OECD, 2013[17]). Resultant legislation can be binding on national authorities (European Commission, 2021[18]). For an order of magnitude, the EU adopted 806 directives and 1042 regulations since 1992 (by basic or amending legislative acts). Uneven information is available on the levels of transposition across EU Member States (EUR-Lex, 2021[19]).

Multilayered IRC engagement in (a) given area(s) to achieve co-operation objectives is common practice across all OECD member countries, often resulting in an overlapping of their features or form continuums (OECD, 2013[17]). Facilitated by the EU framework, the forms of co-operation between EU Member States ("intra-EU IRC") range from harmonisation of rules to more informal dialogues and exchanges on a regular basis, and from the design to the implementation and enforcement of rules – a broad panorama that is rarely visible in a single regional or multilateral co-operation framework and which makes the EU the largest regulatory and economically integrated region worldwide (OECD, 2016[20]). Harmonisation of rules exists in areas where the EU has exclusive legislative competencies, i.e. in areas in which the EU alone is able to legislate and adopt binding acts. Where the EU only has shared competencies, supporting competencies, or no competencies at all, harmonisation of rules between EU Member States is more uneven, leaving space for complementary IRC mechanisms. For instance, mutual recognition agreements (MRAs) are largely used to close gaps in non-harmonised areas, such as pharmaceutical products or medical devices, where technical specifications are regulated and certification is mandatory (OECD, 2013[17]). Facilitated by the EU framework, its Member States also engage with each other in transgovernmental networks and recognise common technical standards. Enhancing co-operation between national energy regulators, for example, is one the primary means through which the EU seeks to fulfil objectives in the energy sector (OECD, 2013[21]).

Second, the EU has the ability to sign international treaties in the areas of its attributed powers or to join international organisations. As such, the European Commission catalyses its Member States' international engagement to the international stage beyond EU borders ("external EU IRC"), that then also adds to EU law and the *acquis* applicable to EU Member States (EUR-Lex, 2022[22]). The European Commission participates in or interacts with multiple intergovernmental organizations or international fora (e.g. International Monetary Fund, World Bank, OECD, G7, G20, and the European Bank for Reconstruction and Development), including the development of joint instruments, memoranda of understanding (MoUs) or other agreements, and engages in constant dialogue and informal exchanges of information such as the Transatlantic dialogues instituted by the EU and the United States through the Transatlantic Economic Council and the EU-Canada Comprehensive Economic and Trade Agreement (CETA) (OECD, 2013[17]). As such, in the areas where the EU has competence and is active in international fora, the European Commission acts as an enabler for IRC between the EU as a whole and non-EU members. In parallel, and de facto, some commentators have qualified the EU as a global regulatory power deploying a "Brussels effect" via market forces, with EU standards adopted at the global level without the EU imposing them on other jurisdictions (Bradford, 2020[23]). Broadly speaking, this "Brussels effect" can result in integration with non-EU jurisdictions.

The EU Better Regulation Agenda includes some elements to support Member States' consideration of "external EU IRC" when new initiatives are prepared and when existing legislation is managed and evaluated at the European level. For instance, the European Commission's *Better Regulation Toolbox* (2021[9]) suggests a "screening of options against the EU's international legal commitments" in external trade and investment when designing policy options, notably the World Trade Organisation (WTO) Agreements and EU trade agreements with third countries (European Commission, 2021, p. 219[9]). Where the European Commission has sector specific international agreements in place with third countries, such as Agreements on Conformity Assessment and Acceptance of Industrial Products (ACAAs) with EU neighbouring countries and Mutual Recognition Agreements (MRAs) with trade partners, the *Better Regulation Toolbox* (2021[9]) suggests to consider them additionally when designing policy options. It also notes that international organisations can provide valuable sources for gathering data and indicators relating to impacts and contextual information of policies (European Commission, 2021, p. 363[9]). The case to consider the international environment also beyond the EU borders when regulating is therefore recognised by the European Commission and paves the way for further efforts to support co-ordination with international peers to work together and avoid duplication. The *Compendium for International Organisations' Practices* (2021[24]) provides some key elements, building on the responses to an international organisations' survey in 2018, to help identify and map potential partners, establish common objectives, and select appropriate instruments, stages and procedures for co-ordination.

Finally, where EU Member States develop their own regulations, they co-operate with EU Member States and non-EU jurisdictions individually ("residual EU Member States' IRC"). EU Member States each engage in "residual EU Member State IRC" of relevance to them for a good reason: although there is a growing number of rules originating from EU legislation, there remains space for regulatory divergence in many areas. This concerns, first and foremost, areas that are not under the exclusive competency of the EU and are thus not fully harmonised. For instance, the EU only has "supporting competency" in the areas of health, education or tourism (European Commission, 2021[18]). Where the EU has exclusive competency (e.g. the customs union, competition in the internal market, or trade policy), the level of harmonisation essentially depends on how the competency is exercised respectively, i.e. what type of EU law is used. Although the adoption of EU directives has declined in the last years (only 5 EU directives have been adopted in 2020 compared to 33 in 2019 and 47 in 2014 (EUR-Lex, 2021[19])), the fact that EU Member States have discretion when transposing EU directives inevitably leads to the issue of how to ensure that domestic regulations implementing EU law are fully coherent with the underlying common policy objectives in protecting citizens and do not create trade barriers (OECD, 2010[25]). While policy coherence and united action is particularly evident to maintain supply chains and protect citizens in times of crisis, initial regulatory responses to the COVID-19 pandemic in EU Member States were still mostly inward-looking (Russack and Blockmans, 2020[26]) (OECD, 2020[27]).

Looking at each EU Member States' engagement in IRC, the following findings from the iREG survey illustrate that EU Member States mostly engage in "intra-EU IRC" and that "residual" EU Member States' IRC efforts still matter, to reap the full benefits of international co-operation for domestic rule-making.

General State of Play in three layers of IRC practice in EU Member States

IRC starts with a systematic whole-of-government policy/strategy and a dedicated governance structure promoting it. This is highlighted in the *2021 OECD Best Practice Principles on International Regulatory Co-operation* (2021[16]) as a *sine qua non* condition to evoke ambitious IRC together with by the embedment of international considerations throughout the domestic regulatory design, development and delivery, and leveraging bilateral and multilateral co-operation on regulatory matters to support national policy objectives (OECD, n.d.[28]). As a broad strategic document or other instrument, a dedicated IRC policy/strategy is an opportunity to build a holistic IRC vision with clearly identified roles and responsibilities that ideally feeds into the broader strategic priorities of the government.

Box 1.3. Examples of IRC policies/ strategies across EU Member States

The Cabinet Regulations No. 707 and 96 in **Latvia** provide a whole-of-government policy/strategy on IRC as they govern the cross-government engagement with international organisations and the institutions of the European Union, respectively. These provide strategic direction to Latvia's IRC activities in these fora, by establishing procedures for the initiation, development, co-ordination, approval and update of regulatory documents.

In **Germany**, Article 25 of the Constitution represents a "partial" legal basis on IRC to the extent that it incorporates certain international instruments, i.e. "the general rules of public international law", as an integral part of federal law. In addition, the German Constitutional Court has developed a principle of *Völkerrechtsfreundlichkeit (*friendliness to international law*)* according to which the German Basic Law "presumes the integration of the state it creates into the international legal order of the community of States". As a result, German Law is to be interpreted as consistently as possible with international law. This illustrates that jurisprudence and legal principles developed by domestic courts can promote IRC in domestic legislation and regulation.

To inform domestic rule making with international evidence, regulators in **Estonia** are required to examine available international practices regarding the issue under consideration during the drafting of legislative proposals. If information from foreign legislation contributed to the preparation of a draft, this must be included in the accompanying explanatory letter.

The One-Stop Shop for New Business Models launched by **Denmark** in 2018 requires the Danish Business Authority (DBA) to collaborate with neighbouring countries to analyse how EU Directives are implemented in different ways across jurisdictions. It has a particular substantive focus on the sharing economy, the circular economy, e-commerce and data and new technology. Anchored in the Strategy for Denmark's Digital Growth, under the pillar of agile regulation, this aims to reduce digital barriers to trade and support an innovation-friendly internal market in the EU.

In **Slovenia**, regulators – when developing laws and regulations – are required to use information from EU regulations, decisions of the Court of Justice of the European Union, analysis of regulation in the EU acquis, analysis of regulation in at least three legal systems of EU Member States, as well as beyond the EU, from international agreements and analyses of regulation in other legal systems.

Source: (OECD, n.d.[28]) (OECD, 2021[1]), see also: Mutual Legal Assistance Agreement between the Federal Republic of Germany and the Republic of Austria on Legal and Administrative Assistance in Customs, Excise and Monopoly Matters, Order of the German Constitutional Court from 22 March 1983 (BVerfGE 63, 343-380 (370)).

OECD data show that IRC policies/strategies may have varying scope and legal underpinnings across countries, ranging from statutory obligations, over established legal principles to more flexible approaches (Box 1.3). In the EU, most Member States have a range of legal provisions in place to frame their participation in the EU, which can be considered as "partial" IRC policies, given their geographical focus on regional partners (OECD, 2021[1]) – with "partial" implying no value judgement on their level of scope or ambition. By virtue of their membership obligations and of various EU treaties, the Member States therefore intrinsically have an active regulatory co-operation mechanism built into their processes (OECD, 2018[29]). In some cases, "partial" IRC policies in EU Member States also apply to certain sectors or to specific types of co-ordination. EU Member States thus tend to focus their IRC engagement to a geographic region or a specific sector (see examples, Box 1.3). In comparison, six OECD member countries have a whole-of-government, cross sector policy on IRC in place (OECD, 2021[1]). Individual IRC approaches of EU Member States to co-operate internationally also beyond the EU when regulating are less common (Figure 1.2).

Figure 1.2. While almost all EU Member States set up legal provisions to frame their participation in the EU, a systematic whole-of-government policy or a legal basis on IRC is still the exception

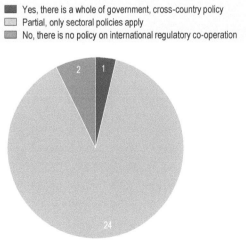

■ Yes, there is a whole of government, cross-country policy
□ Partial, only sectoral policies apply
▨ No, there is no policy on international regulatory co-operation

Note: Data is based on 27 EU Member States.
Source: Indicators of Regulatory Policy and Governance (iREG) Survey 2021.

Facilitation of a whole-of-government strategy around IRC is further impeded through a fragmentation of responsibilities in EU Member States, as the oversight of IRC practices is almost exclusively organised either amongst multiple central government bodies or without any governance structure at all. Similarly, only seven EU Member States reported that the authority in charge of regulatory oversight in general is also in charge of ensuring the consideration of international instruments in the development process of regulations.

The iREG survey results suggest that a number of formal requirements exist in EU Member States to consider recognition and incorporation of international instruments when developing domestic regulations or revising existing ones (Figure 1.3). Such formal requirements are a common way to ensure that international experience and expertise are considered in domestic rule making (OECD, 2021[1]). Leveraging usage and considerations of evidence from foreign policy makers and international organisations may prove valuable in building the body of evidence for a particular regulation, inform a greater range of options for policy action, and help to develop an evidence-based and transparent narrative around the chosen measure (OECD, 2021[16]). The majority of EU Member States have specific formal requirements in place to consider EU regulations and directives when developing or reviewing domestic laws which is particularly beneficial in areas where the EU has exclusive legislative competence and thus a large stock of regulations and directives, most notably in trade (i.e. the customs union). While the increasing use of IRC and good regulatory practices (GRPs) to reduce unnecessary barriers to trade is in line with the general trend in OECD countries, analytical work confirms that IRC offers critical tools for achieving national and international policy objectives well beyond trade liberalisation. The COVID-19 pandemic and climate change are only two examples of complex global challenges whose public management would benefit from better implementation of IRC tools addressing cross-border policy challenges more effectively and efficiently (OECD, 2021[1]). Yet, formal requirements in EU Member States to consider international instruments beyond the consideration of EU law focus on binding international instruments and only a few survey respondents have formal requirements in place for international standards or international instruments as a whole. This suggests that EU Member States often fail to apply their knowledge and experience of systematic IRC practices gained in the EU context (through "intra-EU IRC") beyond the EU framework.

Figure 1.3. Where formal requirements to consider international instruments when developing or reviewing domestic law exist in EU Member States, they rarely go beyond EU legislation and binding international instruments

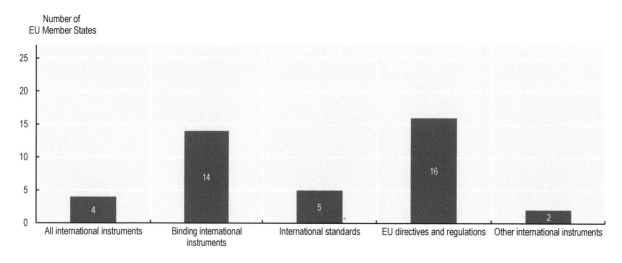

Note: Data is based on 27 EU Member States.
Source: Indicators of Regulatory Policy and Governance (iREG) Survey 2021.

The consideration of international instruments can be supported by practical guidance or databases, as highlighted in the *Best Practice Principles on International Regulatory Co-operation* (OECD, 2021[16]). This may reduce burdens for regulators and to consider more systematically the international environment and engage in fruitful IRC. While EU Member States increasingly provide supporting tools to policy makers and regulators (e.g. specific guidance documents or online databases to underpin regulatory processes with international evidence), in line with the general OECD trend, they are usually sector specific (e.g. on climate change or quality infrastructure) or instrument specific (e.g. for binding international law) and only apply infrequently (Figure 1.4).

The EU's expertise as the most integrated regional framework is reflected in its Better Regulation Agenda that sets out key elements on IRC as an important pillar of regulation. Member States of the EU therefore have the experience and tools to improve individual IRC objectives and practices when regulating, in order to close gaps that emerge from the still significant regulatory divergences across the EU, resulting from discretion that remains in the transposition of directives and areas of national competence. EU Member States also have the opportunity to improve their IRC with non-EU countries, particularly EU neighbouring countries, with whom they lack the same legal and institutional framework as with EU Member States but still share policy objectives. They can therefore work closer with both EU and non-EU members to ensure effective and efficient responses to common policy challenges.

Figure 1.4. Guidance and databases to support the consideration of international instruments in domestic rule making are increasingly common, but usually only for specific sectors or instruments

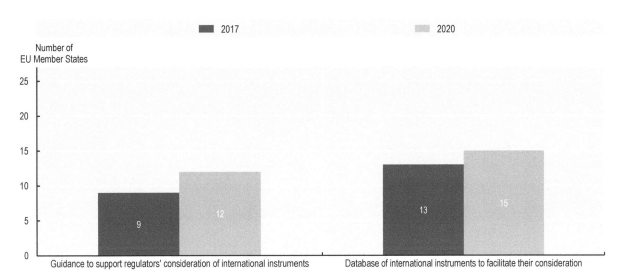

Note: Data is based on 27 EU Member States.
Source: Indicators of Regulatory Policy and Governance (iREG) Surveys 2017 and 2021.

Institutional setting and regulatory oversight across EU Member States

Regulatory oversight bodies (ROBs) are essential to help governments deliver on their Better Regulation goals. They can do so by promoting the systematic and consistent use of evidence and stakeholder engagement in the design and revision of rules, as well as by fostering strong institutional co-ordination and risk-based, forward-looking and innovative approaches to regulation. If they have adequate powers, resources and capacity, ROBs can also help ensure that rules are fit for the future by adopting a holistic perspective in their scrutiny of regulatory management tools and acting as knowledge brokers vis-à-vis ministries and regulatory agencies. The *OECD Recommendation of the Council on Regulatory Policy and Governance* (2012[3]) stresses the importance of establishing mechanisms and institutions to provide oversight of regulatory policy procedures and goals, support and implement regulatory policy, and thereby foster regulatory quality. The recently adopted *OECD Recommendation of the Council for Agile Regulatory Governance to Harness Innovation* (2021[30]) acknowledges the critical role of regulatory oversight in addressing many emerging regulatory challenges.

As this section will show, EU Member States' clear acknowledgement of the importance of regulatory oversight contrasts with the pace of reform measures undertaken to further strengthen and develop oversight systems, which remains slow in key areas such as the quality control of *ex post* evaluations and stakeholder engagement (including across borders). This mismatch is also observed for the OECD membership as a whole.

In line with the *OECD Regulatory Policy Outlook* (OECD, 2021[1]), the present section defines ROB as a body undertaking at least one "core" function of regulatory oversight on a systematic basis. Core functions are: quality control of regulatory management tools; guidance on the use of regulatory management tools; co-ordination on regulatory policy, and systematic evaluation of regulatory policy (see Box 1.4 for more details). The section discusses the institutional organisation of regulatory oversight in EU Member States, with special attention to oversight and quality control mechanisms for regulatory management tools, and identifies priorities for oversight systems in the years to come.

Box 1.4. "Core" functions of regulatory oversight

While previous analytical work by the OECD pertaining to regulatory oversight was broad in scope in order to capture a wide variety of situations, this section focuses on selected core functions. These have been identified in previous work carried out by the Secretariat based on analysis by Andrea Renda and Rosa J. Castro (Renda, Castro and Hernandez, forthcoming[31]) as being essential for effective regulatory oversight.

The functions considered as core are:

- Quality control of regulatory management tools (i.e. reviewing the quality of individual regulatory impact assessments, stakeholder engagement processes, and *ex post* evaluations);
- Issuance or provision of relevant guidance on the use of regulatory management tools;
- Co-ordination on regulatory policy; and
- Systematic evaluation of regulatory policy.

Although relevant actors of regulatory policy, a number of bodies' contribution is ancillary to core regulatory oversight functions. For the sake of consistency, bodies that do not perform core oversight functions or do so only on an *ad hoc* basis are therefore not considered for analytical purposes. Below is a list of bodies that are excluded on those grounds:

- Better regulation units inside ministries/departments;[5]
- Public think tanks and advisory bodies;
- Behavioural Insights Teams;
- Competition authorities;
- Ad hoc task forces;
- Permanent consultation bodies;
- Public training schools for civil servants;
- Budget and investment ministries/agencies;

- Trade ministries/units;
- Ministries of foreign affairs.

Source: OECD (2021[1]), OECD Regulatory Policy Outlook 2021, OECD Publishing, https://doi.org/10.1787/38b0fdb1-en; (Renda, Castro and Hernandez, forthcoming[31]), Defining and Contextualising Regulatory oversight and Co-ordination, OECD Publishing, Paris.

Regulatory oversight landscape in the EU: an overview

All EU Member States continue to have at least one dedicated body in charge of promoting and monitoring regulatory reform and quality in the national administration from a whole-of-government perspective. This arguably reflects their awareness of the importance of robust regulatory oversight for Better Regulation. ROBs also exist at the EU level that play an important role in implementing the Better Regulation agenda.

As of end 2020, EU Member States reported 64 ROBs as being in charge of performing at least one core regulatory oversight function on a systematic basis. This amounts to an average of nearly 2.4 ROBs per Member State, which is comparable to the OECD average. As shown in Table 1.1, this figure conceals, however, important differences. For example, **Denmark** has five ROBs and **Lithuania**, **Poland**, the **Netherlands**, and **Slovenia** have four bodies each, whereas other Member States (e.g. **Portugal**, **Finland**, **Romania**, and the **Slovak Republic**) have a single ROB each. More generally, there continues to be broad variety of institutional settings for regulatory oversight across Member States.

Table 1.1. Number of ROBs in each EU Member States

EU Member State	Number of regulatory oversight bodies in each EU Member State				
	1	2	3	4	5
Austria		✓			
Belgium		✓			
Bulgaria	✓				
Croatia		✓			
Cyprus	✓				
Czech Republic			✓		
Denmark					✓
Estonia		✓			
Finland	✓				
France			✓		
Germany			✓		
Greece		✓			
Hungary	✓				
Ireland			✓		
Italy			✓		
Latvia		✓			
Lithuania				✓	
Luxembourg	✓				
Malta			✓		
Netherlands				✓	
Poland				✓	
Portugal	✓				
Romania	✓				
Slovak Republic	✓				
Slovenia				✓	

EU Member State	Number of regulatory oversight bodies in each EU Member State				
Spain			✓		
Sweden		✓			
European Union			✓		

Note: Data is based on 27 EU Member States and the European Union.
Source: Indicators of Regulatory Policy and Governance (iREG) Survey 2021.

As shown in Figure 1.5, approximately three-quarters of ROBs are located within government. Forty percent of these are at the centre of government, i.e. within a body that provides direct support and advice to the Head of Government and the Council of Ministers, such as Prime Minister's Offices, Cabinet Secretaries, or Secretaries-General of the Government. Bodies at this location are ideally placed to foster a whole-of-government approach to regulatory policy and ensure effective co-ordination.

Figure 1.5. A large majority of ROBs across all EU Member States (in % of the total) are located within government

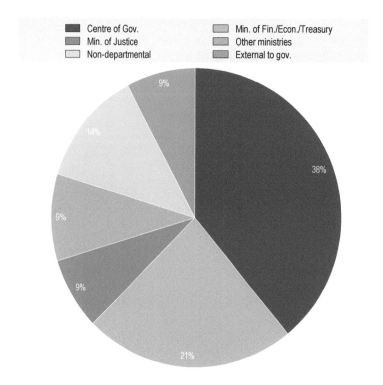

Note: Data is based on 27 EU Member States.
Source: Indicators of Regulatory Policy and Governance (iREG) Survey 2021.

A strong legal anchoring and a stable mandate are important for ROBs' influence and autonomy. In line with findings for OECD members, the mandates of the majority of ROBs in EU Member States are established in either law or statutory requirement or, alternatively, in a presidential or cabinet directive. Twenty two Member States also indicated having a ROB in charge of RIA scrutiny whose mandate is established in a legally binding document. Since the beginning of 2018, several ROBs had their mandate renewed or made permanent. Among OECD members, the latter include **Denmark**'s Government Economic Committee, the two bodies within **Greece**'s Secretariat General of Legal and Parliamentary Affairs, **Latvia**'s State Chancellery, **Portugal**'s Technical Unit for Legislative Impact Assessment, and **Spain**'s Regulatory Coordination and Quality Office. In addition, **Bulgaria**, **Croatia**, **Cyprus**, **Malta** and

Romania have at least one ROB each whose mandate is permanent. In a number of EU Member States, ROBs have also assumed new responsibilities, such as new functions or additional areas for scrutiny. This may signal these governments' willingness to embed oversight further in the wider regulatory policy environment.

An uneven coverage of core regulatory oversight functions in EU Member States

When considering core regulatory oversight functions in EU Member States, there is a contrast between, on the one hand, well-covered functions such as RIA quality control and guidance on regulatory management tools and, on the other hand, equally relevant yet less widespread functions, such as quality control of *ex post* evaluations. In addition, EU Member States have institutional arrangements in place to oversee other elements of regulatory policy that are not covered systematically by the OECD Indicators of Regulatory Policy and Governance, such as the transposition of EU law (OECD, 2019[2]).

Figure 1.6 presents the percentage of ROBs in various locations that are tasked with each core oversight function across all EU Member States. ROBs at the centre of government are entrusted with a relatively broad range of functions, and they are typically tasked with co-ordination-related functions as well as the provision of guidance on regulatory management tools. ROBs at Ministries of Economy, Finance or Treasury tend to focus on quality control of regulatory management tools (chiefly RIA) and guidance provision. ROBs located at Justice Ministries focus on guidance, legal quality review and support to the quality control of RIA. Non-departmental bodies, in turn, have a clear focus on RIA quality control as well as on evaluating regulatory policy. In most cases, these are arm's length bodies, which are not subject to the direction on individual decisions by the executive government but may be supported by government officials (OECD, 2018[32]). ROBs external to government (within Parliament or the Judiciary) have a similar focus. For additional insights on oversight by parliamentary bodies, see Box 1.5 later in this section.

Figure 1.6. ROBs at the centre of government tend to perform a broad range of oversight functions and are by far the preferred choice for co-ordination on regulatory policy

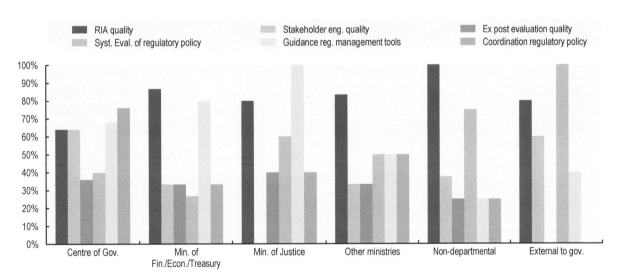

Note: Data is based on 27 EU Member States. Figures refer to the share (in %) of ROBs in a given location performing each core function (across all EU Member States).
Source: Indicators of Regulatory Policy and Governance (iREG) Survey 2021.

Oversight of regulatory management tools: RIA-only is not enough

Out of the four dimensions covered by the OECD composite indicators, *oversight and quality control* of regulatory management tools, which accounts for the role and attributions of ROBs as well as for publicly available evaluations, is the least developed (see Figure 1.7). Over the 2017-2020 period, this dimension has shown the lowest scores in each composite indicator, which highlights the need for stepping up efforts in this area. Particularly in the case of *ex post* evaluations, quality control is not progressing fast enough to ensure that this regulatory management tool is used appropriately and systematically. The significantly lower *oversight and quality control* score for *ex post* evaluations is also related to the latter's low uptake (as shown also by the *systematic adoption* score). Moreover, Figure 1.8 shows that relatively few EU Member States have an oversight body in charge of systematically reviewing the quality of either *ex post* evaluations or stakeholder consultation processes.

Figure 1.7. As a general rule, *oversight and quality control* of regulatory management tools remains weak in EU Member States

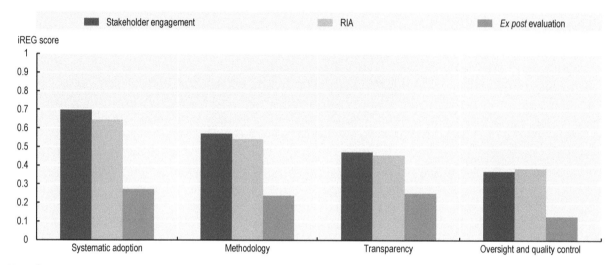

Note: Scores represent the average of primary laws and subordinate regulations. The maximum score per dimension for each regulatory management tool is one. Data is based on 27 EU Member States.
Source: Indicators of Regulatory Policy and Governance (iREG) Survey 2021.

Figure 1.8. Few EU Member States have set up institutions for the quality control of all regulatory management tools

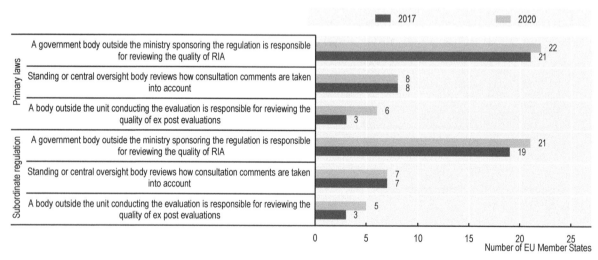

Note: Data is based on 27 EU Member States.
Source: Indicators of Regulatory Policy and Governance (iREG) Surveys 2017 and 2021.

Oversight of ex post *evaluations: still lagging behind*

Even though they are crucial for regulatory quality and despite recent improvements (see Chapter 4 for further information), systematic oversight of *ex post* evaluations continues to be the exception rather than the rule in EU Member States; even more so when considering Member States with a body responsible for reviewing the quality of *ex post* evaluations of packages of legislation (only **Austria**, **Italy** and the **Netherlands**) as well as *ad hoc* reviews of the regulatory stock, such as administrative burden or in-depth reviews (only the **Netherlands** does). Strengthening oversight in these areas is essential to foster a more holistic approach to regulatory analysis.

In the few EU Member States where oversight of *ex post* evaluations does happen, ROBs (generally located at the centre of government) provide feedback or advice during the preparation of *ex post* evaluations and/or issue formal opinions on their quality. These opinions are seldom published (see Figure 1.9).

Figure 1.9. Quality control of *ex post* **evaluation is still the exception rather than the rule in EU Member States**

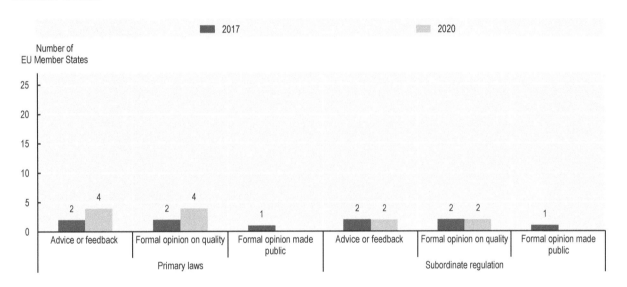

Note: Data is based on 27 EU Member States.
Source: Indicators of Regulatory Policy and Governance (iREG) Surveys 2017 and 2021.

Some EU Member States have however taken steps in recent years to strengthen oversight of *ex post* evaluations of legislation. One of them is **Germany**, which in November 2019 introduced a requirement for independent quality assurance of all *ex post* evaluations of legislative proposals exceeding EUR 5 million in annual compliance costs. In the same vein, in 2020 **Lithuania** institutionalised the *ex post* assessment of regulations and designated the Ministry of Justice as dedicated function for *ex post* evaluation co-ordination.

Oversight of stakeholder consultation

Although nearly two-thirds of EU Member states have formal requirements to consider consultation comments when developing laws and regulations, fewer than one third have a standing or central oversight body whose mandate consists of reviewing how consultation comments are taken into account for rule making. This proportion applies to both primary laws[6] and subordinate regulation.[7] ROBs with this function tend to carry it out together with RIA scrutiny. They are usually at the centre of government although bodies external to government and non-departmental bodies may also be involved. As shown in Figure 1.10, a minority of EU Member States also resort to judicial reviews to hold regulators accountable in this regard. For both approaches, uptake has not progressed compared with 2017.

Figure 1.10. About two thirds of EU Member States do not have an oversight body in charge of reviewing how consultation comments are taken into account for rule making

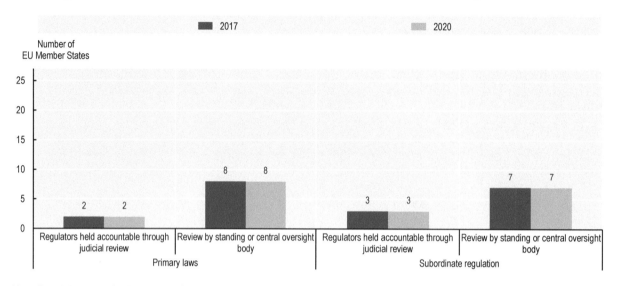

Note: Data is based on 27 EU Member States.
Source: Indicators of Regulatory Policy and Governance (iREG) Surveys 2017 and 2021.

RIA oversight

RIA scrutiny remains the main area of focus of most regulatory oversight systems in the EU. As of end 2020, about 80% of Member States declared to have a body outside the ministry sponsoring the regulation that is responsible for reviewing RIA quality: 21 and 22 for primary laws and subordinate regulation respectively. Most ROBs tasked with RIA quality control are located within government and often share this function with non-departmental bodies.

The ROBs in charge of RIA scrutiny have some sort of gatekeeping function (i.e. they can return a RIA for revision if it deems it inadequate) in 13 and 10 EU Member States for primary laws and subordinate regulations, respectively. This represents an increase compared with 2017 (Figure 1.11). For example, the *Conseil d'État* in **France** has the power to disjoint a legislative provision or even to refuse to give an opinion on a law if the RIA is inadequate. ROB's decision to return a RIA can however be overturned through an active decision (e.g. from cabinet, a minister or a high-ranking official) in nearly all EU Member States. Only **Croatia** reported that, for primary laws, it cannot be overturned (as the competent oversight body can request to postpone the law). In certain cases, however, RIA quality control takes place in more consensus-oriented settings whereby ROB's review suggestions or recommendations are generally adhered to even if legislative proposals cannot be formally prevented from moving forward. For example, the networking efforts of **Portugal**'s Technical Unit for Legislative Impact Assessment within the administration help improve RIAs analytical quality even in the absence of formal sanctions. In **Denmark**, co-operation and consensus plays an important role in the dynamic between the ministries and regulatory oversight bodies, even if the Danish Business Authority's Better Regulation Unit can stop a proposal from being published for consultation. In addition, a recent review concluded that ministries are making significant and increasingly frequent changes to the draft legislative proposal on the basis of the recommendations from the country's Secretariat for digital-ready legislation (Agency for Digitisation, 2021[33]).

Figure 1.11. The share of EU Member States whose ROBs in charge of RIA scrutiny can act as "gatekeepers" has slightly increased compared to 2017

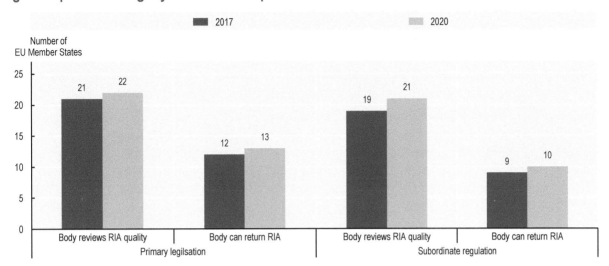

Note: Data is based on 27 EU Member States.
Source: Indicators of Regulatory Policy and Governance (iREG) Surveys 2017 and 2021.

As will be discussed in Chapter 3, there may be cases where exceptions to conducting RIAs can be a proportionate response to significance of a regulatory policy. Excepting a legislative proposal from RIA requirements should however only be undertaken in cases of genuine unforeseen emergencies or when a policy has truly negligible impacts. RIA systems will be ineffective if legislative proposals are arbitrarily exempted from *ex ante* impact assessment or if RIA obligations can be easily avoided. Therefore, decisions to waive RIA must be exceptional, transparent and subject to oversight. A majority of EU Member States contemplate some sort of exemption to RIA. Only **Austria**, **Estonia**, **Finland**, **Germany**, **Lithuania** and **Spain** report that RIA is conducted without exception. In half of them, this applies to both primary legislation and subordinate regulation. However, only approximately one-third of EU Member States have a body responsible for reviewing the decision made by officials about whether a RIA is required – and few of these bodies publish their conclusions in that respect (see Figure 1.12). Exceptions to RIA in the context of proportionate regulatory analysis across EU Member States are discussed in more depth in Chapter 3.

Figure 1.12. There is still limited scrutiny of decisions not to conduct RIA, and those decisions are seldom published

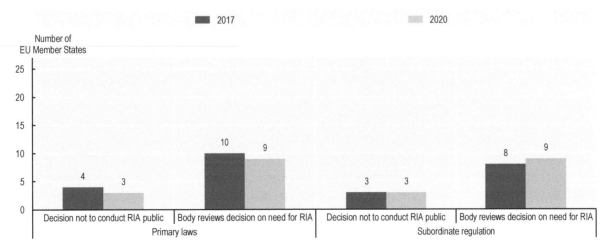

Note: Data is based on 27 EU Member States.
Source: Indicators of Regulatory Policy and Governance (iREG) Surveys 2017 and 2021.

Regulatory oversight by parliaments in EU Member States

Although Parliaments have a crucial role to play in regulatory oversight and Better Regulation more generally (OECD, 2015[34]), their involvement in this respect remains limited. Based on the definition applied in this report, only one ROB located in parliament has been included in the present analysis: **Germany**'s Parliamentary Advisory Council for Sustainable development. Although not considered for analytical purposes, four and six EU Member States also reported having a parliamentary committee in charge of reviewing the quality of individual RIAs and overall RIA systems respectively.

Furthermore, since data for this report focuses and relies primarily on reporting by government entities, bodies outside the executive branch of government may be underrepresented as a result. A comprehensive study by the European Parliamentary Research Service (EPRS) provides complementary insights on the role of national parliaments of all 27 European Union Member States and 11 further Council of Europe countries with respect to RIA and *ex post* evaluation, including regarding oversight. Box 1.5 summarises some of its key findings.

Box 1.5. Better Regulation practices in national parliaments from the EU and Council of Europe countries: an analysis by the EPRS

According to the EPRS' study, there is a wide diversity of settings and approaches across parliamentary bodies engaging in regulatory oversight and regulatory policy more generally. These functions can be carried out either *ad hoc* (e.g. via parliamentary questions, consideration at committee level or resolutions) or systematically (with the help of dedicated tools, methods and capacities). Dedicated regulatory policy structures may be located at the political or administrative level, or include a combination of both.

Depending on the specific setting, parliaments' better regulation engagement may involve the scrutiny of RIAs and *ex post* evaluations prepared by the executive and/or the use of regulatory management tools. Concerning RIA, certain parliaments focus on *scrutiny* of formal and procedural aspects, notably by verifying that the regulatory proposal is accompanied by a complete RIA (e.g. the Italian Senate and the Slovenian Parliament). Legal quality scrutiny is also commonplace. In other cases, parliamentary bodies conduct more substantial scrutiny, such as in-depth checks on RIA quality. The study indicates that this is the case for the EPRS (for nearly all RIAs), as well as the Parliaments in France and Norway (which has power to return a draft legal proposal if the underpinning RIA is deemed inadequate and has used this power in the past). Certain parliaments, in turn, focus on specific elements, such as budget implications (e.g. Canada, Austria, Portugal and Sweden). In addition, some parliaments review the entire regulatory framework or carry out audits, sometimes in co-operation with national audit institutions, as is the case in the UK. Only a few legislatures have embedded RIA in their *legislative function* and assess the impact of either draft legislation initiated by parliament (e.g. Poland) or of selected legislative amendments tabled at the committee stage (e.g. Estonia and the European Parliament).

As a complement to scrutiny, parliamentary bodies can play a valuable information-brokering role by providing parliamentary committees with key elements for informed decision-making in a suitable format, such as synthetic documents summarising the results of scrutiny work. Again, a good example is the EPRS, which, compared to the RSB (the European Commission's scrutiny body), steps in at a later stage in the law-making process by verifying, among other things, coherence and due consideration of RSB remarks. It also provides committees with a condensed assessment of the content and quality of the European Commission's impact assessments, and can provide further impact assessment work upon request by committees.

Turning to the other end of the policy cycle, a number of parliaments, including the European Parliament, make systematic use of *ex post* evaluation as an oversight tool. The scope and depth of parliaments' engagement may vary substantially, from a purely legalistic approach to fully-fledged evaluations. For instance, the Canadian Parliament has a long heritage of formal post-enactment scrutiny, its scope being limited to a legal conformity check on delegated regulations. In comparison, policy evaluation has reached a particularly high degree of institutionalisation in the parliaments of France, Sweden and Switzerland, whose evaluation function is constitutionally mandated. According to the EPRS study, the Swiss Parliament's evaluation system stands out with its wide-reaching rights to obtain information from the executive and related follow-up requirements.

Source: European Parliamentary Research Service (2020[13]), Better Regulation practices in national parliaments, http://dx.doi.org/10.2861/06573 and (2021 MRP Conference, forthcoming), https://www.oecd.org/gov/regulatory-policy/Measuring-Regulatory-Performance-events.htm.

ROBs can help governments to maximise the benefits from regulatory reform by improving monitoring and evaluation

Principle 6 of the *Recommendation* (OECD, 2012[3]) encourages members to monitor and assess regulatory policy reform efforts, including the practical functioning of tools such as RIA, stakeholder engagement and reviews of existing regulations. Despite some progress in recent years, the performance assessment of regulatory management tools in the EU is however not yet fully transparent or systematic.

In this context, ROBs can enhance governments' ability to reap the benefits from regulatory reform and target limited public resources by improving how the performance of regulatory management tools, and regulatory policy more broadly, is assessed and communicated upon. Doing so notably involves promoting the adoption of the OECD's *Framework for Regulatory Policy Evaluation* (OECD, 2014[35]) and ensuring that measurement and assessment efforts encompass all relevant domains of regulatory reform instead of focusing exclusively on certain aspects such as the cost of complying with administrative obligations (Radaelli, 2012[36]). Certain ROBs may also contribute to this goal by engaging in evaluative work in their own right.

As shown in Figure 1.13, only a minority of EU Member States publish online reports on the performance of their *ex post* evaluation system or stakeholder consultation practices on draft regulations – mostly on an *ad hoc* basis. No EU Member State reported evaluating consultation with foreign stakeholders, although the European Union does so. In addition, only **Austria** reported to have assessed the effectiveness of *ex post* evaluations in improving the regulatory stock in the past five years and published the results. Efforts by the EU's Regulatory Scrutiny Board to draw forward-looking conclusions from its scrutiny of *ex post* evaluations illustrate, however, the benefits of conducting this kind of assessment on a systematic basis. Such benefits include identifying recurrent design flaws to improve methodological approaches and helping to prevent potential biases and conflicts of interest (Regulatory Scrutiny Board, 2019[37]).

Reporting on the performance of RIA systems is comparatively more widespread. For example, as of end 2020, 12 EU Member States had assessed the effectiveness of RIA in leading to modifications of regulatory proposals (compared to 10 in 2017). However, despite RIA's prominence in most Member State's regulatory policy frameworks, approximately 40% of them still fail to publish reports on the performance of their RIA system, and only seven do so annually.

A similar picture emerges when considering how indicators are used to monitor the appropriate functioning of regulatory management tools. Indicators on the percentage of RIAs compliant with formal requirements or guidelines are available in a few EU Member States: **Bulgaria**, **Czech Republic**, **Hungary**, **Italy**, **Poland**, **Portugal**, **Slovenia**, **Slovak Republic** and **Sweden**. Five Member States reported availability of indicators on the percentage of compliant stakeholder consultations: **Bulgaria**, **Italy**, **Latvia**, **Lithuania** and **Slovenia**, and none reported compiling equivalent indicators for *ex post* evaluations (although such indicators are available at the EU level). Only the **Netherlands** reported compiling (internally available) indicators based on survey results regarding the usefulness or quality of stakeholder consultations.

Figure 1.13. Efforts to assess and report on the performance of regulatory management tools can contribute decisively to regulatory reform and quality, but they remain limited and unsystematic

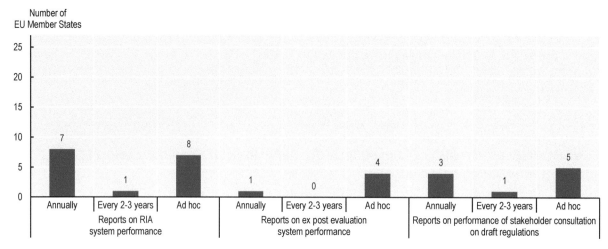

Note: Data is based on 27 EU Member States.
Source: Indicators of Regulatory Policy and Governance (iREG) Survey 2021.

Better performance assessment is essential to strengthen regulatory oversight

Ensuring the effectiveness and continuous relevance of regulatory oversight processes and institutions involves assessing their performance on a regular basis, including, to the extent possible, in terms of regulatory improvement. A majority of EU Member States say they publish reports on the effectiveness of at least one ROB responsible for quality control of regulatory management tools; e.g. containing information on its activities, the fulfilment of its mission, or results of perception surveys on its performance and value added. However, as is the case across OECD members, many ROBs' reporting activity in EU Member States still focuses relatively little on effectiveness and outcomes and prioritises implementation (e.g. number of items scrutinised, turnaround times) and compliance with formal requirements (usually easier to track and measure) instead.

Despite the overall need for improvement, there are valuable examples in the EU and beyond of efforts to monitor and evaluate ROBs' work in greater depth, including through the involvement of external evaluators (see Box 1.6). In addition, new tools and technologies can improve our understanding of ROBs' performance and its determinants. For instance, a recent study uses machine learning to identify major change requests in RSB opinions and text similarity measures to identify changes between draft and final versions of impact assessment reports (Senninger and Blom-Hansen, 2021[38]). In the same vein, **Australia**'s Office for Best Practice Regulation are developing an IT system for RIA that they will notably use to understand what kind of feedback is more effective at each stage of the policy cycle and target their efforts accordingly.

Box 1.6. Selected examples of monitoring and evaluation of ROB's work

In May 2021, **Denmark** published an evaluation of the effort to make legislation digital-ready. This evaluation examines whether regulatory reform efforts deployed in this area have had the desired effect. It includes an assessment of the value added through co-operation with the Secretariat for Digital-Ready legislation, an oversight body set up in 2018 and in charge of screening draft legislation (with a focus on public implementation impacts), and providing guidance and support to ministries.

In its 2019 annual report, **Norway**'s Better Regulation Council published performance indicators seeking to capture, among other aspects, the effect of the Council's statements in which it had deemed RIAs not to be fit for purpose. This report also included and assessment of the general trends and developments regarding RIAs within the Council's remit and any recurring problems, as well as an overview of the Council's guidance and information activities to foster effective regulations. In 2021, the Council underwent an external evaluation concluding that it contributes to improving the quality of regulatory impact assessments for legislative proposals and proposing a number of recommendations.

Sweden's Better Regulation Council surveys, on an ad-hoc basis and with varying scopes, ministries' and government agencies' perception of its opinions and their impacts and publishes results in its annual reports. **The Netherlands'** Advisory Board on Regulatory Burden (ATR) also gathers feedback from mechanisms, e.g. on the fast-track procedure it introduced in 2019.

The **European Commission**'s Regulatory Scrutiny Board publishes key performance indicators including on quality improvements subsequent to interactions with European Commission services in its oversight capacity. In Korea, white papers for Regulatory Reform are published on an annual basis including a regulatory reform satisfaction index. **Mexico**'s CONAMER has, in turn, developed an "indicators for results" approach encompassing indicators to assess its contribution to reducing regulatory burden.

Source: Comisión Nacional de Mejora Regulatoria (2019[39]), Informe de avances en la implementación de la Estrategia Nacional de Mejora Regulatoria y de la Comisión, https://www.gob.mx/conamer/documentos/informe-de-avances-de-en-la-implementacion-de-la-estrategia-nacional-de-mejora-regulatoria-y-de-la-comision-nacional-de-mejora-regulatoria; Agency for Digitisation (2021[33]), Evaluation of the effort to make legislation digital-ready, https://en.digst.dk/media/24344/evaluation-of-the-effort-to-make-legislation-digital-ready-accessible-version.pdf; ATR (2019[40]), Dutch Advisory Board on Regulatory Burden. Annual report 2019, https://www.atr-regeldruk.nl/wp-content/uploads/2020/06/2019-ATR-annual-report.pdf (accessed on 5 March 2021); and OECD (2018[32]), Case Studies of RegWatchEurope regulatory oversight bodies and of the European Union Regulatory Scrutiny Board, https://www.oecd.org/gov/regulatory-policy/regulatory-oversight-bodies-2018.htm.

Looking ahead: regulatory oversight for the 21st Century

The *OECD Recommendation of the Council for Agile Regulatory Governance to Harness Innovation* (2021[30]) and its accompanying Practical Guidance highlight the importance of ensuring that the mandate, capacity and functioning of oversight bodies allow them to effectively support agile and forward-looking regulatory policy and governance. This notably involves embedding anticipatory approaches into ROB's working methods and mandate. The EU has already shown the way by expanding the mandate of its Regulatory Scrutiny Board to include foresight (European Commission, 2020[41]).

Moreover, the *Recommendation* (2021[30]) stresses that addressing emerging regulatory challenges notably requires using regulatory management tools in a more dynamic, adaptive and iterative manner. ROBs in EU Member States can be instrumental in that context by fostering systematic linkages and complementarities between these tools, so that they can meaningfully inform the adaptation of regulatory and policy approaches. Moreover, they can actively ensure that regulatory impacts on innovation are duly taken into account throughout the policy cycle. For example, the Danish Business Authority is in charge of verifying that new regulation does not impose unnecessary burdens on businesses' ability to innovate. The associated Danish Business Regulation Forum performs a similar function with regard to existing regulations.

It will likewise be important to define ROBs' roles and attributions, as well as additional capacity and skills needed, with regard to new regulatory approaches for dealing with innovation, such as regulatory exemptions and experiments (e.g. sandboxes) and soft law instruments (e.g. self-regulation). Regulatory exemptions, for example, are likely to require careful oversight to ensure a reliable assessment of their results and prevent regulatory capture. It may also be useful to explore options to enable closer interaction between ROBs and stakeholders in situations where this can substantially improve regulatory quality (e.g. if access to external knowledge and expertise is required for meaningful scrutiny).

A number of ROBs' mandates already reflect some of these emerging priorities; e.g. eight EU Member States reported having a body in charge of overseeing regulatory quality during a crisis (emergency rule making), and ten have one focusing on innovation-friendly regulation, e.g. by helping ministries and regulators take into account the impacts of regulation on innovation. It should be borne in mind that appropriate execution of regulatory oversight functions, *old* and *new*, will require appropriate capacity and resourcing, especially in light of the increased number and complexity of requests received by ROBs, increased time pressure and additional needs in terms of analytical depth.

Notes

[1] "Stakeholder engagement" refers to the process by which the government informs all interested parties of proposed changes in regulation and receives feedback (OECD, 2018, p. 250[29]).

[2] The term "regulatory impact assessment (RIA)" is defined as a systematic process of identification and quantification of benefits and costs likely to flow from regulatory or non-regulatory options for a policy under consideration. A RIA may be based on benefit-cost analysis, cost-effectiveness analysis, business impact analysis etc. Regulatory impact assessment is also routinely referred to as regulatory impact analysis, sometimes interchangeably (OECD, 2018, p. 250[29]).

[3] "*Ex post* evaluation" refers to the process of assessing the effectiveness of policies and regulations once they are in force. It can be the final stage when new policies or regulations have been introduced and it is intended to know the extent of which they met the goals they served for. It can also be the initial point to understand a particular situation as a result of a policy or regulation in place, providing elements to discuss the shortcomings and advantages of its existence. *Ex post* evaluation should not be confused with monitoring, which refers to the continuous assessment of implementation in relation to an agreed schedule (OECD, 2018, p. 248[29]).

[4] On 25 January 2022 the OECD Council decided to open accession discussions with Argentina, Brazil, Bulgaria, Croatia, Peru and Romania.

[5] While these units are tasked with the oversight of better regulation activities in their own administration and they play a co-ordinating role, they are not responsible for overseeing the quality of the overall

regulatory governance cycle (or any parts thereof) or for co-ordination on regulatory policy from a whole-of-government perspective. They are thus not considered as ROBs.

[6] Primary laws are defined as "regulations which must be approved by the parliament or congress". This category further distinguishes between primary laws initiated by parliament and those initiated by the executive.

[7] Subordinate regulations are defined as "regulations that can be approved by the head of government, by an individual minister or by the cabinet – that is, by an authority other than the parliament/congress". Examples include regulations, rules, orders, decrees, etc. Please note that many subordinate regulations are subject to disallowance by the parliament/congress.

References

Agency for Digitisation (2021), *Evaluation of the effort to make legislation digital-ready*, https://en.digst.dk/media/24344/evaluation-of-the-effort-to-make-legislation-digital-ready-accessible-version.pdf. [33]

ATR (2019), *Dutch Advisory Board on Regulatory Burden. Annual report 2019*, https://www.atr-regeldruk.nl/wp-content/uploads/2020/06/2019-ATR-annual-report.pdf. [40]

Bradford, A. (2020), *The Brussels Effect: How the European Union Rules the World*, Oxford University Press, https://doi.org/10.1093/oso/9780190088583.001.0001. [23]

Business Europe (2018), *Strategy Paper - Transparency of trilogues*, https://www.businesseurope.eu/sites/buseur/files/media/position_papers/internal_market/2018-07-17_transparency_of_trilogues_-_strategy_paper.pdf. [15]

Comisión Nacional de Mejora Regulatoria (2019), *Informe de avances en la implementación de la Estrategia Nacional de Mejora Regulatoria y de la Comisión*, https://www.gob.mx/conamer/documentos/informe-de-avances-de-en-la-implementacion-de-la-estrategia-nac. [39]

EUR-Lex (2022), *Glossary of summaries - The European Union's External Action*, https://eur-lex.europa.eu/summary/glossary/external_responsibilities.html. [22]

EUR-Lex (2021), *Legal acts – statistics*, https://eur-lex.europa.eu/statistics/legislative-acts-statistics.html. [19]

European Commission (2021), *Better Regulation Guidelines*, https://ec.europa.eu/info/sites/default/files/swd2021_305_en.pdf. [8]

European Commission (2021), *Better Regulation Toolbox*, https://ec.europa.eu/info/sites/default/files/br_toolbox-nov_2021_en_0.pdf. [9]

European Commission (2021), *Better Regulation: Joining forces to make better laws*, https://ec.europa.eu/info/sites/default/files/better_regulation_joining_forces_to_make_better_laws_en_0.pdf. [7]

European Commission (2021), *Webpage of the European Commission*, [18]
https://ec.europa.eu/info/law/law-making-process/types-eu-law_en (accessed on
6 December 2021).

European Commission (2020), *Strategic foresight*, https://ec.europa.eu/info/strategy/priorities- [41]
2019-2024/new-push-european-democracy/strategic-foresight_en (accessed on
15 December 2020).

European Commission (2005), *Better Regulation for Growth and Jobs in the European Union*, [6]
https://eur-lex.europa.eu/legal-content/en/txt/pdf/?uri=celex:52005dc0097&from=en.

European Commission (2002), *European governance - A white paper*, https://eur- [5]
lex.europa.eu/legal-content/en/txt/?uri=celex:52001dc0428.

European Court of Auditors (2020), *Law-making in the European Union after almost 20 years of* [11]
Better Regulation, https://www.eca.europa.eu/en/Pages/DocItem.aspx?did=54353.

European Parliamentary Research Service (2021), *Impact Assessment and European Added* [12]
Value, https://www.europarl.europa.eu/eprs/eprs-impact-assessment-european-added-value-
presentation.pdf.

European Parliamentary Research Service (2020), *Better Regulation practices in national* [13]
parliaments, https://doi.org/10.2861/06573.

European Union (2016), *Interinstitutional Agreement of 13 April 2016 on Better Law Making*, [10]
https://eur-lex.europa.eu/legal-content/en/txt/pdf/?uri=celex:32016q0512(01)&from=en.

Goldberg, E. (2018), *'Better Regulation': European Union Style*, [4]
https://www.hks.harvard.edu/centers/mrcbg/publications/awp/awp98.

OECD (2021), *Compendium of International Organisations' Practices: Working Towards More* [24]
Effective International Instruments, OECD Publishing, Paris,
https://doi.org/10.1787/846a5fa0-en.

OECD (2021), *International Regulatory Co-operation*, OECD Best Practice Principles for [16]
Regulatory Policy, OECD Publishing, Paris, https://doi.org/10.1787/5b28b589-en.

OECD (2021), *OECD Regulatory Policy Outlook 2021*, OECD Publishing, Paris, [1]
https://doi.org/10.1787/38b0fdb1-en.

OECD (2021), *Recommendation of the Council for Agile Regulatory Governance to Harness* [30]
Innovation, OECD Publishing, https://legalinstruments.oecd.org/en/instruments/OECD-
LEGAL-0464.

OECD (2020), *International organisations in the context of COVID-19: adapting rulemaking for* [27]
timely, evidence-based and effective international solutions in a global crisis Summary Note
of COVID-19 Webinars of the Partnership of International Organisations for Effective
International Rule-making, https://www.oecd.org/gov/regulatory-policy/international-
organisations-in-the-context-of-covid-19.pdf (accessed on 1 June 2021).

OECD (2019), *Better Regulation Practices across the European Union*, OECD Publishing, Paris, [2]
https://doi.org/10.1787/9789264311732-en.

OECD (2018), *Case Studies of RegWatchEurope regulatory oversight bodies and of the European Union Regulatory Scrutiny Board*, https://www.oecd.org/gov/regulatory-policy/regulatory-oversight-bodies-2018.htm.
[32]

OECD (2018), *OECD Regulatory Policy Outlook 2018*, OECD Publishing, https://doi.org/10.1787/9789264303072-e.
[29]

OECD (2016), *International Regulatory Co-operation: The Role of International Organisations in Fostering Better Rules of Globalisation*, OECD Publishing, Paris, https://doi.org/10.1787/9789264244047-en.
[20]

OECD (2015), *OECD Regulatory Policy Outlook 2015*, OECD Publishing, Paris, https://doi.org/10.1787/9789264238770-en.
[34]

OECD (2014), *OECD Framework for Regulatory Policy Evaluation*, OECD Publishing, Paris, https://doi.org/10.1787/9789264214453-en.
[35]

OECD (2013), *International Regulatory Co-operation: Case Studies, Vol. 2: Canada-US Co-operation, EU Energy Regulation, Risk Assessment and Banking Supervision*, OECD Publishing, Paris, https://doi.org/10.1787/9789264200500-en.
[21]

OECD (2013), *International Regulatory Co-operation: Addressing Global Challenges*, OECD Publishing, Paris, https://doi.org/10.1787/9789264200463-en.
[17]

OECD (2012), *Recommendation of the Council on Regulatory Policy and Governance*, OECD Publishing, Paris, https://doi.org/10.1787/9789264209022-en.
[3]

OECD (2010), *Regulatory Policy and the Road to Sustainable Growth Regulatory Policy and the Road to Sustainable Growth*, OECD Publishing, Paris, https://www.oecd.org/regreform/policyconference/46270065.pdf (accessed on 26 November 2021).
[25]

OECD (n.d.), *OECD Best Practice Principles for Regulatory Policy*, OECD Publishing, Paris, https://doi.org/10.1787/23116013.
[28]

Radaelli, C. (2012), *Radaelli, Claudio and Oliver Fritsch (2012), "Measuring Regulatory Performance – Evaluating Regulatory Management Tools and*, http://www.oecd.org/gov/regulatory-policy/2_Radaelli%20web.pdf (accessed on 1 March 2021).
[36]

Regulatory Scrutiny Board (2019), *Annual Report 2019*, https://ec.europa.eu/info/sites/info/files/rsb_report_2019_en.pdf (accessed on 5 March 2021).
[37]

Renda, A., R. Castro and G. Hernandez (forthcoming), *Defining and Contextualising Regulatory oversight and Co-ordination*, Working Paper No. 17, OECD, Paris.
[31]

Russack, S. and S. Blockmans (2020), *How is EU cooperation on the Covid-19 crisis perceived in member states?*, CEPS, https://www.ceps.eu/ceps-publications/how-is-eu-cooperation-on-the-covid-19-crisis-perceived-in-member-states/ (accessed on 26 November 2021).
[26]

Senninger, R. and J. Blom-Hansen (2021), "Meet the critics: Analyzing the EU Commission's Regulatory Scrutiny Board through quantitative text analysis", *Regulation & Governance*, Vol. 15, pp. 1436–1453, https://doi.org/10.1111/rego.12312.
[38]

Simonelli, F. and N. Iacob (2021), "Can We Better the European Union Better Regulation Agenda?", *European Journal of Risk Regulation*, Vol. 12, pp. 849-860, https://doi.org/10.1017/err.2021.40.

[14]

2 Stakeholder engagement across the European Union

It is important for policy makers to engage and discuss with those affected by regulations. This not only improves the quality of regulations, it also promotes transparency and strengthens both trust in the government and compliance with any resultant rule. Using the results of the OECD 2021 Indicators of Regulatory Policy and Governance, this chapter reviews stakeholder engagement practices in all 27 EU Member States and in the European Union. It assesses the timing and content of stakeholder engagement at various stages of policy development as well as how governments use input received from interested parties. In addition, it further discusses the use of stakeholder engagement when EU Member States negotiate or adopt regulatory proposals of the European Commission.

Key messages

- Only a few EU Member States and the European Commission inform stakeholders in advance of upcoming consultations. EU Member States could benefit from adopting this practice more widely to boost transparency and participation in policy development.

- Policy makers in EU Member States engage with stakeholders systematically at the regulatory draft stage. Opportunities exist for Member States to further engage with stakeholders when discussing policy problems and exploring potential solutions.

- Consultations are generally open and available to the public in most EU Member States. Policy makers most commonly invite stakeholders to participate online. Progressively more EU Member States are systematically listing their consultations on respective single websites.

- EU Member States tend to initially engage with selected stakeholders that are likely to be particularly affected by the problem or that have some type of expertise. Member States use online platforms more systematically to consult on regulatory drafts.

- Most EU Member States have set minimum consultations periods. A few EU Member States have a time interval that policy makers must use as a guide for specific consultations. A minority do not have a fixed time or an interval, but require policy makers to be proportionate when deciding the time available for consultations.

- Views of participants are publicly available online in most EU Member States. Around two-thirds of EU Member States have requirements to make use of comments when developing final regulatory proposals. That said, in practice it is often unclear to stakeholders how their comments have shaped proposals, and more can be done by EU Member States to respond to comments received.

- EU Member States are partly responsible for determining the outcomes of the European Commission's proposals by informing domestic stakeholders of ongoing Commission consultations. In addition, the facilitation role played by EU Member States to engage domestic stakeholders in ongoing European Commission consultations can improve resultant EU policies at both the negotiation and transposition stages. More research is needed to ascertain the extent to which Member States alert stakeholders beyond the "usual suspects" to ongoing consultations by the European Commission.

- Few EU Member States formally require stakeholder engagement to inform their negotiating position on the European Commission's policy proposals. However, when undertaken in practice they are generally open to the public. Some EU Member States use the results of the European Commission's consultation processes as input to inform their negotiating position. EU Member States would benefit from more systematically engaging with affected parties in the formulation of their negotiation position to better understand domestic impacts. This is especially the case for proposed EU regulations, for which the negotiation stage represents the final opportunity to shape such proposals.

- Nearly 90% of EU Member States have formal requirements to conduct stakeholder engagement when transposing EU directives into national law. EU Member States do not generally rely on the results of the European Commission's consultation during the transposition of EU directives. Member States can still benefit from the European Commission's consultation results, particularly where implementation issues were considered, and to potentially identify affected domestic stakeholders.

Introduction

Stakeholder engagement is a critical enabler of improved regulatory quality. Stakeholders can bring their own perspectives and learnt experiences to help shape solutions and to avoid costly mistakes. Stakeholders also possess a potential wealth of data on actual impacts incurred, thus providing governments with valuable information to help improve estimations of likely regulatory impacts. Aside from direct information, involving stakeholders helps to garner trust amongst the regulated community, create buy-in and support for new initiatives, and also to boost compliance with any resultant rules. In particular, when stakeholders feel that their views were considered, they received an explanation of what happened with their comments, and they feel treated with respect (Lind and Arndt, 2016[1]). Perfunctory consultation without any actual interest in the views of stakeholders because a decision has already been made, or failure to demonstrate that consultation comments have been considered may have the opposite effect.

Ensuring that stakeholders are adequately consulted has been formally recognised by the OECD. The *OECD 2012 Recommendation on Regulatory Policy and Governance* (OECD, 2012[2]) provides that member countries should "adhere to principles of open government, including transparency and participation in the regulatory process to ensure that regulation serves the public interest and is informed by the legitimate needs of those interested in and affected by regulation. This includes providing meaningful opportunities (including online) for the public to contribute to the process of preparing draft regulatory proposals and to the quality of the supporting analysis. Governments should ensure that regulations are comprehensible and clear and that parties can easily understand their rights and obligations" (OECD, 2012[2]).

This chapter analyses EU Member States' stakeholder engagement requirements and practices as reported in the indicators of Regulatory Policy and Governance (iREG) survey and its extension to all EU Member States. The first section presents an overview of the results and recent reforms based on the iREG survey. The second section focuses on the domestic requirements and practices of individual Member States and includes information pertaining to those of the European Union where relevant. In particular, it provides information about both the timing and content of stakeholder engagement, and how governments use input received. The final section presents information on stakeholder engagement as it relates to the legislative processes of the European Union. It looks at the extent to which individual EU Member States inform domestic stakeholders of European Commission regulatory proposals of interest. It also examines how EU Member States use the European Commission's stakeholder engagement processes to inform both their negotiating position and on the transposition of EU directives.

General trends in stakeholder engagement across the EU

EU Member States improved their stakeholder engagement practices with respect to primary laws to a greater extent than subordinate regulations. EU Member States are now more often conducting their consultations concerning primary laws over the internet for both early and late stage consultations, and more countries have developed guidance for their policy makers on how to engage stakeholders. Some EU Member States have also improved the transparency of their consultations for primary laws, as they now publish the decision to not conduct a consultation and the reasons as to the decision. There have been slight improvements on the oversight and quality control of stakeholder engagement for both primary laws and subordinate regulations, with more EU Member states having oversight bodies in charge of promoting and scrutinising consultations of stakeholder engagement.

Figure 2.1. Composite indicators: Stakeholder engagement in developing primary laws, 2021

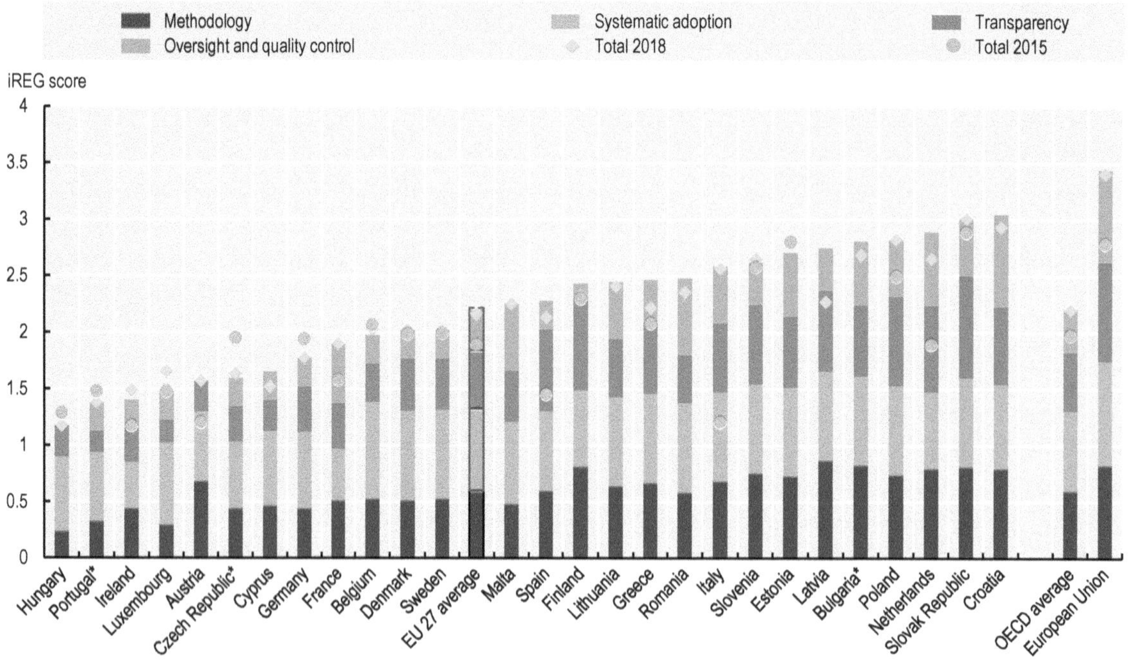

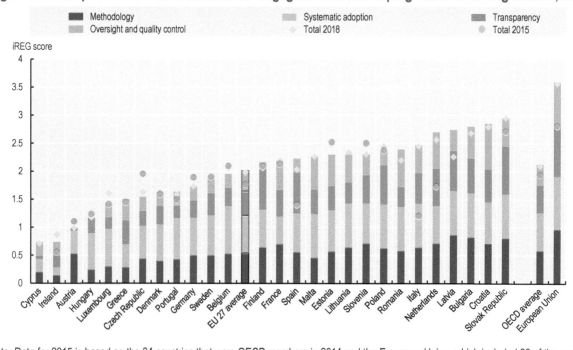

Note: Data for 2015 is based on the 34 countries that were OECD members in 2014 and the European Union, which included 20 of the current 27 EU Member States. The OECD average is based on the 38 member countries at the time of the survey. Data for 2018 and 2021 includes the remaining EU Member States of Latvia, Lithuania, Bulgaria, Croatia, Cyprus, Malta and Romania. The more regulatory practices as advocated in the *2012 Recommendation* a country has implemented, the higher its iREG score. * In the majority of EU Member States, most primary laws are initiated by the executive, except for Bulgaria, the Czech Republic and Portugal, where a higher share of primary laws are initiated by the legislature.
Source: Indicators of Regulatory Policy and Governance Surveys 2014, 2017 and 2021.

Figure 2.2. Composite indicators: Stakeholder engagement in developing subordinate regulations, 2021

Note: Data for 2015 is based on the 34 countries that were OECD members in 2014 and the European Union, which included 20 of the current 27 EU Member States. The OECD average is based on the 38 member countries at the time of the survey. Data for 2018 and 2021 includes the remaining EU Member States of Latvia, Lithuania, Bulgaria, Croatia, Cyprus, Malta and Romania. The more regulatory practices as advocated in the *2012 Recommendation* a country has implemented, the higher its iREG score.
Source: Indicators of Regulatory Policy and Governance Surveys 2014, 2017 and 2021.

Countries that made substantive changes since 2017 include **Greece**, **Latvia**, the **Netherlands** and **Spain**.

- **Greece** is now using its consultation portal more frequently to seek public comments on draft primary laws and it now publishes a list of laws to be prepared or modified in advance. It has also developed written guidance on how to conduct stakeholder engagement for primary laws.
- Public consultations in **Latvia** are now systematically conducted on draft legislation and stakeholders benefit from having a broader range of supporting material to help focus their input into policy proposals.
- **Netherlands** now offers written guidance to policy makers on how to conduct stakeholder engagement. In the past three years policy makers in the Netherlands have begun to carry meetings at an early-stage of policy development with SMEs.
- **Spain** now lists all ongoing consultations on its centralised online platform and allows citizens to engage both before regulatory development starts and at the draft regulation stage.

Stakeholder engagement for the development of domestic regulations

Policy makers in EU Member States engage and consult more systematically with stakeholders on draft regulatory proposals; and less frequently when discussing the policy problem and exploring alternative solutions

The *2012 Recommendation* (OECD, 2012[2]) calls for transparency and participation in the regulatory process to ensure that regulation serves the public interest and is informed by the legitimate needs of those interested in and affected by regulation. Some examples from EU Member States where stakeholder engagement improved the resulting policy are summarised in Box 2.1. Civil society, businesses, non-governmental organisations and the public sector can be affected by policy problems and by the solutions that policy makers find to those problems. It is therefore important that decision makers engage and consult with concerned parties that have expertise, information and interests to help deliver a regulatory or non-regulatory solution that is adequate to the policy issue at hand. Policy makers should engage stakeholders throughout the policy development process, including when they have identified the existence of a public policy problem and are considering various ways to solve it – which is referred to as early stage consultation; and when the decision to regulate has been made and a draft of the regulatory proposal already exists – which is referred to as late stage consultation.

Box 2.1. Selected EU Member States' examples where stakeholder engagement improved the resulting policy

Dialogue and early involvement of stakeholders facilitated the co-ordination of the approach chosen by **Bulgaria** to transpose the Directive on the reduction of the impact of certain plastic products on the environment into the national legal framework. A preliminary consensus on the basic approach and measures to transpose the Directive was reached, while the official procedures for public consultations served to refine concrete texts and provisions.

Croatia launched a consultation on the initiative to ban the use of pyrotechnics (Explosives Substances Act and the Production and Trafficking of Weapons) in 2020. The consultation was conducted through the e-Consultation portal with 788 comments received. Following the comments received and with the aim of protecting human life, the government adopted the Explosives Substances Act with provisions prohibiting the sale, possession and use of firecrackers and weapons to citizens for personal use.

The "Citizens' Climate Convention" (*Convention citoyenne pour le climat*) was held in **France** between 2019 and 2020. A panel of 150 citizens representing the diversity of French society was chosen at random. Following hearings of experts and summaries of the work of researchers, international bodies and civil society organisations, the panel formulated normative proposals, some of which were included in the Climate and Resilience Law adopted in August 2021.

In **Italy**, the Ministry for Disabilities, the Association of Disabilities, and public authorities established a work programme with the aim to promote the application of the principles of the United Nations Convention on the Rights of Persons with Disabilities (CRPD). The programme set-up 13 working groups specialised in different areas (e.g. definition of disability, simplification of sector regulations, social policies or international co-operation) consisting of representatives of the civil society and institutions. The work outputs and consultation results significantly contributed to the formulation of the Government Delegation Law on Disability Matters adopted in October 2021.

In October 2021, The Ministry for Finance and Employment in **Malta** launched a National Employment Policy for 2021-2030. During the drafting of the Policy, a wide and intense consultation process was carried out. Thirty focus groups were held across various industry sectors which were attended by industry leaders and academic experts. Participants provided feedback on their perceptions and expectations of the economy, which were fed into a forecasting model used to gauge future sentiment. A focus group with foreign workers engaged in the Maltese labour market was also carried out. The feedback helped to understand the situation at hand as well as to capture areas of concern and aspects that required addressing by the Policy.

Co-operation with relevant stakeholders in **Poland** at the early stage of development of reforms to the Public Procurement Act helped improve the decision making process by, amongst others, identifying a number of problems, including barriers related to the access of SMEs to the public procurement market. Some of the stakeholders consulted were industry representatives, entrepreneurs, Polish and foreign scientists, local governments, contracting authorities, practitioners, and state champions amongst others.

In **Romania**, a public debate helped policy makers identify the need to regulate internships. Ministry representatives as well as representatives of public institutions and civil society partners were part of the working groups invited to participate in the consultation. The discussions focused on a range of topics related to the organisation and conduct of internships, such as the integration of people into the labour market through internship opportunities, the internship contract and allowance, as well as the Employment Premium Fund for employers (which turns internship contracts into employment contracts).

Source: Supplementary material provided to the indicators of Regulatory Policy and Governance Survey 2021.

Policy makers in EU Member States engage and consult more systematically with stakeholders on draft regulatory proposals; and less frequently when discussing the policy problem and exploring alternative solutions (Figure 2.3). Consulting with citizens, businesses and other relevant stakeholders once there is a regulatory draft is important. Firstly, because stakeholders can provide input on how any resultant regulation could be delivered. Secondly, because stakeholders know how any new rule may affect them before it becomes part of their daily lives. However, when policy makers engage with those who are affected or have some expertise in the topic early, when discussing the issue and its potential solutions, they can get important information to help shape the regulatory or non-regulatory options (OECD, 2020[3]). Stakeholders engaged early in the regulatory process are better able to participate in the development of the proposed policy. The European Commission, **Belgium** and **Italy** consult with stakeholders when a policy problem is being discussed.

Figure 2.3. Most EU Member States and the European Commission tend to systematically engage with stakeholders once there is a draft regulation

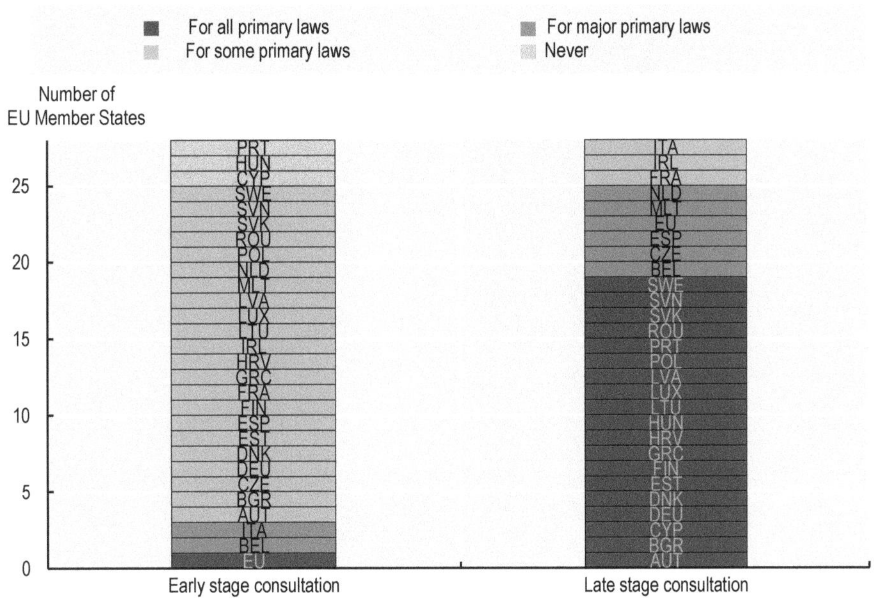

Note: Data is based on 27 EU Member States and the European Union.
Source: Indicators of Regulatory Policy and Governance (iREG) Survey 2021.

Policy makers need to inform stakeholders about upcoming consultations and provide them with enough time to participate

Policy makers should enable stakeholders to provide their feedback in consultations by making them inclusive, timely and accessible (OECD, 2012[2]). Engaging in consultations might not always be a priority for citizens who are pressed with other issues in their day-to-day life, nor for companies, as they might rather spend their time and resources on other activities, such as growing their businesses. At the same time, stakeholders have information and experiences that can contribute to a better regulatory environment that can improve their daily lives. This duality reflects the need to facilitate participation and to obtain public feedback during the policy making process. Part of enabling the public to participate includes three practices: letting stakeholders know in advance of upcoming consultations, being informed when a consultation has started, and granting them enough time to provide their feedback.

More EU Member States would benefit from informing either the public at large or specific stakeholders when a planned consultation is going to take place. Currently only the European Commission, **Croatia**, **Finland**, **Italy**, and **Slovak Republic** systematically do so (Figure 2.4). Knowing in advance of a consultation is generally the first chance that stakeholders have of figuring out whether the issue is relevant to them, and if so, to organise themselves to be able to provide feedback. In particular individuals or groups with fewer resources, such as small businesses and NGOs might not be able to participate in consultations if they learn about them too late in the process.

Figure 2.4. Only a few EU Member States systematically inform stakeholders in advance about upcoming consultations

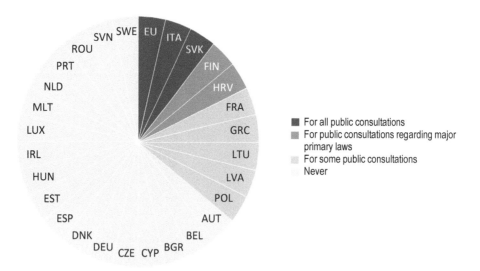

Note: Data is based on 27 EU Member States and the European Union.
Source: Indicators of Regulatory Policy and Governance (iREG) Survey 2021.

The EU Member States that notify the public in advance of upcoming consultations do it through different means such as roadmaps or announcements on a website to ensure that this information reaches relevant stakeholders. This shows these countries' commitment to transparency. **Croatia**, **Finland**, **Italy**, **Latvia** and **Lithuania** publish a road map or early warning document that lists all upcoming consultations in a defined period. In particular, **Croatia** publishes dates of consultations of each public body in the Consultations Plan at the beginning of the year, and **Italy** publishes a document outlining consultations that are planned to take place during a period of six months on the webpage of the Department for Legal and Legislative Affairs (DAGL). Other EU Member States make individual announcements of upcoming consultations. For instance, the **Slovak Republic** shares this information through its central legislative website at least 15 days prior to the consultation starting. The European Commission publishes a timeline of each initiative on their "*Have Your Say*" web portal, which for upcoming consultations shows that the initiative is "*in preparation*" and informs when it is planned to take place (see Box 2.2 below).

A large majority of EU Member States invite stakeholders to participate in consultations once they have started (Figure 2.5). Effectively communicating that consultations are underway to affected parties is crucial to receiving input as part of the development of regulations and for the transparency of the process. The most effective way to inform stakeholders about ongoing consultations is in part dependent on the resources and capacities of those involved (OECD, 2021[4]). Most EU Member States invite stakeholders to participate in ongoing consultations both through ministries' websites and through central government consultation websites. Furthermore, governments use the latter more systematically to invite stakeholders to participate in consultations that pertain to primary laws (Figure 2.5).

Figure 2.5. Most EU Member States invite the public to participate in consultations via central consultation government websites

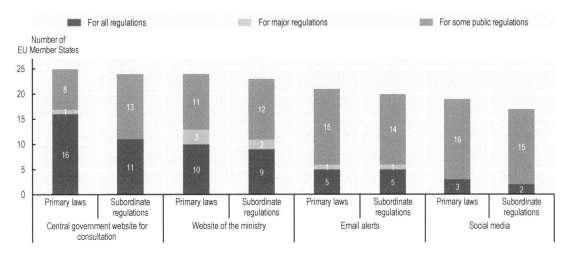

Note: Data is based on 27 EU Member States.
Source: Indicators of Regulatory Policy and Governance (iREG) Survey 2021.

EU Member States are aware that stakeholders may more regularly check their emails and social media than consultation websites, and also take advantage of these means to invite them to participate in ongoing consultations (Figure 2.5). Policy makers can reach participants more easily through these forms of communication, which may also stimulate stakeholder buy-in. As an example, stakeholders that are interested in consultations conducted by the European Commission can subscribe in the 'Have Your Say' web portal selecting specific policy areas to receive an email notification when a consultation has started (see Box 2.2). **Estonia**, **Malta** and the **Netherlands** have a similar subscription system where the public can register to get alerts based on the ministries and topics they are interested on. In other countries, ministries use their social media to invite the public to participate in consultations and in the post provide the link to visit the consultation website.

Box 2.2. The consultation website for the European Commission: "Have your Say"

"Have Your Say" is the European Commission's entry point for contributions to its legislative proposals, evaluations/fitness checks and communications. The European Commission posts and conducts consultations open to the public in the 'Have Your Say' portal. Stakeholders, including members of the public, businesses, scientific and technical experts, can contribute through the portal to initiatives as they are formed before and after the adoption by the European Commission.

The "Have Your Say" consultation portal has several features that make it accessible, comprehensive, user friendly and that can contribute to stakeholders' participation throughout several stages of policy making:

- Stakeholders can participate in the Commission's Call for evidence by providing feedback (including on the definition of the problem) and by participating in public consultations, provide feedback on regulatory drafts, and during the European Commission's adoption of the initiative. Likewise, participants can provide feedback on the simplification of existing regulations through the "Have Your Say: Simplify!" portal.

- Each initiative has a graphic timeline that indicates what stage of policy making the consultation concerns to (i.e. Call for evidence, draft, etc.), and also indicates whether each consultation stage is upcoming, open or closed.

- The home page displays a warning message informing stakeholders about the number of days remaining to provide comments in an active consultation. Some important consultations are showcased in the opening page.

- Stakeholders can filter consultations by stage, topic, type of act, and other criteria, which helps them to visualise the consultations more easily.

- Stakeholders can provide their feedback in 24 languages, which makes consultations accessible to a wide range of public.

- Comments and feedback are made public and visible to everyone after they are posted.

- Stakeholders can subscribe to get e-mail notifications of upcoming and ongoing consultations based on their topic of interest.

Note: To see more access https://ec.europa.eu/info/law/better-regulation/have-your-say_en

Source: European Commission (2021[5]); Better Regulation Guidelines, https://ec.europa.eu/info/sites/default/files/swd2021_305_en.pdf; European Commission (2021[6]), Better Regulation Toolbox, https://ec.europa.eu/info/sites/default/files/br_toolbox-nov_2021_en_0.pdf.

Once consultations are ongoing, in most EU Member States there are minimum periods during which consultations should be open to allow stakeholders enough time to provide their feedback (Figure 2.6). This time enables the public to study the documents made available for discussion and to form an opinion. In one third of EU Member States the minimum consultation period is of at least 30 days or four weeks. However, there are also extreme differences across EU Member States since countries like **Hungary**, **Greece**, **Latvia**, and **Spain** require consultations to be open only for at least two weeks, while **Sweden** and the European Commission require a minimum is 12 weeks (Figure 2.6). In **Romania**, at least 10 days of public consultation must be undertaken within a period of minimum 30 working days prior to the submission of the draft regulation for inter-ministerial approval.

Instead of having a minimum fixed time for consultation, **Bulgaria**, **Belgium**, **Slovak Republic** and **Slovenia** have an interval that guides policy makers to determine for how long a specific consultation should be open for (Figure 2.6). Intervals allow policy makers to be flexible and proportional and give each consultation the appropriate time it needs (OECD, 2021[4]). The choice of the specific time that policy makers will grant for each consultation usually depends on the complexity of the policy draft that is being consulted on. In **Belgium** the minimum consultation period requirement ranges from four to eight weeks; while in **Lithuania** there is a minimum 10 working days which can be extended to 12 working days for voluminous or complex draft legal acts.

In **Czech Republic**, **Denmark**, **Germany**, **Ireland** and **Malta** there is not a mandatory interval or fixed consultation period; however, in **Denmark** and **Germany** policy makers are required to be proportional when deciding on the time for each consultation. Under the principle of proportionality in **Germany**, policy makers are to give appropriate, sufficient and fair time for consultation but it is at their discretion to decide whether public consultations will be carried out, in what format, and for how long. The Joint Rules of Procedure of the Federal Ministries and additional decisions of the Federal Government however recommend four weeks as a standard period. Similarly, in **Denmark**, the consultation period must be adapted to the specific circumstances, but should always be long enough that the parties consulted have the opportunity to prepare an adequate response. A consultation period of four weeks is thus recommended, but not mandated. However, information on whether actual consultations are sufficiently long for stakeholders to provide meaningful input in countries without minimum periods is currently not available.

Figure 2.6. The shortest consultation period in EU Member States is of less than two weeks and the longest is of at least 12 weeks

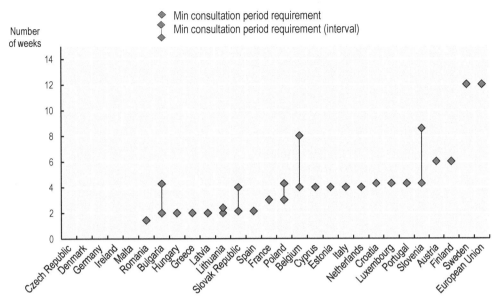

Note: The minimum consultations period requirements refer to primary laws. Data for France and Malta relates to subordinate regulations, since these countries have no formal requirements for minimum period for consultations for primary laws. Data is based on 27 EU Member States and the European Union.
Source: Indicators of Regulatory Policy and Governance (iREG) Survey 2021.

Consultations in EU Member States are generally open to the public

In most EU Member States, as well as in the European Commission, consultations are generally open to the public, which contributes towards their transparency. Only five EU Member States – namely **Austria**, **Czech Republic**, **Finland**, **Germany**, and **Ireland** – have no requirement to conduct consultation open to the general public. However, Austria and Finland regularly undertake consultations open to the general public in practice. Interestingly, in the last few years, more EU Member States are systematically listing their consultations on a single website (Figure 2.7). Having all consultations listed on a single website, or having all links redirecting to other consultation portals on a single website, can reduce stakeholders' search costs, as they know there is a single place to look at to participate in a consultation.

Figure 2.7. More EU Member States now list their ongoing consultations on a single central website

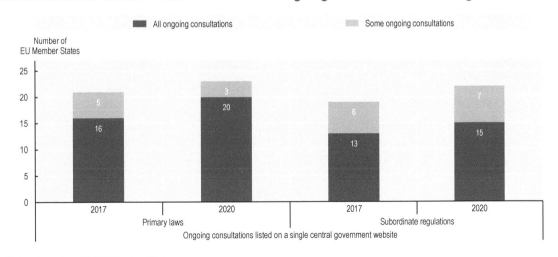

Note: Data is based on 27 EU Member States.
Source: Indicators of Regulatory Policy and Governance (iREG) Surveys 2017 and 2021.

EU Member States enable stakeholders to provide feedback by providing supporting documents and consulting in different ways

Most EU Member States enable stakeholder engagement by providing documents that help prepare their feedback and by undertaking tailored consultation approaches. Member States can further their consultation practices by more frequently using different consultation channels, such as citizen panels, at early stages of policy development and by more systematically providing documents such as green papers or preliminary impact assessments

Policy makers should offer documents and information that are clear, complete, timely, reliable and easy to both find and understand (OECD, 2017[7]). For early stage consultations, stakeholders need to understand the policy problem, while for late stage consultation, in addition, it is important that they also be informed of the implementation of a preferred policy solution.

It is less common for policy makers in EU Member States to share supporting documents during early stage consultations, such as documents describing the problem and soliciting input from the public on possible solutions (Figure 2.8). That said, **Ireland** highlighted that documents can be shared at an early stage of policy development. As part of improving the quality of its education qualifications systems, **Ireland** published a green paper outlining its system and asking stakeholders on possible enhancement opportunities.

Conversely, it is more common that EU Member States share supporting documents with stakeholders once there is a regulatory draft (Figure 2.8). This allows citizens and businesses to better understand the preferred solution, to read the actual draft and its planned implementation, to look at the different costs and benefits that the regulatory proposal entails – with the Regulatory Impact Assessment (RIA) – and overall to be in a position to provide a more informed opinion.

Figure 2.8. During early stage consultation, stakeholders receive less documents, less systematically

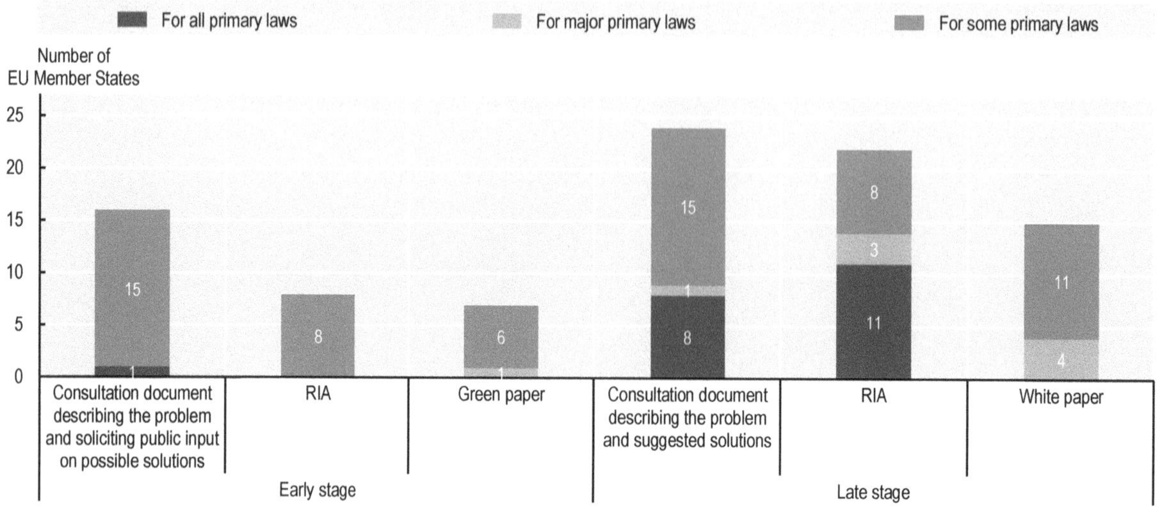

Note: Data is based on 27 EU Member States
Source: Indicators of Regulatory Policy and Governance (iREG) Survey 2021.

As a means of transparency, policy makers in EU Member States could publish the information and evidence gathered as part of informing both early and late stage consultations. Providing, for example, draft RIAs, where a policy problem is identified and where the impacts of various policy options is assessed, enables stakeholders to help assess the feasibility of such options and to raise alternatives that may not have been considered previously by policy makers. This is however dependent on policy makers identifying and assessing a range of regulatory and non-regulatory policy alternatives in RIAs. Publishing RIAs for consultation on regulatory drafts helps to focus stakeholder feedback, especially on potential implementation issues. Only eight EU Member States make RIAs available for some of their early stage consultations, while half of the EU Member States make RIAs systematically available when a regulatory draft exists (Figure 2.8).

Policy makers should use different formats of engagement that facilitate participation, do not create unnecessary burden on those whose input is needed, and also help engage the appropriate stakeholders for the problem at hand. Stakeholders can have different resources, time availability and preferences for particular communication avenues (OECD, 2009[8]; OECD, 2015[9]). At the same time, policy makers are called to create strategies that can help reach out to diverse stakeholders in a way that all voices can be heard (OECD, 2012[2]) (OECD, 2015[9]; OECD, 2021[4]).

The most common format of consultation in EU Member States is online and open to the general public, as well as formal engagement with selected groups of stakeholders such as trade unions or business association (Figure 2.9). EU Member States also conduct both physical and virtual public meetings, citizen panels or workshops, albeit less systematically.

EU Member States more often conduct closed consultations when engaging stakeholders at an early stage (Figure 2.9). Consulting with selected groups in a focused manner at an early stage can be appropriate for situations where input from a specific group or specific experts is needed. This is particularly true of qualified stakeholders, i.e. representative associations of businesses, consumers, employers and so on whose mission it is to articulate the opinions of their members, including on policy and regulatory drafts. Their capacities and ability to represent a range of smaller stakeholders means that they are particularly important to consult. Policy makers in EU Member States also use this focused approach for consultation on regulatory drafts (see Box 2.3). For policy problems of more general nature, it is also advisable to consult more openly (OECD, 2021[4]; OECD, 2021[10]), when inputs from the general public can, for example, help to inform the magnitude policy problem early on.

All EU Member States use more forms of engagement for consultations on draft regulations and use them more systematically (Figure 2.9). As explained before, this diversity of means facilitates stakeholders' participation, but it also contributes towards the transparency and inclusivity of consultations. Policy makers in EU Member States could benefit from more systematic engagement in early stage consultations.

Figure 2.9. EU Member States engage with stakeholders through more open formats at a later stage of policy making

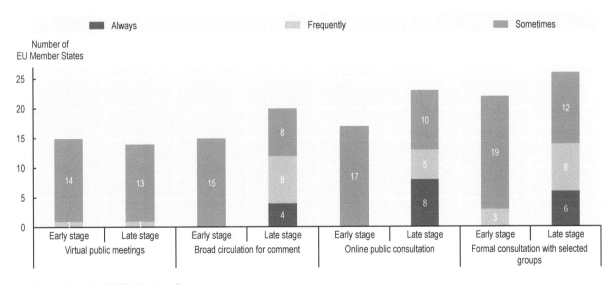

Note: Data is based on 27 EU Member States.
Source: Indicators of Regulatory Policy and Governance (iREG) Survey 2021.

Box 2.3. Consultations can be proportionate and focused on selected stakeholders

Consultations can be burdensome for policy makers as well as for participants. Not all stakeholders are interested in all consultations nor have expertise in all topics. At the same time, policy makers benefit from input of specific stakeholders who have particular expertise or are particularly affected by the policy matter at hand. The OECD Recommendation on Open Government calls for policy makers to have a proportionate approach to consultation. The Recommendation encourages policy makers to be aware of the possibility of consultation fatigue, but also to dedicate specific effort to reach out to "*the most relevant, vulnerable, underrepresented, or marginalised groups in society*" (OECD, 2017[7]). In addition to having open online consultations, which can have low administrative costs, policy makers must also adapt who they consult with to the type of problem that is being discussed and invest time and resources in those consultations.

Some EU Member States already require their policy makers to consult with specific parties depending on the topic of the consultation, for instance:

In **Germany**, when developing a regulation, federal ministries are required to consult with state governments, associations, and experts in the specific field affected by the policy problem or the draft regulation being discussed.

When regulations or policy problems might impact small businesses in the **Netherlands**, the policy maker invites SMEs, entrepreneurs and SME representatives to panel discussions about the problem at hand. During these discussions, the policy makers, together with these groups, consider the feasibility of the legislative proposal and discuss how these proposals might affect SMEs' regulatory pressure.

In **Lithuania**, when regulations pertain to small businesses, policy makers invite to consultations representatives of The Small and Medium-sized Business Council and of the Tripartite council (formed by the tripartite co-operation between the Government, trade unions and employers' organisations).

Policy makers in **Sweden** should ask the opinion of authorities, organisations and municipalities when conducting consultations. In addition, policy makers indicate which stakeholders each published consultation pertains to, even when it is open to the general public.

Source: Indicators of Regulatory Policy and Governance (iREG) Survey 2021; OECD (2021[4]), Regulatory Policy Outlook 2021, https://doi.org/10.1787/38b0fdb1-en; OECD (forthcoming[11]), SME test: Taking SMEs into account when regulating. Annex to the RIA's Best Practice Principles.

Transparency and the use of comments

Most EU Member States publish participants' views (Figure 2.10), which is another example of transparency during consultations. Policy makers sometimes make views of participants public immediately on their interactive websites, which is the case of the European Commission and some EU Member States such as **Bulgaria**, **Croatia**, **Greece** and **Slovenia**. On **Croatia**'s interactive consultation website, each input provided by stakeholders is visible, and other people are able to like or dislike each comment. Website users are also able to order comments by newest to oldest, or for instance, to see the most popular comment first. On **Slovenia**'s interactive consultation website, participants can reply to each other's comments, transforming the consultation into an interactive conversation. In other countries, such as **The Netherlands,** comments are made public on the website, but only after the person providing the feedback authorises it. In other EU Member States, policy makers publish feedback from stakeholders after the consultation is over, either through a summary or together with the RIA for the regulatory proposal (Figure 2.10).

Figure 2.10. The majority of EU Member States publish stakeholders' comments

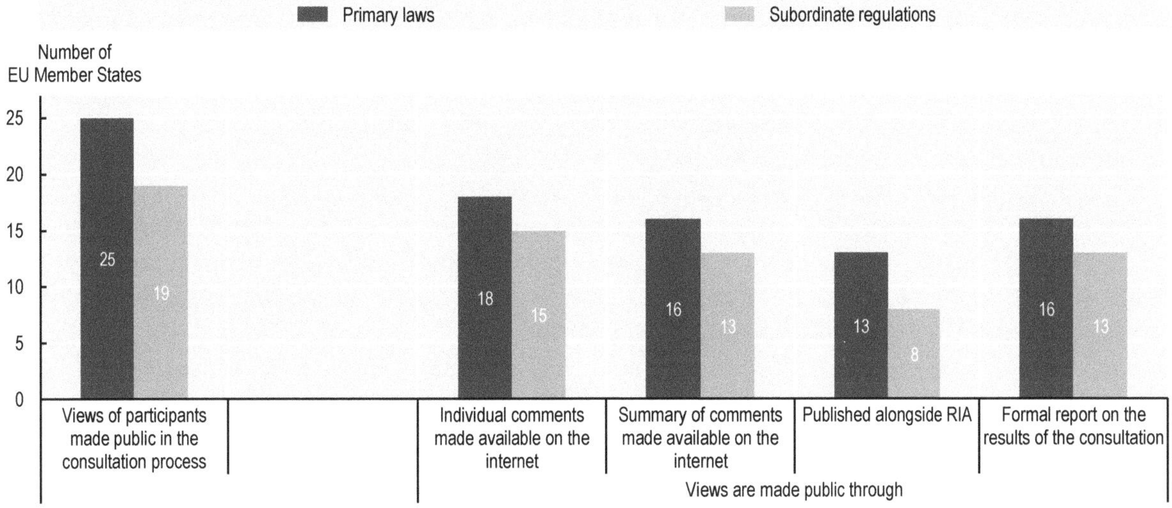

■ Primary laws   ▨ Subordinate regulations

Number of EU Member States

	Views of participants made public in the consultation process	Individual comments made available on the internet	Summary of comments made available on the internet	Published alongside RIA	Formal report on the results of the consultation
Primary laws	25	18	16	13	16
Subordinate regulations	19	15	13	8	13

Views are made public through

Note: Data is based on 27 EU Member States.
Source: Indicators of Regulatory Policy and Governance (iREG) Survey 2021.

Even though consultations in EU Member States are mostly transparent and public, less than a third of Member States have a requirement to respond in writing to comments received which undermines the purpose of consultations (Figure 2.11). Responding to comments shows stakeholders that their effort and opinions are valuable and were taken into account (Lind and Arndt, 2016[11]). This can encourage stakeholder participation in future consultations as it provides a sense of ownership regarding regulations that affect their lives and business. Policy makers responses to consultation comments should not be limited to merely acknowledging receiving a comment, but should also explain how the comment was taken into account. In four EU Member States policy makers are required to respond to each individual comment directly, while another four Member States have a requirement to publish a summary responding to the most significant or important comments received (Figure 2.11). It is important to highlight that even in the absence of an explicit requirement, there are some EU Member States where policy makers do reply to individual comments directly online, for example when consultations are conducted through interactive websites.

Figure 2.11. Only a few EU Member States require policy makers to respond in writing to consultation comments

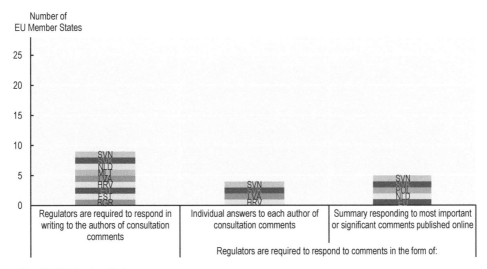

Note: Data is based on 27 EU Member States.
Source: Indicators of Regulatory Policy and Governance (iREG) Survey 2021.

In most EU Member States, the views expressed in the consultation process are made available to decision makers in the RIA report. In **Belgium**, **Estonia**, **Lithuania** and **Luxembourg** comments are summarised in other documents such as an explanatory memorandum or regulatory preamble document. Two-thirds of EU Member States require decision makers to actually consider comments when developing the final regulation (Figure 2.12). Knowing that their comments are seriously considered and potentially used to develop the final regulation can increase stakeholders' trust in the consultation process. It is important to note however that policy makers might not be able and should not be expected to action and incorporate all received comments in the final decision. Policy makers should make the best decision in the public interest whilst considering multiple and sometimes competing stakeholder interests. Stakeholders are by definition biased as they represent specific interests (e.g. trade unions, employer organisations, business representatives, and consumers' associations) and policy makers ought to carefully balance all interests received when treating stakeholder consultation responses.

Figure 2.12. Most EU Member States require decision makers to use consultations comments in any final regulation

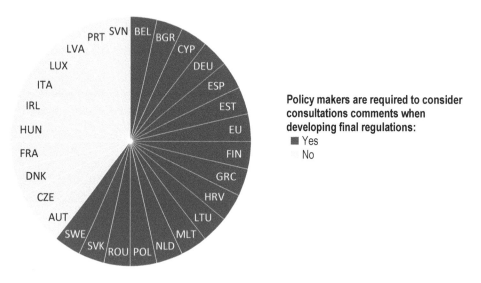

Note: Data is based on 27 EU Member States and the European Union.
Source: Indicators of Regulatory Policy and Governance (iREG) Survey 2021.

There needs to be more transparency when policy makers decide to not conduct consultation

Even though openly engaging with stakeholders is the norm in most EU Member States, in some cases consultation is bypassed. For example, in some EU Member States public consultation may not be considered necessary where regulatory proposals are political and/or sensitive or when policy makers consider that the costs of conducting consultation would outweigh its benefits, or be an ineffective method for reaching target groups (European Commission, 2021[6]; Minister van Veiligheid en Justitie, 2011[12]). In the vast majority of EU Member States, the decision itself requires a high level of approval, as either a minister or the head of the responsible department has to decide to forego a consultation that was required in principle. Policy makers in EU Member States however rarely inform the public of the decision to bypass a consultation (Figure 2.13). The lack of public communication regarding this decision is not in line with the overall transparency and openness policies that EU Member States show in other parts of their consultation process. Only seven EU Member States and the European Commission either publish the decision to bypass stakeholder consultation on a website or as part of the final RIA (Figure 2.13).

Figure 2.13. EU Member States can improve transparency when bypassing public consultation

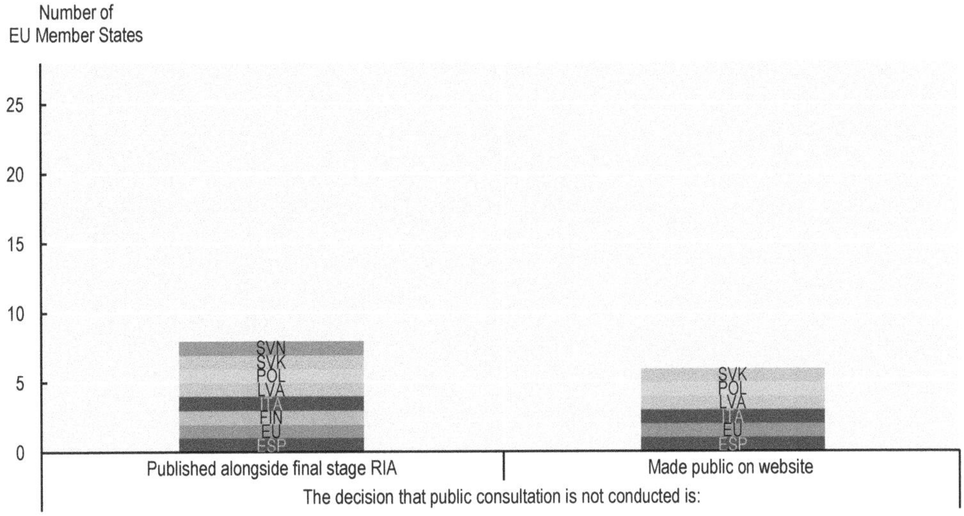

Number of
EU Member States

Note: Data is based on 27 EU Member States and the European Union.
Source: Indicators of Regulatory Policy and Governance (iREG) Survey 2021.

Stakeholder engagement during the negotiation and transposition of EU directives/regulations

Facilitating Member States' domestic stakeholders in EU consultations

Individual Member States play an important role ensuring that their stakeholders are informed about European Commission proposals that affect them. In policy areas where the EU has sole competency all proposals are generated by the European Commission. In practice this means that consultations for these proposals follow the European Commission's processes (Box 2.4). Similarly, standard Member State procedures apply where they have policy exclusivity (see previous section). For areas of shared regulatory competency a mix will apply.

Box 2.4. Stakeholder engagement by the European Commission

Under Article 11(3) of the Treaty on European Union, the European Commission is required to conduct broad consultations with parties concerned in order to ensure that the EU legislation is coherent and transparent.

Stakeholder consultations support policymaking by facilitating the collection of evidence. According to the *Better Regulation Guidelines* (2021[5]), taking into account stakeholders' views and experience helps to improve the Commission's understanding of the issues at stake and leads to better quality and credibility of proposed policies, while also fostering trust and acceptance by the EU citizens.

Consultations should be carried out when preparing initiatives that are accompanied by an impact assessment. For evaluations of policies and programmes of broad public interest and for fitness checks, a public consultation is highly recommended. Where "back-to-back" impact assessments and evaluations are carried out, the mandatory public consultation should cover both the backward- and forward-looking elements, to provide input for the evaluation and the impact assessment. However,

---

consultations on very technical initiatives and of limited interest to the general public tend to be targeted at specific groups of stakeholders, e.g. experts in the field.

Stakeholder engagement in the European Commission is guided by four principles: First, consultations should be inclusive and engage a wide range of stakeholders. Second, the consultation process and the use of the input should be transparent to those involved and to the general public (including those with disabilities). Third, consultations should be conducted when stakeholders' input can still make a difference, while taking into account proportionality and other constraints. Fourth, the consistency of consultation processes, analysis, review and quality control should be ensured across all services.

The European Commission's consultation system is based on the **"Call for evidence"** which combines two elements:

- Feedback to the Call for evidence documents that present key elements of impact assessments and evaluations of broad public interest and fitness checks,
- And public consultation, if it is required.

At the initial stage of policy development, the public has the possibility to provide feedback on the European Commission's policy plans through its "Call for evidence", including data and information they may possess on all aspects of the intended initiative and the initial impact assessment. Feedback is taken into account by the European Commission when further developing the policy proposal or when evaluating several related laws or policies in a single policy area. The feedback period for the "Call for evidence" is four weeks.

For most major policy initiatives and those accompanied by an impact assessment, a 12-week public consultation is conducted simultaneously or not with the Call for evidence through the multilingual "Have Your Say" portal and may be accompanied by other consultation methods (such as targeted consultation, workshops, and small-business panels). The consultation activities allow stakeholders to express their views on key aspects of the proposal and the main elements of the impact assessment or evaluation under preparation.

Stakeholders can provide feedback to the Commission on its proposals and their accompanying final impact assessments once they are adopted by the College. Stakeholder feedback is presented to the European Parliament and Council and aims to feed into the further legislative process. The consultation period for adopted proposals is 8 weeks. Draft delegated acts and important implementing acts are also published for stakeholder feedback on the European Commission's website for a period of 4 weeks. At the end of the consultation work, an overall synopsis report should be drawn up covering the results of the different consultation activities that took place.

Finally, the Commission also consults stakeholders as part of the *ex post* evaluation of existing EU regulations. This includes feedback on evaluation "Call for evidence" for the review of existing initiatives, and public consultations on evaluations of individual regulations and "fitness checks" (i.e. "comprehensive policy evaluations assessing whether the regulatory framework for a policy sector is fit for purpose"). In addition, stakeholders can also provide views and recommendations on how to simplify existing EU legislation via the "Have your say: Simplify!" web portal.

Source: Indicators of Regulatory Policy and Governance (iREG) Survey 2021; OECD (2019[13]), Better Regulation Practices across the European Union, https://doi.org/10.1787/9789264311732-en; European Commission (2021[5]), Better Regulation Guidelines, https://ec.europa.eu/info/sites/default/files/swd2021_305_en.pdf.

Facilitating domestic stakeholder participation in European Commission's consultations helps to ensure that all views are included and taken into account by the European decision makers. Member States' stakeholder input can help to identify feasible alternatives to those proposed by the European Commission; identify and assess potential benefits and costs of various policy options; and raise potential implementation issues. Member States thus have an important role in ensuring that European legislative proposals consider all stakeholder views and are evidence-based (see Chapter 3).

Nineteen EU Member States facilitate the engagement of domestic stakeholders in the European Commission's consultation processes (Figure 2.14). Most EU Member States inform stakeholders of the European Commission's consultations through their individual ministries' websites, where stakeholders are redirected to the relevant Commission consultation page. Some EU Member States (**Denmark**, **Finland**, the **Netherlands** and **Slovenia**) list the European Commission's consultations on their respective central consultation portal that their own stakeholders are already familiar with. Ministries in **France** communicate the European Commission's public consultations to stakeholders through publication on their websites or through direct exchanges relevant parties. **Germany** uses a multi-step process to assist stakeholders prioritise potentially relevant consultations. The Federal Ministry of Economic Affairs and Energy contacts a large range of stakeholder representatives to examine all proposals of the annual Commission Work Programmes with regards to potential SME impacts. The Federal Ministry of Economic Affairs and Energy then publishes a list that includes all proposals of the Commission Work Programme and indicates their importance for SMEs. The list is made publicly available online. It includes regularly updated information on ongoing Commission consultations and aims to encourage domestic stakeholders to actively participate.

Figure 2.14. A majority of EU Member States report informing domestic stakeholder about European Commission consultations

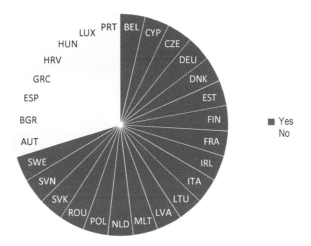

Note: Data is based on 27 EU Member States.
Source: Indicators of Regulatory Policy and Governance (iREG) Survey 2021.

Half of the EU Member States facilitate the co-ordination of domestic government input in the European Commission's consultations. Qualitative evidence suggests that the national ministry in charge of the regulatory agenda co-ordinates with other ministries or officials to submit an official response. For example, government officials in **Latvia** are engaged through a co-ordination mechanism – during the consultation process the competent institution involves the other relevant institutions and government officials to formulate a government response to relevant EU proposals.

The use of stakeholder engagement by EU Member States to inform the negotiation of EU directives and regulations

Engaging with stakeholders at the early stages of policy development helps to identify specific issues and provides the opportunity to citizens to help shape regulatory proposals (OECD, 2021[4]). The types of legislative acts available to the European Union were described in Chapter 1. Two relevant dimensions to consider in the EU context are the extent of substitutable and complementary stakeholder engagement:

- The *substitutionary dimension* relates to EU Member States utilising the input received to the European Commissions' proposals by their domestic stakeholders (irrespective of whether the Member State helped to facilitate that input).

- The *complementary dimension* is when individual EU Member States call for domestic input directly from stakeholders in forming their negotiating position. This may unearth new stakeholders who were either unwilling, unable – or, if not facilitated by the EU Member State – uninformed about the European Commission's own stakeholder engagement on a proposal.

One interesting possibility is that the same stakeholder input can influence policy development differently. For instance a submission to the European Commission that provides detailed disaggregated country level anticipated impacts may not be utilised by the Commission as part of its policy development owing to the fact that the costs may not be representative of the anticipated distribution across the EU. However, such a submission resubmitted to an individual Member State may be viewed as significantly more influential in informing the country's negotiating position. The foregoing highlights that EU Member States can receive stakeholder input through a variety of different means to help inform their respective negotiation positions on the European Commission's proposals.

Despite the potential for Member States to utilise different engagement strategies the reality is more mixed. Only six Member States' governments have systematic requirements to conduct stakeholder engagement to define a negotiating position for the development of EU regulations or directives. Of these, **Italy** and the **Slovak Republic** systematically open stakeholder engagement to the general public (Table 2.1). An additional six Member States require stakeholder engagement to inform their negotiation position for some EU regulations and directives. The approach taken varies significantly across individual Member States (Box 2.5).

Table 2.1. EU Member States use the European Commission's consultations more than requiring stakeholder engagement to form a negotiation position

	Stakeholder engagement is required to define negotiating positions	Stakeholder engagement to define negotiating positions must be open to the public	Results of European Commission's consultations are used to inform negotiating positions
Austria			
Belgium			
Bulgaria			
Croatia			
Cyprus			
Czech Republic			
Denmark	■		
Estonia	■		
Finland	■		
France			
Germany			■
Greece			

	Stakeholder engagement is required to define negotiating positions	Stakeholder engagement to define negotiating positions must be open to the public	Results of European Commission's consultations are used to inform negotiating positions
Hungary	For some regulations/ Sometimes	For some regulations/ Sometimes	For some regulations/ Sometimes
Ireland	For some regulations/ Sometimes	For some regulations/ Sometimes	Never
Italy	Systematic approach	Systematic approach	Never
Latvia	Systematic approach	Never	Systematic approach
Lithuania	For some regulations/ Sometimes	For some regulations/ Sometimes	Systematic approach
Luxembourg	Never	Never	Never
Malta	Never	Never	Systematic approach
Netherlands	For some regulations/ Sometimes	For some regulations/ Sometimes	Systematic approach
Poland	For some regulations/ Sometimes	Never	Systematic approach
Portugal	For some regulations/ Sometimes	For some regulations/ Sometimes	Systematic approach
Romania	For some regulations/ Sometimes	For some regulations/ Sometimes	Systematic approach
Slovak Republic	Systematic approach	Systematic approach	Systematic approach
Slovenia	For some regulations/ Sometimes	For some regulations/ Sometimes	Systematic approach
Spain	For some regulations/ Sometimes	For some regulations/ Sometimes	For some regulations/ Sometimes
Sweden	For some regulations/ Sometimes	For some regulations/ Sometimes	For some regulations/ Sometimes

■ Systematic approach
▨ For some regulations/ Sometimes
▨ Never

Note: Data is based on 27 EU Member States.
Source: Indicators of Regulatory Policy and Governance (iREG) Survey 2021.

Approximately a third of Member States report to systematically use the results of the European Commission's consultation processes as input to inform the national negotiating position for the development of EU regulations or directives, profiting from synergy effects through the stakeholder consultation framework of the European Commission. An additional ten Member States sometimes use the Commission's consultation results to inform their respective negotiating position (Box 2.5).

Box 2.5. Selected Member States' negotiation procedures on European Commission's proposals

In **Slovenia** the relevant ministry prepares the draft position and identifies the most important issues and the relevant stakeholders groups to be included in the consultation process, depending on the content of the proposed regulation. Before presenting the draft position to the stakeholders, intergovernmental consultation takes place to discuss open issues. Beside regular consultation via a ministerial advisory body, consultation is most often carried out in writing. Slovenia's positions for the most important dossiers, for instance regarding the Common Agricultural Policy and Common Fisheries Policy, undergo public consultation and conferences.

While **Poland** has no requirement for open public consultation on European Commission's proposals, government officials in different ministries are usually consulted. The mechanism of consultation and conducting work on EU draft legislative acts is included in the Polish guidelines. The mechanism is generally applicable from the official presentation of the draft EU legislative act by the European Commission to the EU Council and European Parliament. Ongoing consultations and dialogue with stakeholders occurs throughout the whole process. All concerned stakeholder organisations are proactively provided with information obtained from the work of the European Commission committee/working group. In this working group the Commission consults the Member States on the proposal, and leading experts encourage participation in the consultation, in particular to report any reservations, doubts, proposals for more favourable solutions, simplifications, etc.

Source: Indicators of Regulatory Policy and Governance Survey 2021; Radaelli et al. (unpublished[14]), Extending the OECD indicators of Regulatory Policy and Governance (iREG) to all EU Member States of the European Union.

To assist in carrying out stakeholder engagement, five Member States have specific guidance available to government officials to inform the national negotiating position for the development of EU directives and regulations (Box 2.6).

Box 2.6. Finnish and Slovakian stakeholder engagement to define the negotiation position

The formal requirement to carry out stakeholder engagement in **Finland** is triggered with the mandate given, in practice, once the European Commission adopts the proposal. The Finish Government must submit a "Letter" to the Parliament informing the Parliament about a new initiative and the Government stance on it, and seeking the formal mandate by Parliament to negotiate at the EU level. The Letter together with the RIA is submitted for public consultation.

Public consultation occurs in two stages. First, the Government informs and seeks feedback from one or more of the permanent sectoral sub-committees of the Committee of the EU Affairs. This is an informal consultation, and it is carried out mainly via email and by individual contacts for six weeks. This gives stakeholders a possibility to react to a change in the proposal also during the negotiation, not only during the first six weeks. Individual ministries might decide to run additional consultation rounds on the Letter, extending it to selected additional stakeholders, if they deem it appropriate. Second, the Parliament also carries out public consultation after receiving the Letter, largely with the same stakeholders as the Government.

In the **Slovak Republic,** stakeholder engagement is required to define the negotiating position for EU directives and regulations and is required to be open to the general public. Regular Preliminary Opinions (i.e. the assessment of impacts) are publically available on the Slov-Lex legislation consultation portal. This allows the general public and any relevant stakeholders to comment and provide feedback on the Preliminary Opinion. In addition, stakeholders can attend the discussion at the national Commission for European Affairs; however, except for representatives of employees and employers, stakeholders are not actively invited and engaged in these discussions.

Central Authorities can also raise any comments or objections to the Preliminary Opinion via the consultation portal. Any disagreements with the Preliminary Opinion are resolved in the consultation process or with the help of the national Commission for European Affairs. Should this not be successful, the Opinion is then presented to the Government with the disagreement. A Preliminary Opinion approved by the Slovak Government is generally binding and serves as the basis for negotiation positions of the Slovak Republic.

Source: Radaelli et al. (unpublished[14]), Extending the OECD indicators of Regulatory Policy and Governance (iREG) to all EU Member States of the European Union.

Overall results suggest that the majority of EU Member States both facilitate and rely on the consultations of the European Commission. One-third of EU Member States do facilitate the European Commission's consultations – and use the ensuing results – combined with a requirement to conduct their own stakeholder engagement to inform their respective negotiation positions. **Cyprus**, **Germany**, **Ireland**, **Lithuania**, **Malta**, the **Netherlands**, and **Romania** have no requirement to conduct stakeholder engagement on proposals of the European Commission and instead both facilitate domestic stakeholders' input into the Commission's consultation processes, and then utilise the ensuing results to inform their negotiating positions.

Despite the availability of the European Commission's consultation results, some Member States do not have a requirement for the government to conduct stakeholder engagement to define their negotiating position, nor use the results of the Commission's consultation processes. To some extent this could be because the Member State facilitates the European Commission's consultations and considers that this is sufficient – the substitutionary dimension previously discussed. This may be the case in **Belgium** and the **Czech Republic**, however in **Austria**, **Greece**, **Luxembourg**, and **Spain** it appears that little is done to inform domestic stakeholders about consultations of the European Commission, and there are no requirements in place to either conduct stakeholder engagement or utilise the Commission's consultation results.

The lack of both substitutionary and complementary stakeholder engagement is particularly worrying in the development and negotiation of EU regulations. Since these are directly applicable and binding in their entirety without being transposed into EU Member States' national law, there are fewer opportunities to involve stakeholders and to use their feedback in shaping the legislative proposal.

The use of stakeholder engagement by EU Member States to inform the transposition of EU directives

While few member states require stakeholder engagement to define their negotiation position, the vast majority of Member States have a requirement to undertake stakeholder engagement when transposing EU directives into national law (Figure 2.15). There has been no change in the number of Member States undertaking stakeholder engagement at the transposition stage since 2017. **Ireland**, the **Netherlands**, and **Portugal** still have no requirement to do conduct stakeholder engagement at either the negotiation or transposition stages, although both the **Netherlands** and **Portugal** reported that stakeholder engagement at the transposition stage is occasionally done in practice.

Figure 2.15. Stakeholder engagement is more systematically required at the transposition stage than at the negotiation stage of EU directives

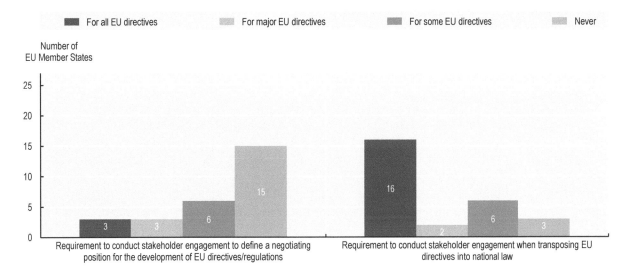

Note: Data is based on 27 EU Member States.
Source: Indicators of Regulatory Policy and Governance (iREG) Survey 2021.

Transposing EU directives involves amending existing or adopting new domestic regulation. As a result, the vast majority of Member States have the same requirements for stakeholder engagement during the transposition of EU directives as they have for regulations originating domestically (Figure 2.16). From a practical perspective it should be noted that consultation at the transposition stage is centrally concerned with assessing various implementation options, since the decision to regulate has already been made. Only **Malta** and the **Slovak Republic** have different stakeholder engagement requirements for transposed EU directives than for regulations originating domestically (see Box 2.7).

Figure 2.16. The vast majority of EU Member States have the same stakeholder engagement requirements domestically as they do for transposing EU directives

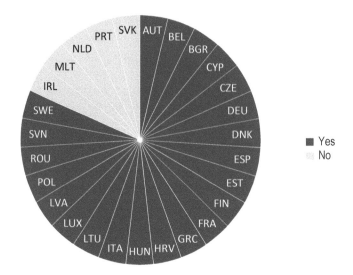

Note: Data is based on 27 EU Member States.
Source: Indicators of Regulatory Policy and Governance (iREG) Survey 2021.

Box 2.7. Differences between stakeholder engagement requirements for laws originating domestically and those originating at the EU level

In **Malta**, MUESAC (the Malta-EU Steering Action Committee) is instrumental at defining a negotiating position and during transposition of major EU directives. MUESAC is responsible for conducting consultation on EU legislative proposals, informing citizens on the latest developments in the EU and issues related to the EU Funding.

In order to optimise resources and prevent consultation fatigue, in co-operation with the Core Group, MEUSAC selects the major EU initiatives with great impact on society, be in, societal, economic and environmental terms, and identifies stakeholders who are likely to be affected the most by the EU directive at hand. This process ensures that the consultation is appropriately targeted and brought to the attention of relevant and affected parties. During the transposition stage, further implementation details, such as timing, training, information support, communication or legal drafting, have to be taken into account. During the consultation process there is a degree of co-ordination between the responsible Ministry and MEUSAC so as not to duplicate efforts.

Slovakia has a well-established public consultation in the implementation phases of policy making. Key stakeholders are consulted during the consultation on the preliminary position (the position and the legislative documents are available on the government's Slov-lex portal).

There are a few differences between consultation requirements for transposed EU legislations and for regulations originating domestically. When transposing EU legislation, the dossier accompanying the proposal must include a correlation table of the legislative proposal by the European Union administration and the List of implementing legally binding acts of the European Union. The correlation table is part of the governmental legislative rules and it monitors and rates the transposition of the EU legislation (the correlation tables are published on the Slov-lex portal).

Source: Indicators of Regulatory Policy and Governance, iREG 2021; Radaelli et al. (unpublished[14]), Extending the OECD indicators of Regulatory Policy and Governance (iREG) to all EU Member States of the European Union.

EU Member States report that they use the European Commission's consultation results less systematically at the transposition stage than at the negotiation stage (Figure 2.17). One reason might be that the results of consultations conducted by the European Commissions are out of date due to changes to draft directives in the Council or the European Parliament (see Chapter 1), or because national adjustments in the transposition including gold plating require additional information (see Chapter 3).

Malta and **Romania** are the only Member States that report to always use the results of the European Commission's consultations. In **Romania**, the results of the European Commission's consultations are processed by the departments for EU affairs and used in the legislative drafting process when transposing the EU directive.

Figure 2.17. The European Commission's consultation results are not systematically used at the transposition stage

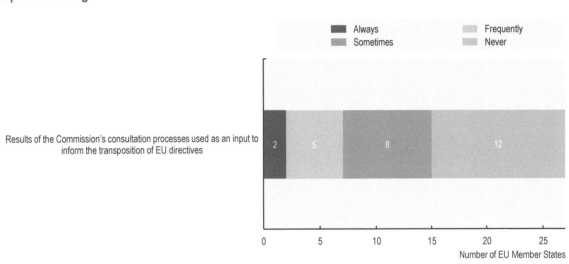

Note: Data is based on 27 EU Member States.
Source: Indicators of Regulatory Policy and Governance (iREG) Survey 2021.

Slovenia uses the results of the European Commission's consultation (including the assessment of the EU directive and reasons for adoption) for preparing the legislative proposal with which the European directives are transposed into national legislation. In **Austria**, the results of the Commission's consultation processes can be integrated into the materials used to draft laws, e.g. by giving reasons and explanations for a draft piece of legislation. In addition to use in transposition, **Croatia** uses the results of the European Commission's consultation including impact assessments and opinions/recommendations of the Regulatory Scrutiny Board during the preparation of national opinions regarding EU regulations.

More than a half of the EU Member States require that consultations on the transposition of EU directives be open to the general public. For example in **Denmark**, all rules, including transposed EU directives, are required to undergo a public and internal consultation process. The consultation on EU proposals is carried out online, via the domestic consultation portal, in addition to taking place through the sectoral EU committees (Radaelli, Dunlop and Allio, unpublished[14]).

In **Germany**, there are different rounds of consultation on transposed directives depending on the ministry concerned – for instance, the Social Affairs and Employment Ministry conducts consultations and public debates that feed into the RIA process on the proposal to transpose the directive. All proposals of the Federal Government are published online together with the statements of the associations involved in the consultation. It is not required that the consultation is open to the general public (Radaelli, Dunlop and Allio, unpublished[14]).

In **Poland**, the draft acts transposing EU legislation available during stakeholder and inter-ministerial consultation should be accompanied by several documents. This includes a "reverse compliance table" that provides a summary of the draft provisions of the Act, which go beyond the implementation, and an explanation of the necessity of including them within the project.

Eight EU Member States report having specific guidance available to government officials for conducting stakeholder engagement to inform the transposition of EU directives.

References

European Commission (2021), *Better Regulation Guidelines*, https://ec.europa.eu/info/sites/default/files/swd2021_305_en.pdf. [5]

European Commission (2021), *Better Regulation Toolbox*, https://ec.europa.eu/info/sites/default/files/br_toolbox-nov_2021_en_0.pdf. [6]

Lind, E. and C. Arndt (2016), "Perceived Fairness and Regulatory Policy: A Behavioural Science Perspective on Government-Citizen Interactions", *OECD Regulatory Policy Working Papers*, No. 6, OECD Publishing, Paris, https://doi.org/10.1787/1629d397-en. [1]

Minister van Veiligheid en Justitie (2011), *Brief van de Minister van Veiligheid en Justitie aan de Voorzitter van de Tweede Kamer der Staten-Generaal*, https://zoek.officielebekendmakingen.nl/kst-29279-121.html. [12]

OECD (2021), *Government at a Glance 2021*, OECD Publishing, Paris, https://doi.org/10.1787/1c258f55-en. [10]

OECD (2021), *OECD Regulatory Policy Outlook 2021*, OECD Publishing, Paris, https://doi.org/10.1787/38b0fdb1-en. [4]

OECD (2020), *Innovative Citizen Participation and New Democratic Institutions: Catching the Deliberative Wave*, OECD Publishing, Paris, https://doi.org/10.1787/339306da-en. [3]

OECD (2019), *Better Regulation Practices across the European Union*, OECD Publishing, https://doi.org/10.1787/9789264311732-e. [13]

OECD (2017), *Recommendation of the Council on Open Government, OECD/LEGAL/0438*. [7]

OECD (2015), *Policy Shaping and Policy Making: The Governance of Inclusive Growth*, OECD Publishing, Paris, http://www.oecd.org/gov/governance-for-inclusive-growth.htm. [9]

OECD (2012), *Recommendation of the Council on Regulatory Policy and Governance*, OECD Publishing, Paris, https://doi.org/10.1787/9789264209022-en. [2]

OECD (2009), *Focus on Citizens: Public Engagement for Better Policy and Services*, OECD Publishing, Paris, https://doi.org/10.1787/9789264048874-en.   [8]

OECD (forthcoming), *SME test: Taking SMEs into account when regulating. Annex to the RIA's Best Practice Principles*, OECD Publishings, Paris.   [11]

Radaelli, C., C. Dunlop and L. Allio (unpublished), *Extending the OECD indicators of Regulatory Policy and Governance (iREG) to all Member States of the European Union*.   [14]

3 The use of regulatory impact assessment across the European Union

Regulatory impact assessment (RIA) provides crucial information to policy makers on whether and how to regulate to achieve public policy goals. RIA examines the impacts and consequences of a range of alternative options and assists policy makers in identifying the most efficient and effective policy before making a decision. This chapter analyses the European Union and the Member States' requirements and use of RIA for both domestic regulations and proposed EU laws. It provides analysis of the application of the proportionality principle of EU Member States' RIA practices in relation to expected impacts, including detailed information collected during a series of interviews with four EU Member States – namely Denmark, Estonia, Germany, and Cyprus.

Key messages

- While all EU Member States have an obligation to conduct impact assessment to inform the development of legislative proposals a gap between requirements and practices remains, particularly for subordinate regulations. The majority of EU Member States apply the principle of proportionate assessment and recognise that the level and depth of analysis should be aligned with proposals' expected impacts.

- About half of the EU Member States have exceptions to conducting impact assessment, particularly where a regulation is introduced in response to an emergency. The consequences of using such mechanisms are however opaque as the exception decisions are most often not scrutinised or published. Exceptions should be used sparingly and, when used, the decision should be transparent.

- Few EU Member States report using threshold tests to determine whether a regulatory proposal warrants more in-depth analysis. EU Member States using threshold tests often use a variety of criteria to guide their decision and impacts on businesses is a factor considered in most of their thresholds. Threshold tests should be inclusive and based on the size of impacts across society rather than focusing on any specific sector or stakeholder group.

- Policy makers in a number of EU Member States can flexibly apply the proportionality principle to determine the depth of the analysis. This is a factor contributing to the significant variation in the format and depth of final RIA across EU Member States. There is however little scrutiny of the correct application of the proportionality principle and the role of regulatory oversight bodies in ensuring that the depth of the analysis is sufficient and proportionate to the significance of the regulation is unclear.

- Identifying and assessing the impacts of the preferred regulatory option is well established in a majority of EU Member States, although assessing alternative policy options, both regulatory and non-regulatory ones, on average seems to be less systematically assessed in EU Member States than in OECD countries. All plausible alternatives, including non-regulatory solutions, should be taken into account by EU Member States.

- It is essential to always identify all relevant direct and important indirect costs as well as benefits that would emerge if the available regulatory options are implemented. EU Member States focus more strongly on identifying and on quantifying the costs of new regulations rather than their benefits. Less than half of EU Member States quantify the costs and benefits of more than one policy option, suggesting that detailed analysis tends to be limited to the option that policy makers prefer to take forward. EU Member States could do more to comprehensively assess the negative and positive impacts resulting from the range of identified policy options.

- EU Member States should collect information about the impacts of EU legislative proposals on the domestic economy and society and should use this information during the negotiation phase at the European Parliament and/or at the Council of the European Union. This is not a systematic requirement in a majority of EU Member States, although some countries report doing so in practice. The short timing between the publication of the European Commission's impact assessment and the beginning of the negotiation can be a barrier to EU Member States undertaking suitable analysis to inform the domestic negotiation position.

- Regulatory impact assessment is more systematically required to be undertaken during the transposition of EU directives into Member States' national law than during the negotiation stage. Almost all EU Member States are required to assess the impacts of EU directives when transposing them.

- Only six Member States report systematically assessing the impacts resulting from additional provisions added to EU directives, suggesting that decision-makers do not always understand the impacts that these impose on their citizens and businesses in most Member States. EU Member States ought to systematically identify and assess the specific impacts resulting from any national provisions added.

- EU Member States appear to use the European Commission's impact assessment to inform the negotiation of EU legislative acts rather than to inform transposition. EU Member States may benefit from using the European Commission's impact assessment more regularly during the transposition stage as it still contains some information and evidence on the types of impacts that countries can collectively expect to encounter when implementing the directive.

Introduction

Regulatory impact assessment (RIA) provides crucial information to decision makers on whether and how to regulate in order to achieve public policy goals. RIA assists in developing efficient and effective policy responses that also maximise societal well-being. It does so by critically examining the impacts and consequences of a range of alternative options and by showing the expected impacts and distributional outcomes of proposals, thereby illustrating the inherent trade-offs. Improving the evidence base for regulation through *ex ante* impact assessment is one of the most important regulatory tools available to governments (OECD, 2012[1]).

RIAs should be integrated into the early stages of policy development to aid the formulation of new regulatory and non-regulatory proposals. They should be used to clearly identify policy goals and to evaluate if regulation is necessary and whether it is the most effective and efficient means in achieving these goals (OECD, 2012[1]). One method of doing so is by analysing the expected costs and benefits of regulation and of alternative means of achieving policy goals and to identify the approach that is likely to deliver the greatest net benefit to society. Policy makers should also examine all feasible policy alternatives as part of RIA, to ensure that a variety of solutions are considered and that the most efficient and effective one is used to attain policy goals. Building on the *OECD 2012 Recommendation of Regulatory Policy and Governance* (OECD, 2012[1]), the *OECD Best Practice Principles on Regulatory Impact Assessment* (OECD, 2020[2]) provide more detailed information and guidance for member and non-member countries on the critical elements required to develop and sustain a well-functioning RIA system (see Box 3.1).

The European Commission has recognised RIA as a centrally important regulatory management tool and it has been at the core of their better regulation practices for 20 years. The current European Commission's *Better Regulation Toolbox* (2021[3]) provides policy makers with an extensive amount of information and guidance on how to carry out an impact assessment. The European Commission has adopted RIA as a key component of its regulatory decision-making process and *ex ante* impact assessments continue to be carried out for major primary laws and subordinate regulation.

This chapter analyses EU Member States' RIA requirements and practices as reported in the indicators of Regulatory Policy and Governance (iREG) survey and its extension to all EU Member States. The section below provides an overview of recent reforms based on results from the iREG survey. The second section discusses the requirements and use of RIA in the domestic legislative process. It focuses on the application of the proportionality principle by EU Member States and is complemented by information collected during a series of interviews with four EU Member States, namely Cyprus, Denmark, Estonia, and Germany, carried out by the OECD as part of this project. In addition, this section reviews the requirements and implementation regarding both the use of alternative options in RIA as well as the assessment of costs and benefits in RIA. The final section of the chapter reviews the RIA requirements and processes as they relate to EU-made laws, including during the negotiation and transposition of EU directives and regulations.

Box 3.1. Summary of the OECD best practice principles for regulatory impact assessment

A well-functioning RIA system can help policy makers identify the potential outcomes of proposed regulations and determine whether regulations will achieve their intended objectives.

RIA should reflect the following critical elements:

- Regulatory impact assessment should be part of the policy implementation process/cycle
- It should start at the beginning of the regulation-making process
- It should clearly and systematically identify the problem and the related regulatory objectives
- Alternative solutions, their costs and benefits are identified and assessed
- It is developed transparently in co-operation with relevant stakeholders
- Its results are clearly and objectively communicated.

The best practice principles relate to the following aspects:

- The role of governments to ensure quality, transparency and stakeholder involvement in the process
- Full integration of RIA in the regulatory governance cycle respecting administrative and cultural specifics of the country
- Strengthened accountability and capacity over RIA implementation
- Using appropriate and well targeted methodology
- Appropriate communication and availability of RIA results to the public
- Continuous monitoring, evaluation and improvement of RIA.

Source: (OECD, 2020[2]), OECD Best Practice Principles for Regulatory Policy: Regulatory Impact Assessment, OECD Publishing, Paris, http://dx.doi.org/10.1787/7a9638cb-en.

General trends in RIA across the EU

On average, EU Member States' RIA practices have improved little in relation to primary laws and subordinate regulations, with marginally more improvements in the former. The largest improvement has been on the oversight and quality control of regulatory impact assessments. There has also been improvement in the systematic adoption of RIA, but to a lesser degree.

Figure 3.1. Composite indicators: regulatory impact assessment for developing primary laws, 2021

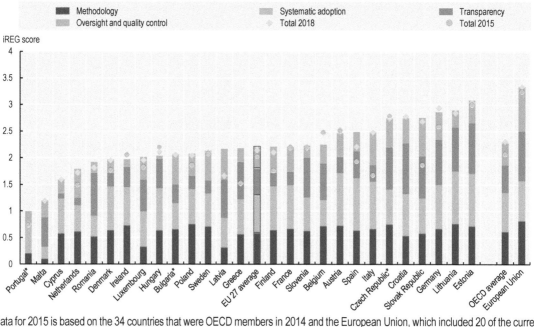

Note: Data for 2015 is based on the 34 countries that were OECD members in 2014 and the European Union, which included 20 of the current 27 EU Member States. The OECD average is based on the 38 member countries at the time of the survey. Data for 2018 and 2021 includes the remaining EU Member States of Latvia, Lithuania, Bulgaria, Croatia, Cyprus, Malta and Romania. The more regulatory practices as advocated in the *2012 Recommendation* a country has implemented, the higher its iREG score. * In the majority of EU Member States, most primary laws are initiated by the executive, except for Bulgaria, the Czech Republic and Portugal, where a higher share of primary laws are initiated by the legislature.
Source: Indicators of Regulatory Policy and Governance Surveys 2014, 2017 and 2021.

Figure 3.2. Composite indicators: regulatory impact assessment for developing subordinate regulations, 2021

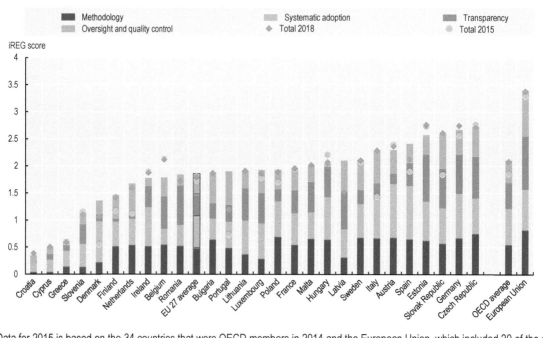

Note: Data for 2015 is based on the 34 countries that were OECD members in 2014 and the European Union, which included 20 of the current 27 EU Member States. The OECD average is based on the 38 member countries at the time of the survey. Data for 2018 and 2021 includes the remaining EU Member States of Latvia, Lithuania, Bulgaria, Croatia, Cyprus, Malta and Romania. The more regulatory practices as advocated in the *2012 Recommendation* a country has implemented, the higher its iREG score.
Source: Indicators of Regulatory Policy and Governance Surveys 2014, 2017 and 2021.

Some EU Member States have nevertheless undertaken recent reforms to their RIA system, including **Greece**, **Latvia**, **Portugal**, and **Spain**.

- Regulators in **Greece** are now required to assess and quantify the impacts of regulations on a large range of factors, including gender equality and social goals.
- **Latvia**'s recent substantive reforms include a requirement to assess a wider range of costs in RIAs, such as financial, budgetary, and administrative costs, as well as an expectation to prepare RIAs early in the policy-making process to later undergo public consultation with the draft law.
- **Portugal** formally established the use of RIA and has since expanded it, particularly for subordinate laws. Portugal has also reinforced the scrutiny of quality of RIA for subordinate regulations.
- **Spain** too has introduced bodies whose functions include watching over the legal quality of regulations initiated by the executive and providing feedback and recommendations on Impact Assessments to regulators.

RIA has the potential to improve resulting policies and this is demonstrated by recent experiences of both OECD members and EU Member States (see Box 3.2). However, nearly a decade of OECD research illustrates that RIA systems across OECD member states continue to experience the same range of fragilities – see OECD (2021[4]; 2019[5]; 2018[6]; 2015[7]). Policy makers appear to focus more systematically on the preferred policy option and generally do not dedicate the same efforts to analyse alternatives, particularly non-regulatory ones. RIAs thus tend to be conducted late in the policy process, when the policy option has been chosen and when the regulatory proposal is already drafted. In such cases, RIA can become akin to a "box-ticking" exercise where the impacts, costs, and benefits of a regulation are calculated *ex post* in order to justify a policy decision that has already been made. These issues are core to the success of RIA within OECD countries as a whole but are also relevant to EU Member States. This chapter attempts to examine some of these topics in more detail, by reviewing the extent to which EU Member States are required to identify alternative policy options, the types of impacts analysed in their RIA, the extent to which regulatory costs and benefits are assessed, and the transparency of their RIA systems.

Box 3.2. Examples of EU Member States and OECD members where RIAs improved the resulting policy

The Ministry of Labour and Pension System, Family and Social Policy in **Croatia** used evidence from the RIA and from relevant policy papers to inform the legislative proposal regarding the introduction of a minimum pension wage. Analysis of the previous pension system and evidence collected as part of the analytical process were key in determining the policy taken forward.

France introduced a new "*Loi relative à la protection des enfants*" (Child Protection Act) in 2022. The accompanying RIA examined a number of policy options and helped policy makers choose the most efficient alternatives. For example, one option considered a referral process to a panel composed solely of juvenile judges. Analysis however highlighted that a large number of judicial courts in France have fewer juvenile judges than would have been necessary under this proposal and the policy option was subsequently discarded for a less stringent alternative.

In **Germany**, the use of RIA when reorganising the national sub-statutory regulations for biocidal products resulted in savings of approximately EUR 50 million. These savings emanated from the decision to follow performance-based regulation, whereby the adopted act prescribed a specific regulatory goal but businesses were free to decide how to implement it to meet the set objectives.

An impact assessment on the opening of the national road maintenance market was carried out in **Latvia**. Two possible models were analysed: one where the market stayed closed and one in which the market was open to competitors and service providers were chosen via public tendering. Each model included financial data, an outline of possible risks and benefits, as well as information about the model in other countries. Based on the analytical results, the government decided that the open market model would result in higher benefits and would be more efficient. The impact assessment allowed the policy makers to make an informed decision and advised stakeholders about its expected benefits.

The Department for Digital, Culture, Media and Sport (DCMS) in the **United Kingdom** sought to establish a policy on the security of consumer connectable products. Due to lack of evidence and data of the cyber security risk that 'internet of things' (IoT) posed, DCMS conducted a series of research projects whose findings informed policy options that fed into the impact assessment on regulating consumer connectable products to ensure they meet basic cyber security standards. Through the research, it became clear that the labelling scheme was not a good option. Research found that consumers already assumed that a device would be secure and thus DCMS instead explored options that removed the burden from the consumer.

Source: Supplementary material to the Indicators of Regulatory Policy and Governance (iREG) Survey 2021.

The use of regulatory impact assessments in domestic legislation

EU Member States have adopted the requirement to conduct impact assessments to inform the development of policy proposals and, in the majority of countries, the depth of the analysis must be aligned with the proposals' expected impacts. Approximately half of the EU Member States have exceptions to conducting impact assessment, particularly where a regulation is introduced in response to an emergency, however their consequences are blurred as the exception decisions are most often not scrutinised or published. Whilst few EU Member States report using threshold test as a filter to decide which regulatory proposal warrant in-depth analysis, there is strong heterogeneity in the way EU Member States apply the proportionality principle. A number of national policy makers throughout the European Union can flexibly choose the level of analysis with little scrutiny. The format and the depth of the final RIA product can thus vary significantly and it is unclear what role regulatory oversight bodies have in ensuring the appropriate application of the proportionality principle. EU Member States have established requirements to identify and assess the impacts of the preferred regulatory option, although such impacts appear to be less systematically required to assess alternative policies, particularly non-regulatory ones. Finally, EU Member States appear to focus their analytical efforts towards assessing the costs of new regulations, rather than their benefits.

The principle and use of proportionate impact assessment across the European Union

EU Member States have recognised the importance of developing RIA requirements and practices that improve the evidence-base underpinning their domestic policy decisions. Almost all EU Member States have requirements – mostly expressed in law, statutory requirements, or in mandatory guidelines – to conduct RIA to inform the development of primary laws, but in practice, some EU Member States do not systematically do so (Figure 3.3). Formal impact assessment requirements can help governments establish foundations for a good and sound RIA. Furthermore, they help to ensure that established regulatory management processes and rules are aligned and followed so that unnecessary duplication is avoided, consistent and good quality RIAs are carried out in practice and their use is maximised. These requirements must however be appropriately applied and enforced, to improve the quality of decision making.

RIAs for subordinate regulations can also significantly impact citizens and businesses but are less systematically required (and conducted in practice) than for primary laws. Fewer EU Member States have a requirement to conduct RIA for subordinate regulations and the gap between requirements and practice is wider than for primary laws (Figure 3.3). Although subordinate regulations are not subject to parliamentary oversight, they represent a substantive part of the regulatory burden faced by citizens and businesses. The impacts of subordinate regulations therefore ought to be systematically assessed to promote policy effectiveness, efficiency, and coherence.

Figure 3.3. Almost all EU Member States require RIAs to be carried out systematically but a gap between requirements and practice remains

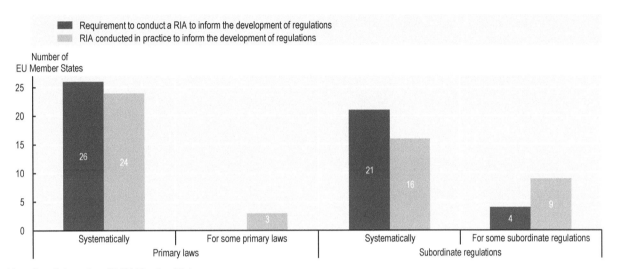

Note: Data is based on 27 EU Member States.
Source: Indicators of Regulatory Policy and Governance (iREG) Survey 2021.

Governments have limited resources and must use them appropriately and judiciously when developing policies as not all proposals have the same anticipated impacts. The OECD recognises that every regulatory proposal is different and does not need the same level of consideration or scrutiny (OECD, 2020[2]). Some proposals are procedural and will result in minor changes, so their development does not warrant as much time and effort as those of proposals that are likely to have major impacts on citizens and businesses. It does take time and resources to conduct *ex ante* analysis, therefore RIA should be undertaken where the costs of doing so are outweighed by the benefits of improving the policy (OECD, 2020[8]).

The *2012 Recommendation* emphasises that RIA should be proportionate to the significance of the anticipated impacts of the policy proposal (OECD, 2012[1]). OECD members' analytical efforts should be targeted towards proposals that are expected to have the largest impacts on society, to ensure that all such proposals are appropriately examined. Sufficient evidence and analysis should also be provided to stakeholders during consultation on such proposals, so they may be informed – and help to estimate – the scope of the potential impacts. The European Commission recognises the significance of the proportionate use of better regulation instruments, acknowledging that "the scope and depth of the analysis should always be proportionate and consistent with the importance and type of initiative and the nature and magnitude of the expected impacts" (European Commission, 2021, p. 81[3]). The principle of proportionality in the context of the European Commission's regulatory practices are covered in more detail in Box 3.3.

The majority of EU Member States recognise that the level and depth of analysis should be aligned with the proposals' expected impacts. Seventeen EU Member States require that impact assessment practices be proportionate to the expected significance of proposals for primary laws (Figure 3.4). Proportionality requirements for primary laws now exist in approximately two-thirds of EU Member States, compared to approximately three-quarters of OECD member countries. The number of countries with such requirements has increased since the previous edition of *Better Regulation Practices across the European Union* (2019[5]) as **Greece** has introduced the requirement that RIAs for primary laws be proportionate to the significance of the proposal in 2019. In contrast, 15 EU Member States require that RIA practices be proportionate to the expected impacts of subordinate regulations, a figure that has not changed since 2017 and that remains below the proportion of OECD members with the same requirements.

Figure 3.4. Most EU Member States have requirements that impact assessment is proportionate to the significance of the regulation

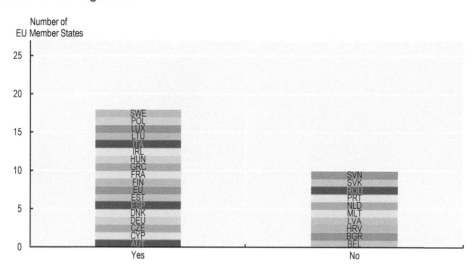

Note: Data is based on 27 EU Member States and the European Union. This figure combines data for both primary and subordinate regulations as all EU Member States, except Cyprus and Greece, have the same requirements for both types of regulations. Cyprus and Greece both require RIAs to be proportionate to the significance of the regulation for primary laws but not for subordinate regulations.
Source: Indicators of Regulatory Policy and Governance (iREG) Survey 2021.

EU Member States' definition of what proportionality is and what the objectives of proportionate RIA are is consistent with the OECD's and the European Commission's definition. Information provided by EU Member States suggest they generally consider that resources and efforts dedicated to a specific regulatory proposal should be proportionate to the type of intervention and the scope of the expected impacts. For example, according to the Government of **Cyprus**, the analytical efforts should be proportionate to the issues addressed by the relevant proposal as well as the intensity of effort required for the carrying out of an impact assessment (collection and analysis of the relevant data and information) (Government of Cyprus, 2016[9]).

Box 3.3. Proportionate RIAs in the European Commission

The impact assessment prepared by the European Commission, in accordance with their guidelines (2021[10]), must be proportionate and consistent with the significance and the type of initiative as well as the nature and magnitude of expected impacts. All expected economic, social and environmental impacts should be considered proportionally to their significance. The proportionality principle not only relates to the impact assessment report but also to all stages of the assessment process.

In order to determine the appropriate depth of the analysis, the following need to be decided:

- The resources and time allocated to the overall assessment process, including data collection, stakeholder consultation and conducting external studies;
- Resources required to answer each of the impact assessment key questions;
- The specific focus of the each step of the analysis – i.e., whether the comparison of policy options should focus on broad options or alternative measures within a given policy option; the level of aggregation at which the assessment should take place; which aspects should be analysed more in depth.

The lead Directorate-General with the interservice group are responsible for determining the depth and level of impact assessment, while taking into account all relevant factors as well as time, resource and data constraints. The depth of the analysis should be determined as early in the planning process as possible and the indication of the level of the analysis should be included in the call for evidence.

The proportionality of the impact assessment report with regard to the measures considered and their impacts is an element in the scrutiny carried out by the Regulatory Scrutiny Board.

Source: European Commission (2021[3]), *Better regulation Toolbox*, https://ec.europa.eu/info/sites/default/files/br_toolbox-nov_2021_en_0.pdf.

Using preliminary threshold tests to decide whether undertaking a RIA at all is necessary for a given regulatory proposal is not a common method to ensure proportionality across EU Member States, as only **Italy** and **Lithuania** do so (Box 3.4). This preliminary reflection takes the form of a threshold test, whereby some assessment is used to determine if the impacts of the regulatory proposal are significant enough to warrant investing resources in conducting a RIA. Using some preliminary assessment to identify whether a RIA is necessary is a less common practice in EU Member States compared to OECD member countries, with approximately one-fifth having such a threshold test in place.

Box 3.4. Threshold tests to determine whether RIA is undertaken in Italy and Lithuania

The new Decree+ Handbook in **Italy** does not fix a single monetary threshold. The proportionality of analysis is met by four conditions, which constitute the set of criteria to be used for determining the "significance" of the expected impacts. This significance may vary. In fact, for each individual regulation/legislation under preparation, a proposal of RIA exemption shall be presented to DAGL by the individual ministry, and DAGL verifies if the decision (of not carrying out RIA) is grounded or not. In other words, on each proposed exemption from RIA, DAGL scrutinises the evidence that demonstrates the low expected impacts of the new legislation/regulation.

> In **Lithuania**, the threshold used to determine whether a RIA ought to be undertaken is based on legal factors rather than analytical ones. Regulatory impact assessments must be conducted when a legislative proposal concerns a policy area that has not been regulated before or when it amends an existing regulation.
>
> Source: Indicators of Regulatory Policy and Governance (iREG) Survey 2021 and OECD (2020[8]), A closer look at the proportionality and threshold tests for RIA. Annex to the OECD Best Practice Principles on Regulatory Impact Assessment, http://www.oecd.org/regreform/Proportionality-and-threshhold-tests-RIA.pdf.

Exceptions to the use of RIA

There are cases, for example in genuinely unforeseen emergencies or when a policy has truly negligible impacts, where not carrying out RIAs can be a proportionate and appropriate way forward. During the COVID-19 pandemic it was sometimes necessary to regulate before undertaking a full RIA. However, policy makers should still attempt to use any information that can be reasonably collected *ex ante* to help inform decision making, and to use it as a basis for later reviews of the policy. There may still be opportunities to undertake *some* impact assessment, for example a focus (perhaps even only qualitatively) on the immediate anticipated effects of the policy. For instance **Canada** adjusted its RIA requirements for COVID-related proposals. Proposals could be developed using adjusted analytical requirements, including cost-benefit analysis and the small business lens analysis. These could be based on qualitative and quantitative data, but the requirement to monetise impacts was relaxed. In addition, proposals could be recommended for exclusion from the one-for-one rule (OECD, 2021[4]). In **Denmark**, COVID-related regulatory proposals were reviewed to assess whether the resulting administrative costs were above the threshold that would have triggered an in-depth RIA under normal circumstances. No COVID-related regulatory measures to date were identified as resulting in impacts above the threshold.

EU Member States have generally adopted exception mechanisms to RIA requirements where it is warranted, and particularly where a regulation is introduced in response to an emergency. In around half of EU Member States such regulations are except from RIA requirements (Figure 3.5). This is in line with the *2021 Regulatory Policy Outlook* that found that nearly half of OECD members have exceptions to conducting RIAs where regulations are introduced in response to an emergency and that several members used this mechanism to bypass their RIA requirements for some of the regulations introduced in response to the COVID-19 pandemic (OECD, 2021[4]).

Figure 3.5. In some instances, regulations are excepted from RIA requirements

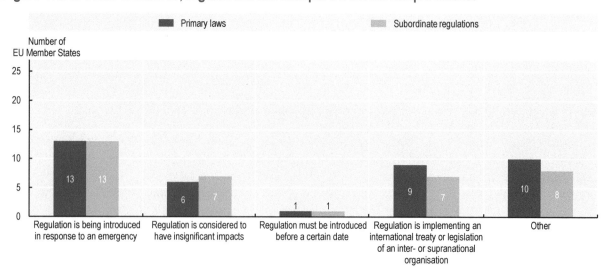

Note: Data is based on 27 EU Member States.
Source: Indicators of Regulatory Policy and Governance (iREG) Survey 2021.

In addition to emergency responses, some EU Member States except regulations from RIA requirements under other circumstances. One-quarter of EU Member States do not require RIAs to be carried out for regulations that are considered to have insignificant impacts whilst one-third report to have exceptions to RIA requirements when a primary law at hand is implementing an international treaty or a legislation of an inter- or supranational organisation (Figure 3.5). These exceptions have not changed since 2017. In **Belgium** the exceptions to RIA apply to legislation concerning co-operation agreements between the federal state and the regional entities and the national security or the public order. In addition, RIA is excepted for autoregulations (i.e. regulations that concern the organisation of the State itself). In the **Czech Republic**, amendments to the Constitution, Acts on State budget, State Final Account, legislation introducing only parametric changes, government resolutions, and legislation that is granted exception by the chairperson of the Government Legislative Council are all excepted from RIA requirements. In **Ireland**, if a legislation is consolidating existing legislation and there are no regulatory changes being introduced, it is excepted from the requirement to undergo a RIA. In addition, legislation drafted as a direct consequence of a Court decision that leaves no discretion to consider alternative options or allow for meaningful consultation are excepted to RIA requirements.

Exceptions to RIA requirements also exist in the EU institutions, as EU policy makers can be excepted from carrying out RIAs when a regulation is being introduced in response to an emergency or is considered to have insignificant impacts. The European Commission recognises that better regulation practices should be applied flexibly and in a proportionate manner that reflect the circumstances of each individual initiative and there can be occasions where the better regulation procedures have to be shortened or simplified (European Commission, 2021[3]). Prior approval is however necessary for such exceptions and must be approved by the European Commission's Secretariat General or by the Vice-President for Better Regulation in more important cases. In addition, all such exceptions should be published in the call for evidence as well as in the explanatory memorandum accompanying the European Commission's regulatory proposal.

Whilst exception mechanisms for RIA are valid and relevant to ensuring that proportionate resources are allocated to the relevant policy proposals, policy makers should be accountable for using them. The events that trigger the exception, such as an unforeseen emergency or the significance of the impacts, must be real and genuine. Transparency of the decision to bypass RIA is an effective way to hold policy makers to account for utilising exception mechanisms and to ensure these are not abused. For example, the *OECD Best Practice Principles on Regulatory Impact Assessment* (2020[2]) calls for the application of thresholds – which includes exceptions to RIAs – to be publicly shared and call for the involvement of regulatory oversight. As such, involving regulatory oversight in reviewing the decision to except a regulation from RIA requirements and publishing said decision not only improves transparency and trust in policy making, it also ensures exceptions and scarce RIA resources are correctly and appropriately utilised.

EU Member States could benefit from providing more transparency around decisions to bypass RIA as scrutiny remains limited. Similarly to the findings from the *OECD Regulatory Policy Outlook* (2021[4]), the transparency surrounding the decisions to except proposals from conducting RIA in EU Member States remains blurred. Only three EU Member States – the **Czech Republic**, **Italy**, and the **Slovak Republic** – currently publish the decision that RIA for a primary law will not be conducted where it ought to have been (Figure 3.6). In addition, only nine EU Member States have a body responsible for reviewing the decision made by officials about whether a RIA for a primary law is required (Figure 3.6). A majority of EU Member States can use the exception mechanisms to bypass RIA with little scrutiny on whether this decision is appropriate or proportionate to the regulatory proposal at hand.

Figure 3.6. EU Member States could benefit from more transparency and oversight in the decision to bypass RIA in case of exceptions

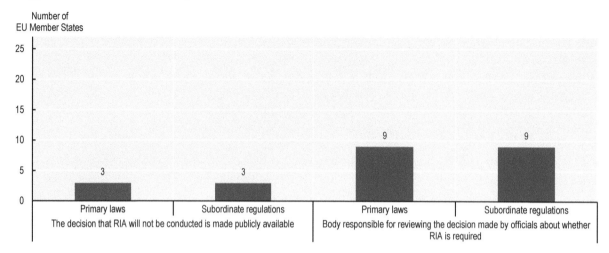

Note: Data is based on 27 EU Member States.
Source: Indicators of Regulatory Policy and Governance (iREG) Survey 2021.

Threshold tests as a method to implement the proportionality principle in EU Member States

Countries can use different practices and methodologies to implement proportionality in their RIA processes. Whilst EU Member States generally recognise that the resources and depth of analysis should be targeted to the proposals with the largest expected impacts, proportionate RIA practices can take various forms. Some of the methodologies used by EU Member States and OECD member countries to establish whether legislative proposals require a certain level of analysis include (OECD, 2020[2]; OECD, 2020[8]):

1. **Setting quantitative threshold tests:** The level or depth of analysis is dependent on the total impacts to society. The policy maker needs to estimate the total impacts quantitatively, usually as part of a preliminary step in the development of a new regulation;

2. **Multi-criteria analysis:** The depth of RIA is based on a mix of quantitative and qualitative criteria in a number of key areas. The criteria may include, for example, the number of affected businesses, a certain level of CO_2 emissions or a subjective assessment of the significance of impacts on key sectors. These impacts are sometimes quantified but usually not monetised;

3. **Single-issue test**: The analytical depth of RIA is based on impacts to one sector or stakeholder group. For example, a full RIA is only required when costs to businesses exceed a certain amount; or

4. **A general principle of proportionate analysis, applied at policy makers' discretion:** The choice of RIA depth is left to the administration itself based on the principle of proportionality. An oversight body could potentially intervene and suggest a deeper analysis where the proportionality principle is deemed to have not been appropriately applied.

A categorisation of the methods used to ensure proportionality in a sample of EU Member States is provided in Table 3.1.

Table 3.1. EU Member States use various methods to apply proportionality in the analysis of the expected impacts of the regulation

A selection of EU Member States where impact assessments are required to be proportionate to the significance of the anticipated/expected impacts.

	Threshold tests			General principle of proportionate analysis, applied at policy makers' discretion
	Quantitative threshold test	Multi-criteria analysis	Single-issue test	
Austria		✓		
Croatia		✓		
Cyprus				✓
Czech Republic				✓
Denmark			✓	
Estonia		✓		
Finland				✓
France				✓
Germany			(informally)	✓
Ireland				✓
Italy	✓			
Latvia			✓	
Lithuania		✓		
Luxembourg				✓
Poland				✓
Spain	✓			
Sweden				✓
European Union				✓

Source: Indicators of Regulatory Policy and Governance (iREG) Survey 2021, OECD (2020), OECD Best Practice Principles for Regulatory Policy: Regulatory Impact Assessment, OECD Publishing, http://dx.doi.org/10.1787/7a9638cb-en, and OECD (2020[8]), A closer look at the proportionality and threshold tests for RIA. Annex to the OECD Best Practice Principles on Regulatory Impact Assessment, http://www.oecd.org/regreform/Proportionality-and-threshhold-tests-RIA.pdf.

In effect, quantitative tests, single-issue test, and multi-criteria analysis can all be considered as part of a two-tiered approach to RIA where a shorter and less rigorous assessment process is used as a filter to identify proposals that should be subject to additional analysis (OECD, 2020[8]). Threshold tests usually take the form of preliminary analysis, either through the use of a "simplified" RIA or through preliminary calculations and measurements. The shorter and less rigorous RIA process might be sufficient in cases of low expected regulatory impacts and may be used to identify proposals where more in-depth analysis is necessary. In other words, if the anticipated impacts of a proposal are above a certain threshold, it must undergo a more thorough and detailed impact assessment process (OECD, 2020[8]). The *Annex to the OECD Best Practice Principles on RIA* (2020[8]) identify elements that policy makers should consider when developing threshold tests and proportionality rules in general (see Box 3.5).

Box 3.5. Annex to the OECD Best Practice Principles on Regulatory Impact Assessment: A closer look at proportionality and threshold tests for RIA

OECD countries should consider the following, when developing proportionality rules or threshold tests:

1. Determining the scope of RIA should start at an early stage when policy makers are evaluating the problem – potentially even before considering the need for intervention – and identifying regulatory and non-regulatory alternatives. Preferably, this process should start already in the phase of legislative planning.

2. An oversight body should assess whether the policy maker has characterised the problem correctly, including its magnitude, when it still has the flexibility in formulating a regulation or policy. The earlier policy makers understand the magnitude of the problem, the better the government may target resources to developing solutions.

3. During the early stage of RIA, policy makers should begin to introduce an economic rationale and data to determine the scope of the issue. This does not mean an in-depth analysis at an early stage (e.g. a well-developed cost-benefit analysis). Policy makers should be broadly scanning an issue, before undertaking an in-depth analysis.

4. The time and resources devoted to the development of regulation and its analysis should relate to the size of the impacts, the size and structure of the economy, the impacts per capita, the flexibility of the policy, and the relative resources of the government.

5. If a country chooses to use quantified thresholds for RIA, they should be inclusive and base the thresholds on the size of impacts across society, rather than focusing on any specific sector or stakeholder group. There may also be a risk in using one single value threshold that captures impacts across society. One stakeholder group may be disproportionately affected but the total impacts are below the threshold, so countries may wish to consider a threshold that also incorporates a per capita or stakeholder threshold.

6. Regulations should only be exempt from completing the RIA process in genuinely unforeseen emergencies, when a significant delay could objectively put the wellbeing of citizens at risk. Oversight bodies should be very critical of ministries that overuse such exemptions. Ministries should also be required to conduct an *ex post* evaluation to establish whether the regulation was effective after a defined period of time.

7. Regulations with limited policy options or flexibility (e.g. transposition of EU directives or supranational laws) might have a less rigorous process. When fewer policy options or instruments are available, even if the impacts may be quite significant, policy makers have less flexibility to improve a policy at this stage. Despite this, governments should be mindful that EU directives or other supranational instruments might still have a degree of flexibility in their implementation.

8. The time and resources for regulation development and analysis should also scale with the capacities of the government. It is important that governments continuously build the expertise of policy makers in RIA and stakeholder engagement to make analysis more effective. Governments must build capacities in ministries before they can require significant levels of analysis.

Source: OECD (2020[8]), A closer look at the proportionality and threshold tests for RIA. Annex to the OECD Best Practice Principles on Regulatory Impact Assessment, http://www.oecd.org/regreform/Proportionality-and-threshhold-tests-RIA.pdf.

Threshold tests are not as common in EU Member States as they are amongst OECD member countries. One-quarter of EU Member States use thresholds to determine the scope and depth of analysis and decide whether more in-depth RIA should be undertaken (Figure 3.7), compared to approximatively half of OECD members. The EU Member States using a two-tiered approach are **Austria**, **Croatia**, **Denmark**, **Estonia**, **Latvia**, **Lithuania**, and **Spain** (Figure 3.7). It is worth noting that **Latvia** and **Croatia** have threshold tests in place even though there are no formal requirements for RIAs to be proportionate to the expected impacts.

Figure 3.7. Two-tiered approaches and threshold tests are not common amongst EU Member States

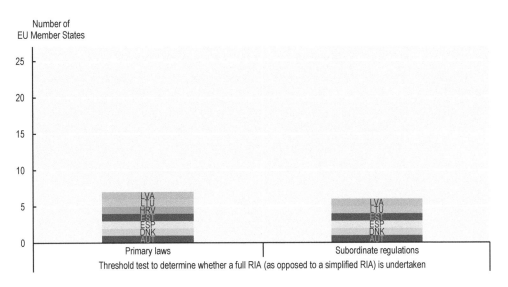

Note: Data is based on 27 EU Member States and the European Union.
Source: Indicators of Regulatory Policy and Governance (iREG) Survey 2021.

There is strong heterogeneity in the methods used to identify regulatory proposals that necessitate more in-depth analysis. As explored in Table 3.1, EU Member States appear to use multi-criteria analysis (as defined above) as a common method to ensure proportionality in RIA practices. By definition, a wide range of factors can be included as part of multi-criteria analysis and this is the case amongst EU Member States, where heterogeneity is so strong that it is difficult to identify a common pattern and to classify countries within specific categories. It is worth noting that the impacts on businesses is a factor considered in the threshold of most of the EU Member States with a two-tiered approach to proportionality. Some countries, such as **Croatia** and **Denmark** use regulatory impacts on particular groups as a guide to define how proportionality should be applied. For example in **Denmark**, in-depth RIAs are triggered when regulatory proposals result in a certain level of costs on businesses. In **Croatia**, it is the impact on citizens and on the population that defines the depth of the analysis. In contrast, other EU Member States such as **Austria**, **Lithuania**, and **Spain** consider a wider range of factors that are more representative of the economy and society as a whole to determine the scope of analysis. In addition, threshold tests can be adapted as RIA practices in countries evolve. This is for example the case in **Estonia** where formal threshold tests and in-depth RIAs have been replaced by more comprehensive analysis that includes core regulatory elements. Further examples of multi-criteria analytical practices across EU Member States are explored in Box 3.6.

Two-tiered approaches are sound methods to implement the proportionality principle, but some important points must be considered when developing and utilising threshold tests:

- First, as noted in the *Annex to the OECD Best Practice Principles on RIA* (2020[8]), thresholds for RIA should be inclusive and based on the size of impacts across society rather than focusing on specific sector or stakeholder group. Policy makers should also consider what happens when regulatory proposals have a large impact on factors that are not considered in the definition of a threshold test. This is particularly relevant for those EU Member States and OECD member countries where the proportionality principle is applied on the basis of a narrow set of criteria. For example, in countries where the threshold test is driven by the impacts on businesses, policy makers must ensure that legislative proposals that have a minor impact on businesses but a major impact on other factors, say the environment, are also appropriately and proportionately assessed. Applying the proportionality principle means that the depth of analysis should be proportionate and appropriate to the significance of *all* impacts, not only those reviewed in the threshold test. Policy makers in countries with narrower proportionality methodologies and with a focus on the impacts on businesses must ensure that they do not neglect proposals that have a major impact on factors that are excluded from the threshold test.

- Second, threshold tests should not be viewed as an opportunity to bypass RIA requirements. They should guide policy makers to apply the most appropriate level of resources given a proposal's significance, but should not motivate shaping the regulation in such a way that avoids stricter RIA requirements. There is a potential role for regulatory oversight bodies to ensure that threshold tests, and the proportionality principle in general, are appropriately and correctly applied, as will be explored at the end of this section.

Box 3.6. Multi-level criteria approaches to proportionality and differences between "lite RIAs" and "full RIAs" from selected EU Member States

Austria

For all new laws and regulations, an impact assessment is mandatory. The regulation underpinning this instrument provides an explicit list of impact dimensions that have to be assessed. Nevertheless, only impacts above a certain threshold have to be assessed in further detail. Thresholds are mostly quantitative and vary depending on:

1. Financial impacts and impacts on access to finance (if financial impact is expected to exceed EUR 2.5 million or affects more than 10 000 enterprises);
2. Impact on the environment (if CO_2 emissions exceed 10 000 tons per year);
3. Impacts on the labour market;
4. Impact on the business (if more than 500 enterprises are affected); or
5. Impact on federal annual budget.

The RIA accompanying the regulatory proposal that fall below all the thresholds have much lighter requirements. Policy makers only have to provide a short (1-2 pages) description about the intent of the new or amended regulation, instead of a full-scale assessment. In addition, such RIAs do not include outcome indicators to measure progress and do not require mandatory *ex post* evaluation five years after their implementation.

The threshold test in Austria was reformed in 2015 to reflect the fact that a large number of minor amendments to laws and regulations that have no significant impact are introduced every year, such as for example renaming a regulatory agency. Such legislation have no significant impact that can be assessed *ex ante* or evaluated *ex post*. As a consequence, only approximately 35% of new laws are accompanied by a full scale RIA and resources can be directed to proposals where in-depth impact assessments are needed.

Croatia

In order for an impact assessment in Croatia to progress from a simplified RIA (Preliminary Assessment) to a full RIA (RIA report), the Preliminary Assessment must fall within at least three combinations that determine the combination of likely direct impacts and effects on the population:

1. Large expected direct impacts and large effects on population;
2. Small expected direct impacts and large effects on population; or
3. Large expected direct impacts and small effect on population.

Denmark

Denmark uses threshold tests to determine whether a full or simplified RIA should be undertaken. Danish RIAs combine different elements: One part focusing on other compliance costs for businesses and another part focusing on administrative burdens. Each part has individual threshold tests based on the level of both anticipated one-off costs and regulatory costs, which determines whether a more in-depth assessment is required.

1. For administrative burdens, an in-depth measurement (including interviews with affected companies) must be undertaken if a regulatory proposal is expected to have administrative consequences for businesses over DKK 4 million annually.
2. An in-depth assessment of business economic impacts is triggered if the regulatory compliance costs are expected to be above DKK 10 million.

The concept of proportionality in Denmark is explored in more detail below.

Estonia

Formally, thresholds to differentiate between "simplified" and in-depth RIAs exist in Estonia and are based on the following criteria:

1. The scale of the impact;
2. The frequency of the occurrence of the impact;
3. The size of the affected target group; and
4. The risk of accompanying undesirable impacts.

In reality, however, "simplified" RIAs have become increasingly exhaustive and include more of the elements that should be assessed in in-depth analysis. As a result, the practices in Estonia have evolved as the simplified RIAs include more evidence than originally required, thereby making in-depth RIAs increasingly irrelevant and rarely done. The concept of proportionality in Estonia is explored in more detail below.

Latvia

Latvian policy makers are allowed to bypass a section of the RIA that includes an assessment of the administrative costs in the RIA if the annual costs are expected to be under EUR 200 for citizens and EUR 2,000 for businesses.

Lithuania

In 2020, The Office of Government in Lithuania introduced several criteria for the selection of draft legislation of a higher impact. These include:

1. Impact on public finances higher than EUR 1 million per year or a change to the tax system;

2. Impact on innovation;

3. Impact on competition;

4. Impact on business, defined as additional regulatory or administrative burdens above EUR 1 million and/or impacts on SMEs;

5. Impact on regional development;

6. Impact on employment;

7. Impact on the structure of the state institutions or on the number of public sector employees.

Spain

Simplified RIAs can be carried out in Spain if the regulatory proposal does not or insignificantly impacts:

1. The economy (including business, competition, competitiveness);

2. Budget;

3. Administrative burdens;

4. Gender;

5. Family and childhood;

6. Environment.

A simplified RIA is also possible for primary laws that are adopted by the executive in case of extraordinary and urgent public need, as allowed by the Spanish Constitution. The minimum content of a simplified RIA should at least include the following sections:

- Policy issues, objective, and alternatives;

- Explanation of content;

- Legal basis;

- Assessment of the regulatory impacts on the budget and on gender;

- Description of the procedure carried out (including consultations, reports, etc.).

Source: Indicators of Regulatory Policy and Governance Survey, 2021 and OECD (2020[8]), A closer look at the proportionality and threshold tests for RIA. Annex to the OECD Best Practice Principles on Regulatory Impact Assessment, http://www.oecd.org/regreform/Proportionality-and-threshhold-tests-RIA.pdf.

Proportionality in the depth of the RIA analysis

A number of EU Member States rely on the principle of proportionality in their analysis, without the use of methods such as threshold tests to apply it, as demonstrated in Table 3.1. In such cases, the scope of the analysis is at the discretion of the policy makers in individual ministries, who have the choice of deciding how much effort and resources should be allocated to analysing the various regulatory impacts. Public officials may, in some cases, be required to assess a specific range of regulatory impacts but the depth and comprehensiveness of this assessment is their choice. This is, for example, the case in **Germany** where RIAs are required for all legislative proposals and there is no formal threshold to determine the depth of RIA. Whilst policy makers are required to assess how the proposal affects a range of factors such as competition, SMEs, and the environment amongst others for all primary and subordinate regulations, ministerial officials can choose the scope and depth of analysis. The example of Germany is explored in the next section, whilst the application of the proportionality principle at policy makers' discretion in the **Czech Republic** is highlighted in Box 3.7.

Box 3.7. How the general principle of proportionate analysis is applied at policy makers' discretion in the Czech Republic

Regulatory impact assessment in **Czech Republic** is based on the principle of proportional analysis, which is related to the different depth and scope of the impact analysis and the whole assessment process – the scope of data collection needed for impact assessment, the scope of consultation of stakeholders and number of options assessed. The analysis evaluates and quantifies the potential impacts of the proposed regulation/solution. It is in the hands of the ministry proposing the regulations to carry out the proportionality analysis and determine the level/depth of the impact assessment. When determining the level of analysis, it is always necessary to take into account the significance and extent of the problem to be solved and its expected impacts.

Source: Indicators of Regulatory Policy and Governance (iREG) Survey 2021.

The fact that the depth of analysis varies across EU Member States also signifies that the format of final RIAs can vary significantly. RIAs as "final products" can range from a checklist in which policy makers tick whether the regulatory proposal results in certain impacts to more in-depth reports where individual effects are comprehensively identified, reviewed, and quantified. Amongst EU Member States that use threshold tests, informal evidence suggests that in-depth RIAs in some countries will, in fact, be considered as simplified RIA in others. Whilst a majority of EU Member States are systematically required to assess how the regulatory proposal affects a range of impacts, it is unclear how Member States decide on the depth of analysis and how the level of assessment for each type of factor varies with the significance of the regulatory proposal. Evidence from a series of interviews with **Cyprus**, **Denmark**, **Estonia**, and **Germany**, carried out by the OECD as part of this project and summarised in the following sections, suggest that the depth of analysis is at the discretion of policy makers and ministerial officials in charge of RIA, with little involvement from regulatory oversight bodies.

Regulatory oversight bodies (ROBs) could be involved in reviewing whether the proportionality principle has been correctly applied in the RIAs scrutinised and whether the depth of the analysis is proportionate to the anticipated impacts. As the *Annex to the RIA Best Practice Principles* (OECD, 2020[8]) suggests, as part of ensuring an appropriate allocation of resources, proportionality rules are often considered as a way to align with the capacity of the ROB to scrutinise the quality of RIA. ROBs are thus also impacted by the proportionality principle and reviewing its correct application could be added to their mandates. RegWatchEurope, a network of European regulatory oversight bodies, argues that independent scrutiny can help ensure that ministerial officials apply the proportionality principle appropriately (RegWatchEurope, 2020[11]). It is crucial for the success of RIA to ensure that policy makers do not abuse threshold tests or take advantage of the discretion offered by the proportionality principle and that it remains an appropriate and efficient evidence-based process. Similarly to the role of some ROBs in reviewing the correct use of RIA exception mechanisms, this is particularly relevant for those EU Member States that use threshold tests to implement the proportionality principle, as policy makers may be incentivised to underestimate the impacts of a proposed regulation so that they fall below the threshold in order to avoid triggering RIA requirements (OECD, 2021[4]).

There are no comprehensive data on the number EU Member States with ROBs involved in ensuring that the depth of the analysis is sufficient and proportionate to a given proposal's expected impacts (or the exact role of those ROBs). As discussed in Chapter 1, there are 21 and 22 EU Member States with a ROB responsible for reviewing the quality of RIAs for primary laws and for subordinate regulations, respectively. In addition, ROBs in 13 EU Member States are able to return RIAs for a primary law for revision where it is deemed inadequate, versus 10 for subordinate regulation. RIAs can generally be returned on the grounds of lack of effective consultation, incorrect assessment of compliance or administrative costs, or inadequate justification for the regulatory intervention. Anecdotal evidence, including from the survey questions on regulatory oversight bodies included in the indicators of Regulatory Policy and Governance (iREG) survey 2017, suggests that discussions on proportionate analysis can sometimes occur informally in meetings between ROBs and the policy officials in charge of the regulatory proposals.

Proportionality in Germany

Germany's RIA system scores highly amongst the EU Member States, as seen in Figure 3.1 and Figure 3.2. RIAs in Germany are required and undertaken for all primary laws and subordinate regulations prepared by the Federal Government. There are no exceptions as all legislative initiatives (of Government) include a proportionate impact assessment and analysis of the resulting compliance costs, even in cases of emergency, and the vast majority of adopted laws are initiated by the Federal Government. Proportionality in the legislative process is grounded within the Basic Law for the Federal Republic of Germany,[1] which provides that regulatory instruments are considered lawful only if they pursue a legitimate purpose and if they are necessary, suitable, and appropriate. The principle of proportionality in Germany is understood in both a broader sense – i.e. to ensure that a law or regulation is necessary, suitable and pursues a legitimate purpose – as well as in a narrower sense, to ensure that the measure is appropriate. The principle of proportionality is thus rooted in the Basic Law and applies to all activities of official bodies and particularly to the legislative powers, to the judiciary, as well as to the public administration including policy makers in charge of RIA. The initiatives introduced by the Parliament (*Bundestag*) and by the legislative body representing the Federal States (*Bundesrat*) must also abide to the principle of proportionality.

There are no formal threshold tests in Germany to determine the depth of RIAs, as policy makers have the discretion to choose the scope of the assessment and the depth at which the various regulatory impacts should be analysed. There is however an informal rule whereby regulatory proposals for which annual compliance costs are expected to be below EUR 100 000 are considered as resulting in minor changes. Therefore, these proposals do not require a detailed quantitative assessment of compliance costs and of other regulatory impacts, such as costs and benefits on citizens. The decision to bypass the quantitative assessment must be based on an estimation of the regulatory compliance costs and must be approved by the *Normenkontrollrat* (NKR) (National Regulatory Control Council).

German policy makers tend to focus their analysis on regulatory costs rather than benefits. They are required to include assessments of a wide range of impacts (competition, SME, environmental, poverty, gender equality etc.) for all primary and subordinate regulations. Policy makers in the ministries decide on the depth of the analysis. In addition, regulators in the Federal Government are required to quantify costs (i.e. compliance costs, which includes administrative costs) for all primary and subordinate regulations – including quantifying costs on individuals, citizens, businesses and the government. These requirements were introduced in the 1990s and their implementation has been improved since. Identifying or assessing benefits is not required in Germany. The State Secretary Committee recommended in 2019 to present the benefits of planned regulations, depending on the political significance of the regulatory proposal.

The NKR is an independent arm's length body that has the legal mandate to review the quality of RIA, including the appropriate assessment of impacts. Where the NKR deems a RIA inadequate, it works with the competent ministry to find a solution to improve it. Where no positive outcomes are reached, the NKR expresses its methodological concerns in an official statement that is presented to the Council of Ministers (i.e. *Bundesregierung*) and published with the RIA. The lead ministry must also prepare a responding statement that must be adopted by the Council of Ministers and subsequently published.

Stakeholder engagement in Germany is formally required for all primary laws and subordinate regulations initiated by the Federal Government as, according to the Joint Rules of Procedures of the Federal Ministries (GGO), federal ministries must consult with state governments, associations, and experts in the specific field affected by the regulation at hand. Consultations are however not required to be open to the general public. Stakeholder engagement appears to be more systematically undertaken when the text of the regulation has been drafted or proposed. Stakeholder engagement is reportedly subject to the principle of proportionality and, like RIA, federal ministries are formally at liberty to decide what entails proportionate consultation for a regulatory proposal. It is also at their discretion to decide whether public consultations will be carried out, in what format, and for how long.

The consultation period during the development of Government initiatives depends on the draft law being consulted. The decision regarding the required consultation period has to be in line with the proportionality principle of the German Basic Law, and as such, ministries are required to give sufficient time for consultation without defining one period of time for all cases and situations. There is however no formal requirement for a minimum period for consultations with the public, including citizens, business and civil society organisations. The GGO and additional decisions of the Federal Government however recommend four weeks as a standard period. The Better Regulation Unit, a regulatory oversight body located in the Federal Chancellery, has the capacity to review whether stakeholder comments have been considered. In addition, if the format or the depth of consultation and stakeholder engagement is found to be inadequate, the regulatory proposal may be rejected by the *Bundestag*.

The principle of proportionality also applies to the *ex post* evaluation requirements in Germany, which are determined in part by threshold tests as all regulations where annual compliance costs are more than EUR 1 million per annum for citizens, businesses or the administration must be evaluated three to five years after their implementation. Compliance costs are not however the only element in determining whether a regulation must be evaluated, as factors such as political relevance and the level of political risk are also deciding factors. Policy makers have the prerogative to decide which initiatives are considered as politically relevant, although this may also be decided by the Federal Chancellery.

All *ex post* evaluations are required to contain an assessment and quantification of costs, but only an assessment of benefits. *Ex post* evaluations regarding major primary and subordinate laws are also required to include a comparison of the actual versus predicted impacts of the regulation being reviewed. In November 2019, the German government introduced additional requirements for independent quality control of *ex post* evaluations which the NKR is performing.

Proportionality in Denmark

Regulatory impact assessment and use of regulatory management tools overall tend to anchor around business impacts in Denmark. RIAs are required and undertaken in practice for all primary laws. Denmark has introduced exceptions to conducting RIAs if a regulation is introduced in response to an emergency and if there is insufficient data to undertake the analysis, but there are otherwise no exceptions to the RIA requirements. In such cases where it is decided that a RIA will not be conducted, this decision is neither reviewed by a regulatory oversight body nor is it made publicly available.

RIAs practices in Denmark are required to be proportionate to the significance of the regulation, (i.e. the expected impact). In line with the findings from the *Annex to the Best Practice Principles on RIA* (OECD, 2020[8]), proportionality, and particularly thresholds, are seen as a way to allocate resources of the oversight body appropriately, to ensure that it scrutinises relevant proposals and to identify which proposals should be subject to a full RIA. It also helps assess whether the implementation and enforcement strategy is proportionate to the perceived risks of regulation.

Threshold tests are used in Denmark to determine whether a full or simplified RIA should be undertaken. The format of RIA and the depth of the analysis is guided by the impacts, and particularly the costs, on businesses. Danish RIAs combine different elements, with one part focusing on other compliance costs for businesses and another part focusing on administrative burdens. Each part has an individual threshold test based on the level of both anticipated one-off costs and recurring costs, which determines whether a more in-depth assessment is required.

- For the administrative burden assessment, an in-depth measurement (including interviews with affected companies) must be undertaken if a regulatory proposal is expected to have administrative consequences for businesses over DKK 4 million annually; and

- An in-depth assessment of business economic impacts is triggered if the regulatory compliance costs are expected to be above DKK 10 million.

The two thresholds are assessed independently. As a result, in-depth assessment on the administrative burdens can be triggered independently of the other compliance costs resulting from the legislative proposal. If a legislative proposal is found to impact only one of the two threshold tests, then this individual section of the RIA will be longer and more in-depth than the other sections. In a full RIA, the consequences for businesses are more thoroughly assessed on the basis of interviews and of cost-benefit analysis, as per the standard cost-model.

Danish policy makers are required to include assessment of a range of impacts (competition, SME, public sector, environmental, poverty, gender equality, regional, UN Sustainable Development Goals, etc.) for all primary laws. In addition, policy makers are required to quantify costs (including administrative burdens and compliance costs) for all regulatory proposals, with particular emphasis on the impacts on businesses. The assessment of regulatory benefits is subject to the same requirements as the assessment of costs and are thus also required to be identified and quantified. The relevant ministry decides on the depth of analysis based on co-operation and dialogue with other relevant ministries and extensive co-operation between the various ministries takes place informally. The depth of analysis of the impacts on businesses is however decided or at least approved by the regulatory oversight body.

Regulatory oversight in Denmark is organised around the impacts on businesses and particularly around regulatory costs. The Danish Business Authority's Better Regulation Unit (BRU) is involved in reviewing the quality of business RIAs for regulations that have an impact on the business community. The Danish Business Regulation Forum (DBRF) is reported to also ensure that regulations are proportionate, in the sense that they do not go beyond what is strictly necessary to resolve the policy issue identified. The business-focus on the DBRF but also of the Better Regulation agenda in Denmark in general is the result of the organisation of membership within the Forum, which does include a majority of business representatives. It is crucial to note that the DBRF however does include members from consumer organisations, from labour organisations, and from non-business groups and that consensus amongst the various members is key to the functioning of the DBRF. The DBRF will not make recommendations on improving the Danish business environment that come at the expense of consumers or workers.

Stakeholder engagement in Denmark is required and must be open to the public for all primary laws. Stakeholder engagement is done systematically when the text of the regulation has been drafted or proposed as part of the public consultation, while formal and informal consultations are held before a preferred policy option has been identified, although there is no requirement to do so. There are no formal requirements for a minimum public consultation period, as the online consultation period must be adapted to the specific circumstances surrounding the legislative proposal. It should however be long enough to enable stakeholders to adequately prepare, so a consultation period of four weeks is recommended under normal circumstances. Other than a requirement for public consultation to be systematically held over the internet, policy makers have discretion to engage with stakeholders how they see fit. There is currently little information on how bilateral engagement with stakeholders, either formally or informally, is undertaken and on what basis policy makers decide to engage and with whom.

Ex post evaluation is required for some laws and there are no thresholds or factors used to identify regulations that will be evaluated. It is at the discretion of the party undertaking the evaluation – either the ministry itself or the DBRF – to decide which regulation will be evaluated. Ministerial officials' decision to undertake an *ex post* evaluation is reportedly based on the political importance of the legislation, but they have the liberty to decide what regulation ought to be evaluated as well as the depth of the evaluation analysis. The DBRF is also completely independent to undertake evaluations on any issue they wish to review, to evaluate regulations as well as their implementation and interpretation. Their decision is reportedly influenced from a bottom-up approach, as the DBRF identifies regulations (or implementation thereof) to evaluate based on feedback from businesses on what they experience as burdensome. In addition, if the Better Regulation Unit, which is responsible for some of the core regulatory oversight functions, considers that an *ex ante* RIA is not adequate, it has the mandate to call for an *ex post* assessment to be undertaken by ministries.

Proportionality in Estonia

RIAs in Estonia are required for all legislative proposals and in practice are carried out for all primary laws but only for some subordinate regulations. RIAs are used early in the policy development process as Estonian policy makers are required to publish documents of legislative intent (i.e. roadmaps) that set out the policy problems, the regulatory objectives, and that highlight a range of suitable policy alternatives. The document of legislative intent is used to guide stakeholder engagement and to gather feedback to guide the development of the legislative proposal. In addition, there are no exceptions to conducting RIA as an impact assessment of the final policy must always be included in the explanatory memorandum that accompanies the legislative text.

RIA practices are required to be proportionate to the significance of the proposed regulation both for primary laws and subordinate regulations and, formally, threshold tests have been in place since 2014 to apply this requirement. The significance of the regulation is officially identified through a qualitative assessment of the impact on target groups using four criteria:

1. The scale of the impact;
2. The frequency of the occurrence of the impact;
3. The size of the affected target group; and
4. The risk of accompanying undesirable impacts.

If the legislative proposal is found to have a significant impact on any of the four criteria, policy makers are required to undertake a more thorough assessment and must collect more information about the expected impacts. In-depth RIAs must also include further information on the regulatory objectives, the assessment methodology, the costs and benefits from a regulatory proposal, how the policy option achieves the regulatory objectives, and set out obligations regarding monitoring and *ex post* evaluation.

In practice, however, simplified RIAs have become increasingly exhaustive and include more of the elements that should be assessed when the threshold test triggers more in-depth analysis. RIA practices in Estonia have evolved since their inception and have adapted to the realities of the legislative system, to such an extent that the procedural norms are no longer aligned with the requirements and that the threshold system has not been as effective and useful as initially expected. Simplified RIAs now include more evidence than originally required and have come to replace in-depth RIAs, which have become largely irrelevant and rarely done. In the past, the decision not to conduct in-depth RIA would always be published and reviewed by the regulatory oversight body, however in practice this is no longer the case as in-depth RIAs have become redundant and since simplified RIAs are conducted without exception. Currently, the four criteria that supposedly trigger in-depth RIAs are instead used as a guide to policy makers' analytical reasoning and are considered as evidence that should be covered in the RIA.

The analysis of regulatory impacts is ensured through a checklist that must be completed and, in practice, a qualitative assessment is included in all RIAs. The depth of the analysis is, however, at the discretion of the ministerial officials in charge of developing the RIA. Estonian policy makers are required to assess regulatory impacts on a wide range of factors such as competition, poverty, environment, etc. for all primary laws and subordinate regulations. Regulatory costs of the preferred policy option, particularly costs for the government, are supposed to be identified and quantified for all legislative proposals. The benefits must be identified for all legislative proposals but only quantified in some cases. The depth of the analysis depends on each individual ministry and its analytical capacities. Informal evidence suggests that, in the majority of cases, the numbers of parties impacted by the regulation is calculated but the extent of the impacts is less systematically measured as it depends on availability of evidence. For example, ministries in charge of financial, economic, and social affairs are able to analyse regulatory impacts in more depth thanks to the availability of suitable data. Ministries in charge of other policy areas, such as health or environment, reportedly do not have access to as much data and therefore undertake a more qualitative assessment.

Guidance material listing the different regulatory impacts that policy makers should explore is available. The regulatory oversight body in Estonia, the Legislative Quality Division located in the Ministry of Justice, scrutinises the explanatory memorandum accompanying the legislative text to ensure that the relevant regulatory impacts and affected parties have been correctly identified, although it is not able to comment on whether the depth of the analysis is sufficient. If the Legislative Quality Division determines that the RIA inadequately assesses regulatory impacts, it will return the RIA and work with policy makers to improve the analysis.

Stakeholder engagement in Estonia must be undertaken and open to the public for all primary laws and for major subordinate regulations once the legislative text has been drafted. Whilst all legislative proposal must be openly consulted with the public (including citizens, business and civil society organisations) for a minimum of four weeks, there are no rules regarding bilateral discussion between stakeholders and policy makers. Ministerial officials thus have discretion to choose if and whom they engage with and with whom the draft legislation will be shared. Policy makers can be subject to criticism for carrying out inappropriate stakeholder engagement but there are no formal consequences. For example, the Legislative Quality Division can voice its opinion in instances of inappropriate stakeholder engagement, but has no formal power to return the legislative proposal if this is the case.

Ex post evaluation of existing regulations in Estonia is mandatory for some primary laws and subordinate regulations. There exists a threshold test to determine whether *ex post* evaluations should be undertaken, but only for primary laws. The requirement for undertaking *ex post* evaluation was originally dependent on the threshold test for in-depth RIA, whereby legislative proposals that triggered an in-depth assessment would also trigger *ex post* evaluation. In practice however, the threshold test has also become redundant for *ex post* evaluation and the four criteria test described above are not used to identify legislation whose efficiency and effectiveness must be evaluated. Estonia is instead currently developing a new *ex post* evaluation strategy whereby legislative proposals introduced in response to an emergency must always be evaluated. Currently, it is at the discretion of the ministerial officials to decide whether an *ex post* evaluation should be carried out, although the Legislative Quality Division plays an important role in ensuring appropriate *ex post* evaluation as they can make suggestions regarding which laws and regulations should be reviewed. If the line ministry is of the view that *ex post* evaluation is unnecessary, then the reasons for it have to be shown in the explanatory letter of the draft law.

Proportionality in Cyprus

A new RIA framework was established in Cyprus in 2015. RIAs are required for all primary laws but only for some subordinate regulations, as impact assessments must accompany all draft bills submitted to the House of Representatives, although there are some exceptions to conducting RIA. Indeed, a draft law can proceed to the House of Representatives without a RIA if, amongst others:

- If it is being introduced in response to an emergency;
- If it is considered to have insignificant impacts, that is, it does not introduce substantial additional or new provisions;
- When the bill is implementing an international treaty or legislation of an inter- or supranational organisation (e.g. EU);

- For legislations related to the budget, to the management of public finance, to procedural content, or to defence policy;
- Other provisions for exceptions as outlined in the *Impact Analysis Guidelines and Questionnaire* (Government of Cyprus, 2016[9]).

The Law Office of the Republic of Cyprus and the House of Representatives are aware which draft legislation may proceed without a RIA. If it is however decided that a RIA will not be conducted, this decision is not made publicly available and this decision is not reviewed.

Impact assessments in Cyprus are required to be proportionate to the significance of the proposed regulation for primary laws. According to the Government of Cyprus, the analytical efforts should be proportionate to the issues addressed by the relevant legislation as well as the efforts required to undertake an impact assessment (i.e. the collection and analysis of the relevant data and information). Some factors that policy makers should consider in determining the scope of analysis include:

- The level of interest and sensitivity surrounding the legislative proposal;
- The policy development stage and whether the policy is innovative, controversial or irreversible
- The scale and duration of the expected impacts;
- The availability of data; and
- Available resources, time and capacity for further analysis.

There are no threshold tests in Cyprus as it is at the discretion of policy makers to decide the depth of the analysis, however they are bound by the framework established in the *Impact Analysis Guidelines and Questionnaire* (Government of Cyprus, 2016[9]). The guidelines establish the following levels of RIA analysis:

- Level 1: Description of the main groups expected to be affected by the proposal (such as businesses, public sector, consumers);
- Level 2: Full qualitative description of the regulatory impacts (e.g. positive or negative), the magnitude of the impacts, and their intensity for each group;
- Level 3: Quantification of regulatory impacts, such as the number of affected parties and estimation of the compliance costs and administrative burdens;
- Level 4: All cost categories and benefits are monetised.

At a minimum, the analytical depth observed in all RIAs should reach level 2, where a qualitative description of all regulatory impacts is provided. Levels 3 and 4 require a quantitative and monetary analysis that might not be feasible for all legislative proposals and policy makers have the discretion to choose whether the regulatory impacts of the legislative proposal warrant such levels of analytical depth. In cases where analysis at levels 3 and 4 does not take place, a more in-depth analysis of levels 1 and 2 should be undertaken.

There is no body outside of the ministry sponsoring the regulation which is responsible for reviewing the quality of the overall RIA and that examines whether the depth of the analysis is proportionate. Whilst the inclusion of an impact assessment as part of the package accompanying legislation for their introduction to the House of Representatives is verified by the Legal Quality Service (Law Office of the Republic of Cyprus), there is no scrutiny on the quality of RIA.

One exception is the involvement of the SME Envoy Cyprus (under the Ministry of Energy, Commerce, and Industry), which is responsible for reviewing the SME Test for regulations that are expected to affect small and medium enterprises. The SME Test and the analytical methodology underpinning it are thoroughly described in the Guidelines (2016[9]), and it details the various analytical stages that policy makers should follow. The SME Envoy reviews whether policy alternatives and mitigation measures have been appropriately identified, whether the analysis of the impacts on SME is adequate, and whether stakeholders have been appropriately consulted. The SME Envoy is not involved in reviewing any assessment unrelated to SMEs and does not comment on the depth of the analysis of non-SME impacts. In addition, specific environmental impact assessment is carried out for proposals that are likely to significantly affect the environment.

Stakeholder engagement in Cyprus must be undertaken for all primary laws and tends to be more systematically carried out once a legislative draft exists. In addition, stakeholder engagement must be open to the public and a central e-consultation platform is currently being constructed. Stakeholder engagement in Cyprus is sometimes proportionate to the significance of the regulation, as policy makers are reported to undertake additional rounds of consultation for legislative proposals with expected high impacts. Stakeholder engagement is at the discretion of the civil servant in charge of developing the legislative proposal and there is no formal oversight. The House of Representatives does however invite stakeholders to provide their opinion during parliamentary debate, in cases where the House finds that stakeholders were not appropriately consulted in the initial stages of the legislative process.

Ex post evaluation of existing regulations is not required in Cyprus and is not undertaken in practice. There is therefore no established framework for *ex post* evaluation in Cyprus.

The policy options considered in EU Member States' analysis

Considering all feasible options when potentially embarking on regulating is crucial to ensure that the broadest possible range of alternatives are genuinely considered by policy makers. This was recognised in the *OECD Recommendation* (2012[1]) and complemented by the *OECD RIA Best Practice Principles* (2020[2]) noting that RIA is more generally an iterative process. This is certainly the case for the consideration of alternative options, as options are gradually ruled out as more information on their potential impacts becomes available; or where stakeholders identify that certain options proposed are not feasible – and also the possibility that stakeholders may raise alternative options not considered by policy makers, as discussed in Chapter 2.

A majority of EU Member States systematically focus on identifying and analysing the preferred regulatory option (Figure 3.8). Identifying and assessing the impacts of the preferred regulatory option for at least some primary laws is almost universally required across the European Union and the results have not changed since 2017. Considering the baseline or 'do nothing' option (i.e. the status quo) also seems relatively well established as around 70% of EU Member States are systematically required to do so (Figure 3.8), although some EU Member States would benefit from systemising this practice more. The European Commission requires its policy makers to identify and assess the impacts of the preferred policy option as well as the impacts of the baseline or 'do nothing' option for major primary laws or subordinate regulations. In practice however, there is still scope for improvement as the Regulatory Scrutiny Board finds that the set of options analysed in RIA is not always complete. The European Commission's impact assessments tend to focus only on the preferred (political) choice, without including alternate ones supported by the main stakeholder groups (Regulatory Scrutiny Board, 2020[12]).

Alternative policy options,[2] both regulatory and non-regulatory ones, are less systematically assessed in EU Member States than in OECD member countries. Countries would benefit from systematically incorporating the assessment of non-regulatory options in their RIAs to avoid prejudging that regulatory intervention is warranted and to provide stakeholders with more information, in order to improve decision making. In the European Commission, the assessment of more than one alternative regulatory option and of one alternative non-regulatory option is mandatory for major primary laws and subordinate regulations. However, policy makers in approximately two-thirds of EU Member States are required to systematically identify and assess alternative regulatory options for primary laws (Figure 3.8), compared to 80% of OECD members (OECD, 2021[4]). This suggests that decision makers generally benefit from having information about alternative regulatory paths that could be taken to solve the policy problem at hand, albeit RIAs are slightly less likely to contain this information when compared with the preferred regulatory option. In addition, just over half of EU Member States for primary laws – and less than two-fifths for subordinate regulations – have a requirement that proposals systematically identify and assess the impact of alternative non-regulatory options (Figure 3.8). Around 70% of OECD members for primary laws and just over half for subordinate regulations have similar requirements (OECD, 2021[4]). Results for both EU Member States and OECD member countries have experienced little change since 2017. The specific assessment of regulatory costs and benefits for the identified policy options is explored in the next section.

Figure 3.8. Most EU Member States identify and assess the impacts of the preferred regulatory option, but fewer do so for non-regulatory options

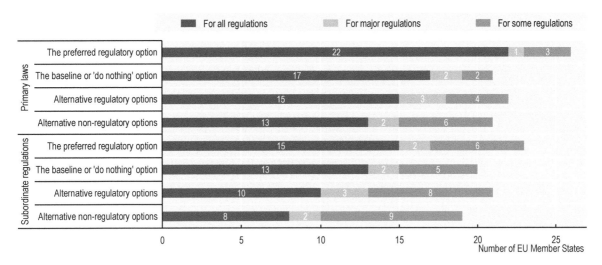

Note: Data is based on 27 EU Member States.
Source: Indicators of Regulatory Policy and Governance (iREG) Survey 2021.

Types of impacts, costs and benefits assessed in EU Member States

Overall, policy makers appear to focus more on economic impacts and on identifying and measuring regulatory costs than benefits, particularly for subordinate regulations. Only a minority of EU Member States quantify the costs and benefits of more than one policy option, suggesting that this detailed analysis tends to be limited to the option that policy makers prefer to take forward. In turn, this risks converting RIA into an analytical exercise that is used to justify an established policy choice instead of a process that is used to inform decision making.

The *OECD RIA Best Practice Principles* (OECD, 2020[2]) calls for policy makers to identify all relevant direct and important indirect costs as well as benefits. It is necessary for policy makers to go beyond direct economic impacts and assess various other types such as impacts on the environment, social impacts (jobs, public health, gender equality, poverty, inequalities and their reduction, working conditions, etc.), the Sustainable Development Goals, impacts on innovation, cross-border impacts and also second-round effects and unintended consequences, etc (OECD, 2020[2]). Wherever partial impact assessments are conducted separately, they should be integrated into one crosscutting integrated impact assessment. The European Commission requires RIAs to assess a broad range of economic, environmental, and social impacts in line with the proportionality principle. In addition though it also requires policy makers to consider issues relating to compliance and enforcement, distributional impacts, as well as identifying a process by which the objective of a regulatory proposal will be assessed.

Policy makers from EU Member States are generally required to assess the impacts of regulatory proposals on a large range of factors (Figure 3.9). Compared to the previous report (2019[5]), there continues to be a strong focus on analysing the economic impacts of regulatory proposals, with the effects on competition and the budget being universally required to be assessed in all Member States. The regulatory impacts on the public sector, on small and medium-sized companies and on the environment are also commonly assessed amongst EU Member States. In line with the findings from the *Regulatory Policy Outlook* (2021[4]) for OECD member countries, the requirement to analyse regulatory impacts on foreign jurisdictions however remains the lowest amongst all assessments. If this trend continues, this may have consequences on the quality of RIA and may result in significant impacts (both positive and negative) being omitted from the analysis, as the magnitude of impacts on foreign jurisdictions will be expected to continue to grow in an ever increasingly interconnected world. This is particularly relevant in the context of the EU, where regional integration via different forms of international regulatory co-operation (IRC) is key to support the four liberties – i.e. free flow of people, goods, services and capital – as discussed in Chapter 1.

Figure 3.9. EU Member States assess regulatory impacts in various areas

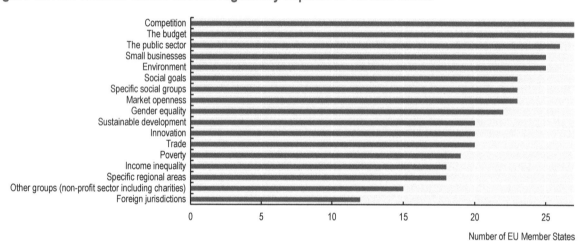

Note: Data is based on 27 EU Member States.
Source: Indicators of Regulatory Policy and Governance (iREG) Survey 2021.

Policy makers should assess the anticipated costs and benefits of a regulatory proposal in order to have an accurate picture of the total impacts of all policy options. RIAs are central to policy makers' decision-making, by helping to provide as much objective information as possible on the likely benefits and costs that would emerge if the available regulatory options are implemented. RIAs thus enable a more meaningful comparison of regulatory options and help policy makers identify which one is the most appropriate to resolve the policy issue at hand. It is therefore crucial to identify, direct costs (i.e. administrative, financial and capital costs), indirect costs (e.g. opportunity costs), as well as benefits for the preferred policy option but also for alternative policy options (OECD, 2020[2]).

The benefits of a regulatory proposal are particularly important to identify, as this provides information on whether the policy option will achieve its objectives as well as on who will gain from it and how. Any significant regulatory intervention is bound to result in costs due to the burdens that it introduces. Policy makers must therefore demonstrate that the benefits resulting from the proposal justify the costs and that it will have a positive net impact on society as a whole. In addition, a reduction in costs could be considered and calculated as part of the anticipated benefits from a policy, thus placing the assessment of the expected benefits at the centre of the assessment methodology.

Quantitative estimation of the costs and benefits provide policy makers with crucial information on the extent of the impacts of the proposal, even if fully-fledged cost-benefit analysis is not proportionate or appropriate for all regulatory proposals. The *OECD RIA Best Practice Principles* (2020[2]) suggest that the goal of governments should lie in making quantitative estimation integral to a RIA as it not only helps identify who may gain or lose from a regulatory proposal, it also provides a point of comparison to discern the costs and benefits arising from various policy options. This contributes to providing policy makers with sufficient evidence to choose which policy option to implement and helps demonstrate whether the benefits of introducing a new regulation justifies its costs.

Qualitative analysis can be informative, particularly when data is not available or reliable. EU Member States are more likely to identify the costs of new regulations over their benefits and put more emphasis on quantifying regulatory costs than benefits (Table 3.2). This trend was already highlighted in the previous edition of this report (2019[5]) and continues to be the case for a number of EU Member States. Almost all EU Member States have a requirement to identify the costs of primary laws, but less than three-quarters of EU Member States have a systematic requirement to identify the benefits. This gap further increases when it comes to quantification: 23 EU Member States require a systematic quantification of regulatory costs for primary laws, compared to 15 for quantification of benefits (Table 3.2). In contrast, policy makers in the European Commission face the same requirements for both regulatory costs and benefits, which must be assessed and quantified for both major primary laws and major subordinate regulations. Despite the importance of assessing benefits, a number of EU Member States continue to focus their analytical efforts on assessing and measuring regulatory costs without understanding the full benefits that may result from a policy proposal.

Table 3.2. EU Member States are more commonly required to identify and quantify regulatory costs than benefits

	Regulators are required to *identify the costs* of a new regulation		Regulators are required to *identify the benefits* of a new regulation		Regulators are required to *quantify the costs* of a new regulation		Regulators are required to *quantify the benefits* of a new regulation	
	Primary Laws	Subordinate regulations	Primary Laws	Subordinate regulations	Primary Laws	Subordinate regulations	Primary Laws	Subordinate regulations
Austria								
Belgium								
Bulgaria								
Croatia								
Cyprus								
Czech Republic								
Denmark								
Estonia								
Finland								
France								
Germany								
Greece								
Hungary								
Ireland								
Italy								
Latvia								
Lithuania								
Luxembourg								
Malta								
Netherlands								
Poland								
Portugal								
Romania								
Slovak Republic								
Slovenia								

	Regulators are required to *identify the costs* of a new regulation		Regulators are required to *identify the benefits* of a new regulation		Regulators are required to *quantify the costs* of a new regulation		Regulators are required to *quantify the benefits* of a new regulation	
	Primary Laws	Subordinate regulations	Primary Laws	Subordinate regulations	Primary Laws	Subordinate regulations	Primary Laws	Subordinate regulations
Spain								
Sweden								
European Union								

■ For all primary laws/ subordinate regulations
■ For major primary laws/ subordinate regulations
■ For some primary laws/ subordinate regulations
□ Never

Note: Data is based on 27 EU Member States and the European Union.
Source: Indicators of Regulatory Policy and Governance (iREG) Survey 2021.

The discrepancy between the requirements to assess regulatory costs and those to assess benefits is more prominent for subordinate regulations. Systematic identification of costs for subordinate regulations is required in approximately 85% of EU Member States and systematic identification of benefits in approximately 60% of them (Table 3.2). The same is true for the quantification of impacts for subordinate regulations: it is systematically required to quantify costs of subordinate regulations in 21 EU Member States but in only 10 EU Member States for benefits (Table 3.2). Many EU Member States therefore appear to have less stringent requirements for subordinate regulations than for primary laws, particularly regarding the identification and assessment of benefits for subordinate regulations.

Less than half of EU Member States quantify the costs and the benefits of more than one policy option, suggesting that policy makers are not provided with evidence on the impacts of alternative policy options. Costs and benefits should not be identified for the preferred policy option only, but should also be done for all policy alternatives in order to help policy makers identify the regulatory option that lead to the best societal outcomes. When it comes to the quantification of costs and benefits, 12 EU Member States quantify the costs of more than one policy option for primary laws, while 10 EU Member States quantify the benefits of more than one policy option. This suggests that a vast majority of EU Member States do not collect detailed evidence on the impact that alternative policy options might have. The European Commission quantifies both the costs and benefits of more than one policy option.

EU Member States appear to focus their analytical efforts on estimating the costs and benefits on governments and businesses, with fewer requirements to estimate the impacts on citizens and on NGOs or charities (Figure 3.10). A similar trend is observed amongst OECD member countries. The impact on NGOs and charities seem to be rarely assessed in this type of analysis: If EU Member States have the requirement to quantify costs and benefits of a regulatory proposal on NGOs and charities, it is usually only required for some laws and regulations (Figure 3.10). Additionally, and in line with the above findings, costs are quantified across all interest groups more often than benefits and such estimation and less systematically required for subordinate regulations than for primary laws. In contrast, the European Commission mandates that the costs and benefits for citizens, businesses, public administrations, NGOs/charities and for the European Union be quantified for major legislative proposals. Focusing the analysis exclusively on the impacts of one or two societal actors may point to a weakness of EU Member States' RIA systems. Indeed, this may present a risk that the analysis – and thus the developed regulatory proposal – is biased towards the impacts one of a limited number of parties and may fail to understand how other key members of society are affected and how such impacts could be mitigated if necessary.

Figure 3.10. Requirements to quantify costs and benefits of new regulations are more common for government and businesses than for individuals and NGOs

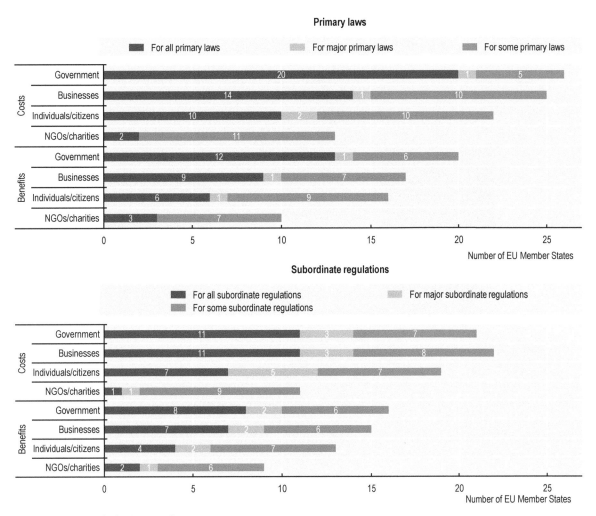

Note: Data is based on 27 EU Member States.
Source: Indicators of Regulatory Policy and Governance (iREG) Survey 2021.

Transparency of RIA procedure in EU Member States

Governments have to ensure transparency of decision making to enable public scrutiny of the RIA process. Transparency is a core feature of the *2012 Recommendation*, with Principle 4.4 stating that "RIA should as far as possible be made publically available along with regulatory proposals" (OECD, 2012, p. 13[1]). Consultation on the draft RIA document is particularly useful since it can focus on the data used, the alternative options selected, the criteria applied for comparing options, and the overall quality of analysis to select a preferred policy option (OECD, 2020[2]). In addition, a transparent decision making process helps ensure that citizens and businesses feel included in the policy making process, accept regulatory decisions and, ultimately, trust their government (OECD, 2018[6]).

RIA practices for EU Member States are more transparent when it comes to laws that are approved by parliament than for those that are approved by the government. The majority of EU Member States make all RIAs regarding primary laws publicly available whilst only half of EU Member States make RIAs regarding subordinate regulations systematically publicly available (Figure 3.11). The majority of EU Member States that make RIAs publicly available publish them on central registries, whilst some also make

RIAs publicly available on ministry websites but this practice is less common. Making RIAs publicly available facilitates access to information for citizens and businesses and improves the transparency of decision-making processes.

Figure 3.11. The majority of EU Member States publish their RIAs online

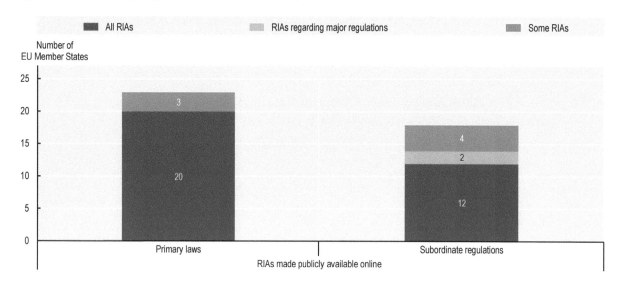

Note: Data is based on 27 EU Member States.
Source: Indicators of Regulatory Policy and Governance (iREG) Survey 2021.

The discrepancy in transparency between primary laws and subordinate regulations is unsurprising but can point to a weakness in EU Member States' regulatory systems. Primary laws are, by definition, adopted by Parliaments and thus subject to parliamentary debates. Members of Parliaments request a wide-range of information, prompting policy makers to publish policy documents, including RIAs, to potentially be scrutinised in open parliamentary debate. Policy makers thus have strong incentives to ensure that the RIAs for primary law proposals are transparent and publicly available. In contrast, subordinate regulations are adopted by a range of institutions in the executive and may not be subject to open debate. There may thus be less direct consequences for policy makers if the RIAs are not published and thus less incentives to do so.

The *RIA Best Practice Principles* (OECD, 2020[2]) call for transparency and clear communication of the results of RIA. RIAs should not only be made publicly available, they should also be written in a clear and understandable manner that maintains a reasonable level of simplicity and conciseness. In addition, it is important to ensure that the level of analytical rigour is at least commensurate with the anticipated impacts resulting from the regulatory proposals and that the RIA is not written in a way that obscures important information or that distorts the assessment to support a particular policy (OECD, 2020[2]).

Requirements and practices regarding RIA for the negotiation of EU directives and regulations and for the transposition of EU directives

EU Member States should be informed about the *domestic* impacts of a proposed EU regulation or directive when they engage in the negotiation stage. Many countries are however under no obligation to conduct a domestic RIA to define a negotiating position, although it is worth noting that some undertake such analysis in practice even if they are not required to do so. The short timing between the publication of the European Commission's impact assessment and the beginning of the negotiation can impede the development of suitable analysis to inform the domestic negotiation position. EU Member States can use the impact assessment produced and published by the European Commission and which provides complementary evidence on the legislative proposal. Many EU Member States report sometimes using the European Commission's impact assessment during the negotiation phase but there is scope for them to do so more systematically.

Regulatory impact assessments are more systematically required to be undertaken during the transposition of EU directives than during the negotiation stage. EU Member States generally understand the importance of assessing the impact of EU directives on domestic citizens and businesses, as almost all countries are required to undertake this analysis at the time of transposition and have the same requirements and processes in place as for legislation originating nationally. Few EU Member States however report assessing the impacts resulting from any additional national provisions added to the directive, suggesting that, if decision-makers do engage in gold plating, they may not systematically understand the impacts that these impose on their citizens and businesses. Finally, evidence from the European Commission's impact assessment appears to not be systematically used during the transposition phase, despite the fact that it includes evidence on the types and range of impacts that EU Member States can collectively expect to encounter when implementing a directive.

The use of RIAs by EU Member States to inform the negotiation of proposed EU directives and regulations

EU Member States should ground their amendments of proposed EU directives and regulations during the negotiation phase on evidence and on an understanding of the anticipated impacts in individual countries. EU Member States can directly amend proposed EU directives or regulations during the negotiations undertaken by the European Parliament and the Council of the European Union. Given that negotiation can result in substantial changes to a proposal before it becomes an EU legislative act, EU Member States ought to prepare evidence on the impacts of the proposed legislation on their individual countries and use it in the debate. This is particularly important for EU regulations as these are directly applicable and binding in their entirety without being transposed into Member States' national law. The negotiation stage is thus crucial as, once regulations are adopted, EU Member States do not have another opportunity to amend them. Impact analysis is a critical tool to use in the context of negotiation as they can help EU Member States base their arguments on evidence and to alleviate any information deficiencies faced when countries commence negotiation.

The analysis at this stage of the legislative process does not necessarily have to be as detailed as the RIAs produced when developing domestic legislation or as impact assessments produced by the European Commission. Member States however ought to undertake proportionately lite analysis that would provide them with some evidence on the types and potential scope of the regulatory impacts on the domestic economy, businesses, and citizens, during the negotiations.

Despite the gains from analysing the domestic impacts of a proposed EU regulation or directive ahead of the negotiation, many EU Member States are under no obligation to conduct RIA to define a negotiating position and evaluate the potential policy impacts at the early stages of a European Commission proposal. This suggests that EU Member States' negotiation positions are not systematically informed by analysis and may fail to consider how the European Commission's proposals may affect their citizens and businesses. In fact, just over half of the EU Member States have a requirement to carry out RIA to define the negotiating position for the development of at least some EU directives and regulations (Figure 3.12), with the **Netherlands** having newly introduced this requirement since 2017. Carrying out domestic impact analysis is particularly relevant when the original impact assessment of the European Commission does not necessarily include an assessment of the impacts on individual countries.

Figure 3.12. A significant number of EU Member States do not have a requirement to conduct RIA to define the negotiating position for the development of EU directives and regulations

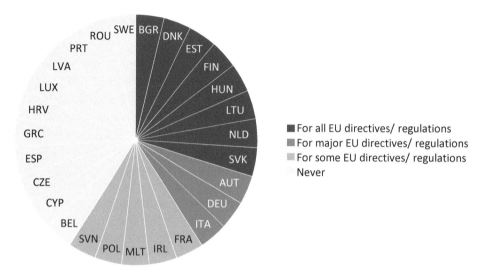

Note: Data is based on 27 EU Member States.
Source: Indicators of Regulatory Policy and Governance (iREG) Survey 2021.

Five of the EU Member States that have requirements to carry out RIA to inform the negotiating position for EU regulations report to have the same RIA requirements as for regulations originating domestically. These EU Member States are **Estonia**, **Hungary, Italy**, **Lithuania** and **Malta**. Most of the EU Member States report to have different RIA requirements for domestic legislation than for laws initiated by the European Commission. Examples of practices of EU Member States when undertaking analysis to inform the negotiation of EU legislative proposals are explored in Box 3.8.

Some EU Member States consider it important to use evidence to inform the negotiation stage, even though they are not formally required to do so. This is, for example, the case of **Croatia**, **Latvia** and **Sweden**, which all have procedures in place to include some assessment of domestic impacts in the negotiation stage. Member States undertaking a RIA without being formally required to do so demonstrates the value of assessing the impacts of EU legislative proposals ahead of the negotiation. The practices followed by some of these Member States are included in Box 3.8.

Box 3.8. Some EU Member States have specific analytical practices to inform the negotiating position of EU legislative proposals

There are no formal requirement in **Croatia** to conduct RIA in the process of drafting the national negotiating positions, however it is encouraged to indicate whether the EU legislation will have national legal and financial consequences. The depth and scope of the analysis depends on the capacities of the ministries responsible for the policy area affected by the EU legislative proposal.

In **Finland**, ministries are encouraged to conduct impact assessment at the time when the European Commission is preparing a new initiative. This is particularly relevant for political files of special interest for Finland. Within 6 weeks upon approval by the European Commission of its proposal and the related notification, the Government (ministries) must submit so-called "U" or "E" Letters to national Parliament to inform it about the new European Commission initiative and the Government stance on it; and to seek the formal mandate to negotiate / deliberate at the EU level. The Letter includes a basic, short

---

RIA. This is not sophisticated as it basically points out the most relevant of the proposal and of the European Commission's impact assessment.

The domestic RIA in **Italy** provides evidence to support the activity of the government and its representatives in the relevant Council formations. The Italian RIA starts within 30 days from the publication of the European Commission's Work Programme. This RIA should look at domestic effects and types of impacts that have not been considered by the European Commission but may be relevant for Italy. It is then part of the normal dialogue between the Member State and the EU institutions.

In **Poland**, the preliminary positions with elements of RIA are prepared obligatorily by the relevant ministries following the publication of the draft legislative act. The positions must be approved by the Committee for European Affairs operating on behalf of the Council of Ministers. In addition, the draft government positions are also reviewed by the relevant parliamentary committee. This acts as a preliminary verification of the impact assessment proposed by the Government.

The European Commission's proposal is distributed to the Permanent Mission of the **Slovak Republic** to the EU, to all Slovak Central Authorities and to the Parliament Office. A primary decision is made by the Ministry of Foreign Affairs together with the Government Office on the basis of the responsibility for given Working Group of the Council of the European Union. A Preliminary Opinion on the European Commission's proposal is then prepared within four weeks upon availability of the Slovak official text. The Preliminary Opinion may be "regular" (for the more important proposals) or a lower level one (non-legislative materials). Regular Preliminary Opinion includes information on the Draft Act, its content and goals, type and time frame of the approval process for given Draft Act in the EU, subsidiarity and proportionality assessment, analytical Impact Assessment for the Slovak Republic regarding the political, economic, legislative, social and environmental impacts.

In **Sweden**, to inform the National Parliament, the *Riksdag*, about an upcoming EU legislative, a document is drafted that includes information on the impacts of the proposed regulation, including the estimated impacts on the budget.

Source: Indicators of Regulatory Policy and Governance (iREG) Survey 2021 and Radaelli et al (unpublished[13]), Extending the OECD indicators of Regulatory Policy and Governance (iREG) to all EU Member States of the European Union.

EU Member States use various methods to identify European Commission legislative proposals that will undergo a domestic RIA. The identification of laws that will be subject to RIA is predominantly based on proportionality, and particularly on the significance of their impacts in general, their impacts on national and EU budgets, or their non-budgetary domestic impacts. For example, in **Germany,** European Commission proposals have to fulfil two conditions (i.e. the double condition) to be subject to a domestic RIA at the time of the negotiation. First, the threshold of EUR 35 million of expected compliance costs across the EU as per the RIA of the European Commission has to be met. The second condition is fulfilled if there is insufficient information on the proposal already available, e.g. via studies carried out in Germany. When the double condition is met, an impact assessment covering the compliance costs for German businesses is carried out by the competent department (Radaelli, Dunlop and Allio, unpublished[13]). In **Estonia**, a preliminary impact assessment is done for all EU directives and regulations. If the preliminary impact assessment identifies significant impacts, a full RIA is ordered and financed by the Government. EU proposals that have a significant impact in **Malta** are required to undergo specific analysis: In order to determine whether a RIA should be carried out at the negotiation stage, the significance of the regulatory impacts is considered. In addition, the number of individuals and businesses affected by the regulation, and matters of strategic national importance (e.g. the protection of national competitive advantages) are considered when evaluating the significance of an EU legislative proposal on Malta.

A minority of EU Member States have analytical guidance used specifically for the negotiation phase. In total, 11 EU Member States report having specific guidance available to government officials for conducting RIA to inform the national negotiating position for the development of EU legislation. In most cases, such guidance is included within the main domestic RIA guideline document although there are some countries where this guideline is separate and specifically directed at officials preparing the negotiation position of EU directives or regulations.

All EU Member States reported carrying out RIAs to inform the development of domestic regulations but in contrast, only around two-thirds reported carrying out RIAs in practice during the development or adoption of EU directives and regulations. This suggests that countries have relevant tools required for carrying out an impact assessment in practice but that such instruments may not be utilised as systematically for laws originating from the EU. Further research and comprehensive data – particularly around the timing difficulties experienced between the publication of the proposal and the start of the negotiation (see below) – is necessary to assess the EU Member States' actual practices regarding the use of impact assessment during the development and negotiation of EU directives and regulations.

The timing between the publication of the European Commission's impact assessment and the beginning of the negotiation can make it difficult for EU Member States to undertake an analysis of domestic impacts. The main difficulties countries report on the interface between the EU and the national processes is the length of time it would take for EU Member States to analyse and quantify the domestic impacts of the EU regulation. Even though the assessment of expected impacts of proposed regulations is crucial in order to carry out evidence-based and well-informed decisions, conducting a more in-depth analysis may not be always possible at the negotiation stage. Time is a variable that is affected by administrative challenges, i.e. how EU affairs are processed with their own deadlines (Radaelli, Dunlop and Allio, unpublished[13]). The deadlines may or may not allow for time invested in in-depth RIA and stakeholder engagement. Evidence provided by some EU Member States suggests that the issue of timing creates friction in the system – there are instances where analytical time to produce quantification of costs or subject RIA content to stakeholder scrutiny is inconsistent with political timing. In addition, it may often be the case that the nature of an EU proposal is uncertain, which makes it difficult to undertake analysis. The inability to carry out RIA can, for example, lead to difficulties optimising future burdens, and the timing pressures may also generate analytical capacity gaps (Radaelli, Dunlop and Allio, unpublished[13]).

The majority of EU Member States could better use the European Commission's impact assessments to inform their negotiating position

EU Member States are able and ought to use the information provided in the European Commission's impact assessment as a starting point for making their own analysis and to improve the evidence that is brought to the negotiation table. Using the information provided in the European Commission's impact assessments is an especially relevant "low-hanging fruit" for the EU Member States that do not undertake their own analysis, as this may be the only source of evidence that they can use when developing their negotiating position. The European Commission's impact assessments are a functional and published resource that EU Member States can easily use and that is available several weeks in advance of the negotiation. Whilst they generally do not provide evidence on the impact of the proposed legislation on individual Member States, the European Commission's impact assessments contain comprehensive and robust information on the objectives and on the types of impacts likely to result from the proposed directive and regulation. Further information on the content of the European Commission's impact assessment is provided in Box 3.9.

Box 3.9. The European Commission's impact assessment

Impact assessments are required for all of the European Commission's initiatives when the expected economic, environmental or social impacts of EU action are likely to be significant and there are available options. The lead European Commission service should establish as early as possible in the European Commissions' internal political validation process whether a RIA is required. Once a decision has been made that a proposal will be prepared, the European Commission publishes a call for evidence in which it is makes clear whether the proposal will be subject to an impact assessment. The call for evidence document presents an outline of the policy problem, an initial mapping of the policy options as well as preliminary assessment of expected impacts. Where no impact assessment is prepared, this is made clear in the call for evidence, which nonetheless provides key elements of the analysis that will be subject to feedback from stakeholders.

The public feedback period on the Call for evidence document and the public consultation (see Chapter 2), contributes to the impact assessment process, including data collection, public and stakeholder consultations, expert hearings and/or seeking additional scientific evidence. The results of the impact analysis will be summarised in an impact assessment report and sent to the Regulatory Scrutiny Board (RSB) for a quality assurance review. Following potential revisions of the impact assessment and based on a positive opinion from the RSB, the RIA is subject to internal consultation between the European Commission's departments together with the legal proposal. Once a regulatory proposal has been adopted by the College of Commissioners, the proposal – accompanied by the impact assessment as well as the opinions of the Regulatory Scrutiny Board – will be published online for feedback and sent to the co-legislators for the negotiation of the European Commission's proposals.

Source: European Commission (2021[3]), *Better Regulation Toolbox*, https://ec.europa.eu/info/sites/default/files/br_toolbox-nov_2021_en_0.pdf.

Many EU Member States understand the importance of using the European Commission's impact assessment during the negotiation phase but there is scope for doing it more systematically. Over 80 percent of EU Member States have reported using the European Commission's impact assessment as input to inform their national negotiating position for the development of EU directives and regulations, although few report doing so systematically (Figure 3.13). There is however no evidence that the European Commission's impact assessment is used at all in several EU Member States, such as **Greece**, **Portugal**, and **Spain**, even though they are not required to prepare a domestic RIA for the negotiation. This suggests that some EU Member States do not systematically arrive at the negotiation table with more complete information, which could potentially lead to poor representation of the interests of their citizens. Using the results of domestically carried out RIA as well as those carried out by the European Commission can help countries form a comprehensive negotiating position to inform better decisions by taking into account robust and available information on the impacts of a proposed regulation.

Anecdotal evidence from several EU Member States suggests that they recognise the European Commission's impact assessment as a relevant source of qualitative information about a proposed directive or regulation. Member States however note that the European Commission's impact assessment cannot and does not provide a sufficiently accurate picture of the regulatory impacts that could be expected at the national level. As such, the European Commission's impact assessment is often an initial starting point to inform more specific domestic analysis. Some EU Member States suggested more clarity regarding which impacts result from the specific provisions in the proposed directive or regulation to help them in developing their own analysis and to inform their negotiation position.

Figure 3.13. A majority of EU Member States use the European Commission's impact assessments during negotiation but few do so systematically

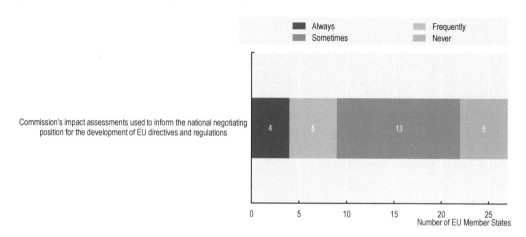

Note: Data is based on 27 EU Member States.
Source: Indicators of Regulatory Policy and Governance (iREG) Survey 2021.

The use of RIA to inform the transposition of EU directives

Transposition is the process that individual EU Member States undertake to incorporate adopted EU directives into national law. Unlike regulations, which are directly applicable to all EU Member States and binding in their entirety, directives offer flexibility to choose the method and form of implementation into national law. Transposition is the very last step of the EU legislative process for directives and takes place after the adopted policy is published in the Official Journal of the EU. EU Member States are bound by the terms of the directive as to the result to be achieved and the deadline by which transposition should take place (European Parliament, 2018[14]). They can however use the transposition process to add national provisions that go beyond the actual requirements set-out in the directive.

It is important for EU Member States to assess the impacts that the directive, in its final adopted form, will have on the domestic economy and society. As mentioned earlier in the chapter, the original impact assessment of the European Commission does not necessarily include an assessment of the impacts on individual countries. In addition, the European Commission's analysis is drafted before the directive is amended by the Council of the European Union and by the European Parliament during the readings and negotiation of the legislative proposal and, as discussed in Chapter 1, the impacts of such amendments are not systematically assessed by the other two EU institutions. The directive adopted may thus differ from the one originally developed by the European Commission and, as a result, the European Commission's original impact assessment may no longer fully reflect the resultant directive.

Requirements to assess the domestic impacts of directives when they are transposed into domestic law are well established across EU Member States. Almost all countries have formal requirements to conduct RIA when transposing at least some EU directives into domestic laws and this has not changed since 2017. In fact, more than three-quarters of EU Member States systematically require RIAs to be carried out during the transposition stage of EU directives (Figure 3.14). Only **Romania** does not require RIA to be carried out during the transposition of EU directives, as EU directives are explicitly exempted from RIAs at the transposition stage (Article 6 of Government Decision No. 561/2009).

Figure 3.14. Most EU Member States systematically require RIAs to be carried out when transposing EU directives into national law

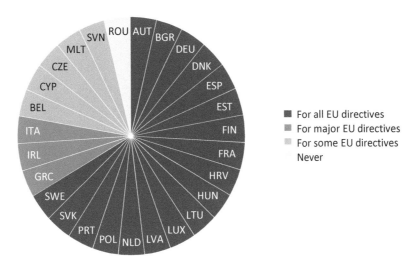

Note: Data is based on 27 EU Member States.
Source: Indicators of Regulatory Policy and Governance (iREG) Survey 2021.

When EU Member States assess the domestic impacts of directives, they usually follow the same processes as when analysing the impacts of their respective domestic proposals. In fact, the vast majority of EU Member States have the same RIA requirements for transposing EU directives as for laws originating domestically and there have been no changes since 2017 (Figure 3.15). As transposing EU directives involves amending existing or developing new domestic regulations, the transposition in EU Member States almost always goes through the same legislative process as laws originating domestically. As such, it is understandable and logical that the RIA requirements for laws originating at the EU level are identical to those originating domestically. The depth of the analysis in some sections may differ as policy makers have less flexibility to improve the policy when transposing EU directives (OECD, 2020[8]). For example, the assessment of the baseline 'do nothing' options or of alternative non-regulatory options may be less in-depth for RIAs accompanying EU legislative proposals because the decision to regulate has already been made. When fewer policy options or instruments are available, even if the impacts may be quite significant, policy makers have less flexibility to improve a policy at this stage. Despite this, governments should be mindful that EU directives or other supranational instruments might still have a degree of flexibility in their implementation (OECD, 2020[8]).

Cyprus, the **Czech Republic** and **Estonia** are the only EU Member States that have a requirement to undertake RIA for EU directives and where the RIA process is slightly different from that of regulations originating domestically. In **Cyprus**, policy makers have a different RIA questionnaire for transposing EU directives and the RIA procedure differs slightly. In the **Czech Republic**, policy makers are excepted from carrying out RIAs when there is no discretion on how to implement the EU legislative act and when no additional provisions going beyond the requirements of the EU directives are added by the Czech Government. In **Estonia**, it is not mandatory to compose a legislative intent document, i.e. an early-stage roadmap, for legislations that transpose EU directives. Examples of RIA practices for the transposition of EU directives in a sample of EU Member States is provided in Box 3.10.

Figure 3.15. Almost all EU Member States have the same RIA requirements for transposed EU directives as for domestic regulations

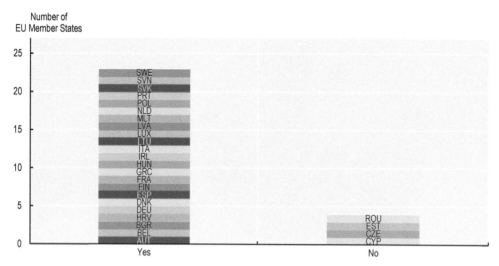

Note: Data is based on 27 EU Member States.
Source: Indicators of Regulatory Policy and Governance (iREG) Survey 2021.

Box 3.10. Examples of RIA practices at transposition stage

The RIA process in **Estonia** kicks off when the deliberations of the Council of the European Union are close to adopting a legal text. The responsibility lies with the Department of Justice and the Government Office. The process follows a series of steps that are carried out by default, meaning that there are no thresholds or exceptions.

In **Denmark**, the Danish Business Regulation Forum advises the government on the implementation of new business-oriented EU legislative acts by commenting on the relevant ministry's Implementation Plan. The responsible ministry must prepare Implementation Plans for all EU legislation (directives, regulations, implementing legislation and delegated acts) that have consequences for business and that must be implemented in Danish law. The Implementation Plan must be drawn-up immediately after the adoption of the legislative act and its publication in the Official Journal of the European Union. In their implementation scheme, the ministries have to explain how they have taken the recommendations from the DBRF into account or why it has chosen not to do so.

In **Finland**, the decision-making process during the transposition stage of EU legislation follows the same procedural steps as legislative initiatives originating domestically. While the RIA follows the standard procedure and format, it takes the European Commission's impact assessment as a starting point. Therefore, the RIA is to a certain extent less elaborated and comprehensive than a RIA on a domestically originated laws, since for example, the problem definition is already defined by the requirement to transpose an EU directive, or directly implement a regulation. On the other hand, the RIA is more elaborated than the impact assessment accompanying the EU Letter

The **Italian** government prepares an annual bill (the "*european delegation law*") that contains the provisions of legislative delegations necessary for the transposition of the directives and other acts of the European Union into Italian law with further legislative decree. This bill contains an appendix with all the legislative decree. Each legislative decree contains the national impact assessment. There is no difference between RIAs of EU legislation and other RIAs. The RIAs of EU legislation are carried out by individual departments and Ministries. They are scrutinized by the central RIA unit which could provide a negative opinion. In that case the opinion is integrated in the documents supporting the final decision of Council of Ministries.

The process in **Poland** is equal to the legislative process of domestic originated drafts acts. The leading ministry submits the application for the introduction of the draft act to the Government Work Plan. The RIA should be attached to that application.

The responsibility for transposition in **Slovak Republic** is allocated by the Government Office. Key stakeholders are consulted during the commenting procedure on the preliminary position which is available at the Slov-lex portal. Relevant European Commission regulations (mainly of higher importance) are subject to impact assessment during the preliminary commenting procedure governed by the Ministry of Economy of the Slovak Republic. The impact on public finances, budget, and businesses, social and environmental impact must be indicated in the "preliminary position" paper.

Source: Indicators of Regulatory Policy and Governance (iREG) Survey 2021 and Radaelli et al (unpublished[13]), Extending the OECD indicators of Regulatory Policy and Governance (iREG) to all EU Member States of the European Union.

Eight EU Member States have reported having specific guidance for conducting RIA to inform the transposition of EU directives. In most cases, such guidance is included within the main domestic RIA guideline document, with only a small sub-section discussing RIAs for the transposition of EU directives. A notable exception is **Cyprus**, where the RIA questionnaire for EU legislation differs slightly from the one for domestic legislation. The country thus has an additional and separate guideline to inform officials drafting legislation and accompanying impact assessments.

EU Member States generally assess the impacts of EU legislation on national economies and societies once the legislation is adopted instead of during the negotiation when it can still be amended. Comparing the number of EU Member States with requirements to carry out RIA to inform the negotiation (Figure 3.12) versus those with a requirement to carry out RIA during transposition (Figure 3.14) suggests that countries use RIAs at a later stage in the legislative process. This issue was highlighted in the previous edition of this report (OECD, 2019[5]) and has not evolved since. The flexibility offered by directives is limited, as the requirements and provisions from the EU directive are already set and Member States are under strict obligations to implement them. The fact that domestic impact assessments are more systematically undertaken once the EU legislative text is adopted raises concerns on the capacity of EU Member States to ground the negotiation and ensuing amendments of EU directives on solid evidence regarding the regulatory impact on *domestic* citizens and businesses. Further evidence and data would be necessary to fully understand why the EU Member States do not have as stringent RIA requirements and practices for negotiations as for transposition and what are some of the factors that drive this discrepancy.

Requirements to assess gold plating

Gold plating is a term specifically used in the European Union to describe over-implementation of a directive through the imposition of national provisions going beyond the actual requirements established by the directive. EU directives set minimum requirements that EU Member States must implement in order to safeguard the Single Market and the level playing field across the Union (European Commission, 2021[10]). Directives also allow EU Member States to choose how to meet the objectives set out, adapting their approach to their own institutional and administrative cultures (OECD, 2009[15]). EU Member States thus sometimes introduce additional provisions that are not directly prescribed by the directive. These can go beyond the requirements set out in the directive, which can result in extra impacts and burdens to citizens and businesses (OECD, 2009[15]).

When EU Member States engage in gold plating, they ought to analyse the impacts ensuing from the national provisions added. Given that provisions are added at the discretion of each EU Member State, the impacts introduced are not considered in the European Commission's impact assessments. In addition, divergence in implementation of EU directives, unless justified, can have important consequences for businesses, particularly those that operate in multiple EU Member States. It is thus crucial that, where gold plating occurs, EU Member States concerned identify and assess the impacts that these will have on its citizens and businesses. Special attention should be given to the additional provisions added at the national level, which ought to be transparently outlined and subject to an individual and specific assessment. This analysis is necessary for EU Member States to make informed decisions about whether such provisions and their impacts are essential to the efficiency of the transposed policy. In addition, there is scope and motivation for EU Member States to undertake this analysis, given that they must report how they transpose directives and may also indicate which national measures go beyond the requirements of EU directives (European Commission, 2021[10]), which is currently not systematically done.

Few EU Member States report assessing the additional impacts that national provisions added to EU directives through gold plating impose on domestic citizens and businesses. Six EU Member States report to systematically conduct specific assessments of potential provisions added at the national level going beyond the requirements set out in the EU directives (Figure 3.16). A further 10 EU Member States report to sometimes conduct gold plating assessments (Figure 3.16). This suggests that whilst almost all EU Member States are required to undertake RIA when transposing EU directives, few systematically conduct a specific assessment of the impacts resulting from any additional provisions. The RIAs undertaken during transposition thus appear to analyse the aggregated regulatory impacts, i.e. cumulating those imposed by the EU and those additionally levied by the respective individual EU Member State, without differentiating the impacts resulting from the directive and those resulting from the domestically added provisions. Indeed, out of the 16 EU Member States reporting to at least sometimes assess gold plating, only nine report assessing the marginal impact that the gold plating provisions have had. In other words, only nine EU Member States distinguish between impacts stemming from the EU requirements versus those resulting from additional national implementation measures in their RIAs. Since 2017, **Finland** has updated its RIA guidelines to now require a specific gold plating assessment, whilst **Slovenia** has reported no longer doing such assessment in 2020. More information of some of the practices of EU Member States related to gold plating are explored in Box 3.11.

Figure 3.16. Approximately two-fifths of EU Member States report that they never conduct specific assessments to estimate the impacts of gold plating EU directives

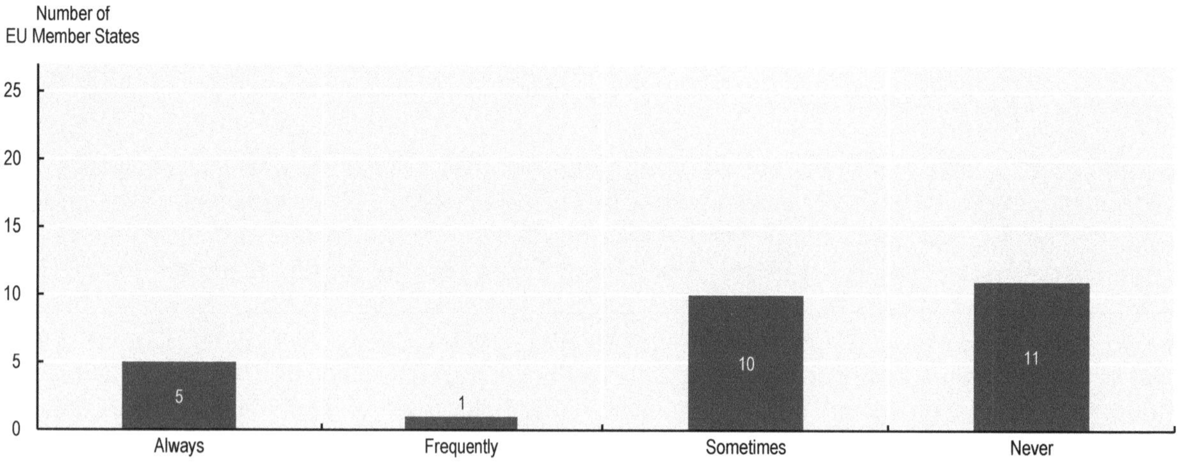

Note: Data is based on 27 EU Member States.
Source: Indicators of Regulatory Policy and Governance (iREG) Survey 2021.

Box 3.11. Gold plating practices across EU Member States

When transposing EU directives in **Czech Republic**, the draft regulation is checked by the Department of Compatibility with EU Law at the Office of the Government that also issues its opinions for the consideration of the Government Legislative Council (LRV). Additionally, there are several provisions in the RIA Guidelines that specifically require regulators to assess the compatibility with the EU law. Moreover, there are several methodological guidelines, such as Methodical Instructions for Fulfilment of Legislative Obligations arising from the Czech Republic's Membership in the EU or Methodical Tool for Prevention of Excessive Regulatory Burden in the Implementation of EU Law that encourage regulators to assess unnecessary measures going beyond the EU requirements as well as to avoid gold plating.

In **Denmark**, the Danish Business Regulation Forum advises a Government Committee on the implementation of EU-legislation and operates within a framework of five principles for good implementation to minimize gold plating in business regulation. The five principles are:

1. National regulation should as a general rule not go further than the minimal requirements in European legislative acts;
2. Danish businesses should not be disadvantaged compared to international competitors, and therefore the implementation should not be more burdensome than expected in comparable EU countries;
3. Flexibility and the exemptions in EU legislative acts should be used;
4. When possible and meaningful, EU legislative acts should be implemented through alternatives to regulation;
5. Burdensome EU legislative acts should commence latest possible with the national common commencement dates taken into consideration.

The process of transposition in **Estonia** is not particularly concerned with gold plating issues. This is not because the matter is not relevant. It is because all gold plating issues are examined at the routine stage of co-ordinating on draft legislation, of any type. The main tool adopted is the zero bureaucracy project.

In 2017, **France** directed an inter-agency mission to identify national transposition measures that deviate from the directive's minimum requirements and that may have penalised business competitiveness, employment purchasing power, or efficiency of public services. Out of the 137 directives identified by the mission as having a transposition gap with a penalising effect, in-depth analysis highlighted that 40 legislative measures no longer constituted over-transposition in view of the subsequently introduced directives.

There is a requirement to assess gold plating in the joint rules of procedure of the Federal Government of **Germany**. Enforcement is a matter left to the Länder and, for certain matters, to the local authorities. The German government provides comprehensive information on compliance costs – including those coming directly from the European legislative proposal. When there is gold plating in the domestic regulation that accompany a wider EU directive, the government applies the one-in-one-out rule.

All initiatives that transpose and implement EU acts in **Italy** should not go beyond what is necessary for the delivery of the minimum level envisaged by the EU legislative act. There is a requirement to be explicit when, in exceptional circumstances, implementation goes beyond the standards envisaged by the EU. These circumstances must be empirically supported and evidenced in the RIA.

In the **Netherlands**, an IAK-analysis is generally required and conducted to inform the development of regulations for all primary laws and subordinate regulations. The detail of the answers to the impact assessment questions must be proportional. Therefore, the analysis can vary per proposal, depending, for example, on the nature of the proposal, the scope and extent of the expected impacts of a proposed regulation. Instruction 9.4 of the Drafting instructions for regulation contains the general provision that implies that no other rules are included in the implementation regulation than necessary for implementation – a separate RIA for added provisions at the national level is therefore not required.

Draft acts transposing EU legislation in **Poland** sent to stakeholders and interministerial consultation should be accompanied by several documents including a so-called "reverse compliance table" that provides a tabular summary of the draft provisions of the Act, which go beyond the implementation, together with an explanation of the necessity of including them within the project. The Ministry of Foreign Affairs in its opinion on conformity of the draft law with the EU law consider possible instances of gold plating.

The issue of gold plating is not considered as a great concern in **Slovak Republic** if correctly justified. That said, the gold plating initiative is being carried out by the Ministry of Economy of the Slovak Republic. The assessment on gold plating is made by the proposing authority. Should it conclude that there is gold plating in the new draft regulation, the authority is obliged to explain the reasons for such gold plating in a Reasoned Report accompanying the draft regulation in the national approval process.

In 2019, the *Riksdag* (Parliament) in **Sweden** called the government to work to ensure that EU directives are implemented in Swedish legislation in a manner that does not impair companies' competitiveness. A starting point should be that EU directives be introduced at a minimum level in the national legislation. When there is cause to exceed the minimum level, the impact on companies should be clearly accounted for and reported.

Source: Indicators of Regulatory Policy and Governance (iREG) Survey 2021; Radaelli et al (unpublished[13]), Extending the OECD indicators of Regulatory Policy and Governance (iREG) to all EU Member States of the European Union; Sveriges Riksdag (2019[16]), Beslut EU-direktiv bör inte försämra företagens konkurrenskraft (NU7), https://www.riksdagen.se/sv/dokument-lagar/arende/betankande/naringspolitik_h601nu7.

A minority of EU Member States report using the European Commission's impact assessments to inform transposition of EU directives

EU Member States could use the European Commission's impact assessments when assessing the domestic impacts of the adopted directive, as they continue to provide helpful information and evidence to the domestic policy maker in charge of transposing the EU directive. There is value in using the European Commission's impact assessment as a source of information when EU Member States are assessing the impact that a directive has on the domestic economy and society. Whilst the European Commission's impact assessments provide evidence aggregated at the EU level, they still contain crucial information on the types of costs and benefits that EU Member States collectively can expect to face. This information can be a solid starting point for EU Member States to build on when developing their own assessment of the domestic impacts.

Approximately half of EU Member States report to use the results of the European Commission's impacts assessment to inform the transposition of EU directives (Figure 3.17). Generally, Member States occasionally use the results of Commission's impact assessment, rather than on a systematic basis (Figure 3.17). Only **Malta** and **Poland** report to always use the results of Commission's RIA to inform their transposition of EU laws. For example, in **Malta**, the results of Commission's analysis and findings are used in comparing with Malta's national situation and to provide options for strategic direction and assist regulators with the implementation of EU laws. In **Poland**, the draft legislative act and staff working documents are used to assess the impact on the national economy.

Figure 3.17. Only six EU Member States report systematically using the European Commission's impact assessments to inform the transposition of EU directives

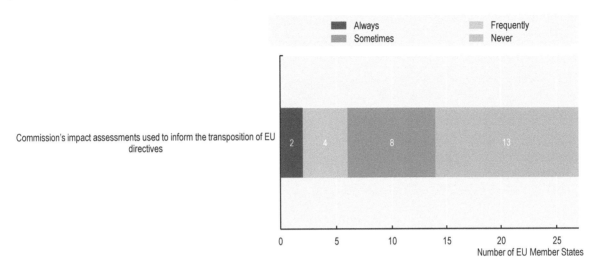

Note: Data is based on 27 EU Member States.
Source: Indicators of Regulatory Policy and Governance (iREG) Survey 2021.

Use of "foreign" data in EU Member States' RIA

Policy makers do not operate in silos, particularly in the context of the European Union, and thus need to collaborate with their counterparts in other EU Member States when developing domestic legislation and when transposing EU directives. Collaborating with parties outside national boundaries is an essential feature of embedding international regulatory co-operation (IRC) in domestic rule making, as highlighted in the *OECD Best Practice Principles on International Regulatory Co-operation* (OECD, 2021[17]).

Collaboration and evidence exchange with other EU Member States can be a relevant practice during the development, negotiation, or transposition of EU legislative acts. Member States would benefit from sharing information on the impacts of EU legislation, as it would allow them to learn from each other, improve their impact assessments and better inform their decision making. Particularly in light of the often-limited time before negotiation takes place, short deadlines might prompt EU Member States to partner to collect or to utilise evidence from one another when preparing their national position in the negotiation phase or when shaping the transposition of EU directives (Radaelli, Dunlop and Allio, unpublished[13]). Similarly, EU Member States can use other Member States' RIAs to supplement their own analysis in addition to the European Commission's, when transposing EU directives and into domestic laws.

EU Member States report not engaging systematically with each other despite the potential gains from collaboration during the negotiation and transposition of EU legislative acts. Four EU Member States – **Denmark**, **Germany**, **Latvia**, and **Malta** – report having systematic mechanisms in place for sharing or exchanging information and evidence on potential impacts of EU directives and regulations with other EU Member States and the European Commission. More information on their practices concerning information exchange with regards to EU legislative acts is provided in Box 3.12. Only six EU Member States report using information from the RIA conducted by other EU Member States when transposing a directive and this appears to be done on an ad-hoc basis.

Box 3.12. Examples of EU Member States with systematic mechanisms for sharing or exchanging evidence on EU legislative acts

Latvian regulators systematically engage with other EU Member States at the European Union Council and European Commission working group meetings during which EU Member States exchange their views. Counsellors exchange with each other possible implications for the legal systems. Furthermore, for the Ministries of Justice there is a network which allows exchanges among ministries about various legal system issues including potential impacts of EU legislation.

Malta engages with other EU Member States on the base of ad-hoc mechanisms. In particular, Maltese regulators engage with like-minded EU Member States to push and advocate for its interests in line with those of other EU Member States.

In **Germany**, the impact of all new regulations of EU law is required to be assessed. Information and evidence on the potential impacts of EU directives and regulations is informally shared with other Member States and with the European Commission during the negotiation of the proposed act through the interactions in various working groups.

According to the **Danish** Guidelines on Legal Quality it is required that line ministries assess the impacts of proposed regulations on foreign jurisdictions. In particular, if the proposed legislation has a significant impact on other Nordic countries it is required that the impacts on these countries are evaluated and that they are described in detail in the comments. With respect to the implementation of EU directives, where appropriate, the relevant Ministry of Industry must ensure that the comments on a legislative proposal include a description of the legislation in other Nordic countries.

Source: Indicators of Regulatory Policy and Governance (iREG) Survey 2021.

It is noteworthy that beyond EU Member States' well-established practice regarding RIA to inform the transposition of EU directives, 11 EU Member States have a requirement in place to conduct a RIA when adopting international instruments beyond EU law. This may be a useful experience for EU Member States more broadly to learn from to conduct RIA to assess the benefits and costs of following non-EU international instruments, particularly when these are non-binding and several parallel instruments exist on the same subject (OECD, 2021[17]). In so doing, they could verify if the international instrument was already the subject of an IA by the international organisation or another member thereof, to draw on it as useful evidence (OECD, 2021[18]). Nevertheless, if the instrument is binding and its implementation is mandatory, it may be more relevant to conduct the assessment before the adoption of the instruments to consider alternative options.

Notes

[1] Basic Law for the Federal Republic of Germany (1949), available at: http://www.gesetze-im-internet.de/englisch_gg/englisch_gg.html#p0111.

[2] See Box 2.5 on pages 25 and 26 of the *OECD Best Practice Principles for Regulatory Policy: Regulatory Impact Assessment* (2020[2]) for a typology of policy alternatives to "command-and-control" regulations

References

European Commission (2021), *Better Regulation Guidelines*, [10]
https://ec.europa.eu/info/sites/default/files/swd2021_305_en.pdf.

European Commission (2021), *Better Regulation Toolbox*, [3]
https://ec.europa.eu/info/sites/default/files/br_toolbox-nov_2021_en_0.pdf.

European Parliament (2018), *Transposition, implementation and enforcement of Union law*, [14]
https://www.europarl.europa.eu/cmsdata/226403/EPRS_ATAG_627141_Transposition_imple
mentation_and_enforcement_of_EU_law-FINAL.pdf.

Government of Cyprus (2016), *Impact Analysis Guidelines and Questionnaire*, [9]
https://issuu.com/presidency-reform-
cyprus/docs/   ecabe30ece8d29.

OECD (2021), *Compendium of International Organisations' Practices: Working Towards More* [18]
Effective International Instruments, OECD Publishing, Paris,
https://doi.org/10.1787/846a5fa0-en.

OECD (2021), *OECD Best Practice Principles for Regulatory Policy: International Regulatory Co-* [17]
operation, OECD Publishing, https://doi.org/10.1787/5b28b589-en.

OECD (2021), *OECD Regulatory Policy Outlook 2021*, OECD Publishing, [4]
https://doi.org/10.1787/38b0fdb1-en.

OECD (2020), *A closer look at proportionality and threshold tests for RIA: Annex to the OECD* [8]
Best Practice Principles on Regulatory Impact Assessment, OECD Publishing,
http://www.oecd.org/regreform/Proportionality-and-threshhold-tests-RIA.pdf.

OECD (2020), *OECD Best Practice Principles for Regulatory Policy: Regulatory Impact* [2]
Assessment, OECD Publishing, https://doi.org/10.1787/7a9638cb-en.

OECD (2019), *Better Regulation Practices across the European Union*, OECD Publishing, [5]
https://doi.org/10.1787/9789264311732-e.

OECD (2018), *OECD Regulatory Policy Outlook 2018*, OECD Publishing, [6]
https://doi.org/10.1787/9789264303072-e.

OECD (2015), *OECD Regulatory Policy Outlook 2015*, OECD Publishing, [7]
https://doi.org/10.1787/9789264238770-en.

OECD (2012), *Recommendation of the Council on Regulatory Policy and Governance*, OECD [1]
Publishing, Paris, https://doi.org/10.1787/9789264209022-en.

OECD (2009), *Better Regulation in Europe: An OECD Assessment of Regulatory Capacity in the* [15]
15 Original Member States of the EU, Project Glossary, OECD, Paris,
https://www.oecd.org/gov/regulatory-policy/44952782.pdf.

Radaelli, C., C. Dunlop and L. Allio (unpublished), *Extending the OECD indicators of Regulatory* [13]
Policy and Governance (iREG) to all Member States of the European Union.

Regulatory Scrutiny Board (2020), *Annual Report 2020*, https://ec.europa.eu/info/sites/default/files/rsb_report_2020_en_1.pdf. [12]

RegWatchEurope (2020), *Conclusions of RWE Workshop on Proportionality Requirements*, https://www.regwatcheurope.eu/wp-content/uploads/2021/06/Conclusions-RWE-workshop-Proportionality-Requirements-002.pdf. [11]

Sveriges Riksdag (2019), *Beslut: EU-direktiv bör inte försämra företagens konkurrenskraft (NU7)*, https://www.riksdagen.se/sv/dokument-lagar/arende/betankande/naringspolitik_h601nu7. [16]

4 *Ex post* evaluation

The actual impacts of laws and regulations are only known after they have entered into force. Such effects may also change over time so regulations that at one time were appropriate may become outdated. It is crucial for governments to regularly review their stock of existing regulations so as to ensure that they continue to deliver for citizens. This chapter assesses the use of *ex post* evaluations across EU Member States. It discusses the types of evaluations commonly conducted, the general approaches taken by EU Member States to regulatory stock management, the role of regulatory oversight in *ex post* evaluation, and the engagement of stakeholders when undertaking evaluations. Finally, it also reviews the use of *ex post* evaluation by EU Member States in the EU legislative process.

Key messages

- Despite recent improvements in some EU Member States, *ex post* evaluations remain heavily underutilised as a regulatory management tool. To maximise the benefits that evaluations offer, EU Member States need to make stronger commitments to review the ever-growing stock of rules and integrate these better in the regulatory cycle.

- Evaluations that look at administrative burdens or competition issues tend to be the most frequently conducted by EU Member States. The results from such evaluations may help to improve the regulatory environment for businesses and citizens but they could go further by assessing whether the regulation is working as intended.

- Few EU Member States have thresholds in place to determine whether evaluations should be undertaken. Selecting which regulations to evaluate is important to ensure that scarce review resources are allocated to priority areas, especially for smaller Member States.

- Fundamental regulatory stock management tools do not exist in a quarter of EU Member States, suggesting that many regulations once made are not systematically checked to ensure that they continue to deliver benefits to the community.

- Given the lack of evaluations across the EU, it is perhaps unsurprising that their oversight is weak. Despite recent improvements, less than one-fifth of EU Member States have an oversight body responsible for checking the quality of evaluations. This result suggests that even where evaluations are conducted, their quality is likely to be highly variable. This is further compounded by a stark lack of training in conducting *ex post* evaluations.

- Stakeholders are usually not informed about forthcoming *ex post* evaluations. That said, two-thirds of EU Member States do consult with stakeholders on some of their evaluations. Stakeholders are more likely to be involved in identifying regulatory issues through ongoing opportunities, for example, through permanent dedicated websites.

- Despite the fact that around 85% of EU Member States undertook at least one *ex post* evaluation in the past five years, less than 15% shared their results with the European Commission. As a transparency measure reviews should generally be published and shared with relevant parties. When the European Commission undertakes *ex post* evaluations, the majority of EU Member States do not use the results to inform either their negotiation position or for the transposition of newly made EU directives.

Introduction

The stock of laws and regulations has grown rapidly in most countries, even more so recently due to new rules being introduced to combat the COVID-19 pandemic. However not all regulations are rigorously assessed when they were originally made – and this is especially the case for those made in haste in response to emergency needs – and even where they have, not all effects can be known with certainty beforehand. Moreover, many external factors influence the attainment of regulatory objectives, demonstrating a need to periodically undertake checks to establish whether rules are working as intended.

The *2012 OECD Recommendation on Regulatory Policy and Governance* calls on governments to "[c]onduct systematic programme reviews of the stock of significant regulation against clearly defined policy goals, including consideration of costs and benefits, to ensure that regulations remain up to date, cost justified, cost effective and consistent, and deliver the intended policy objectives." (OECD, 2012[1]). In some circumstances, the formal processes of *ex post* impact analysis may be more effective than *ex ante* analysis at informing ongoing policy debate. This is likely to be the case for example, if regulations have been developed under pressure to implement a rapid response (OECD, 2018[2]). *Ex post* evaluations should have a level of symmetry with *ex ante* impact assessments: through verifying that stated objectives have actually been met, determining whether there have been any unforeseen or unintended consequences, and considering whether alternative approaches could have done better. Reviews that in addition also encompass proposals for change and revisit the original regulatory objective and its ongoing appropriateness or legitimacy are particularly useful to improve the stock of regulations (OECD, 2020[3]).

This chapter presents a systematic and up-to-date assessment of requirements and practices in place for conducting *ex post* evaluations for primary laws and subordinate regulation across all 27 EU Member States and the European Commission. The first section provides a snapshot of country's systems based on the iREG composite indicator on *ex post* evaluation for primary laws and subordinate regulations. The second section discusses *ex post* evaluations across the EU Member States. It provides information on the types of evaluations commonly conducted, general approaches to regulatory stock management, regulatory oversight, and the engagement of stakeholders when undertaking evaluations. The final section presents results from new survey data on the use of *ex post* evaluations in the EU legislative process.

General trends in *ex post* evaluation across the European Union

EU Member States have improved their *ex post* evaluation practices since 2017 for both primary laws (Figure 4.1) and subordinate regulations (Figure 4.2), with a more significant increase in the former. The largest improvements have been in oversight and quality control of *ex post* evaluations, since more oversight bodies now scrutinise *ex post* evaluations and assist officials in conducting them than in 2017. EU Member States have improved their *ex post* evaluation methodologies, especially for primary laws, as more countries are now assessing the costs, benefits and other impacts of existing regulations; are assessing whether regulations are achieving their intended goals; and have guidance available to officials on how to conduct these evaluations. There has been some improvement in the transparency of evaluations conducted.

Figure 4.1. Composite indicators: *Ex post* evaluation for primary laws, 2021

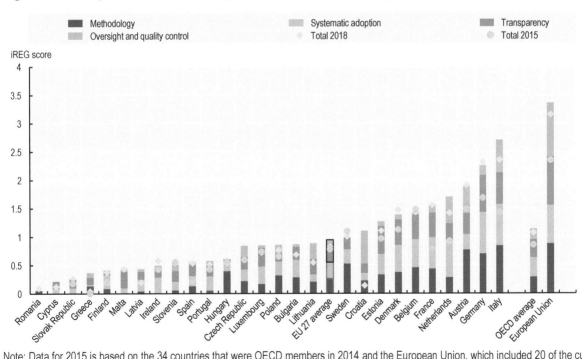

Note: Data for 2015 is based on the 34 countries that were OECD members in 2014 and the European Union, which included 20 of the current 27 EU Member States. The OECD average is based on the 38 member countries at the time of the survey. Data for 2018 and 2021 includes the remaining EU Member States of Latvia, Lithuania, Bulgaria, Croatia, Cyprus, Malta and Romania. The more regulatory practices as advocated in the *2012 Recommendation* a country has implemented, the higher its iREG score.
Source: Indicators of Regulatory Policy and Governance Surveys 2014, 2017 and 2021.

Figure 4.2. Composite indicators: *Ex post* evaluation for subordinate regulations, 2021

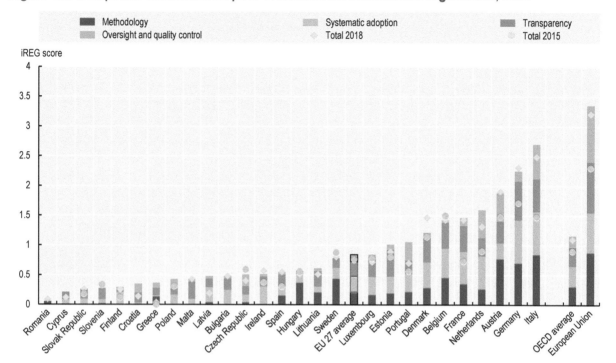

Note: Data for 2015 is based on the 34 countries that were OECD members in 2014 and the European Union, which included 20 of the current 27 EU Member States. The OECD average is based on the 38 member countries at the time of the survey. Data for 2018 and 2021 includes the remaining EU Member States of Latvia, Lithuania, Bulgaria, Croatia, Cyprus, Malta and Romania. The more regulatory practices as advocated in the *2012 Recommendation* a country has implemented, the higher its iREG score.
Source: Indicators of Regulatory Policy and Governance Surveys 2014, 2017 and 2021.

EU Member States that have had substantive changes to their *ex post* evaluation systems since 2017 include **Croatia**, **Greece**, **Italy**, **Latvia**, **Lithuania**, the **Netherlands**, **Portugal** and the **European Union**.

- Since 2018, **Croatia** requires *ex post* evaluations on primary laws two years after their enactment and policy makers are mandated to assess whether those laws are meeting their objectives. The Government Legislation Office is the oversight body in charge of reviewing the quality of the *ex post* evaluations and signing off on the evaluation reports. The Ministry of Economy and Sustainable Development reviews the quality of administrative burden reductions as part of the SME test processes for primary laws and subordinate regulations.

- **Greece** introduced Law 4622 in 2019. Amongst other topics, it made periodic *ex post* evaluations mandatory for all primary laws and for major subordinate regulations, and it now requires all *ex post* evaluations to contain an assessment of costs and benefits. Evaluation techniques and oversight functions related to *ex post* evaluations were also strengthened.

- In **Italy**, new non-binding guidance on *ex post* evaluation was issued in 2018. Initial steps have been taken to plan *ex post* evaluations when preparing RIAs for major legislation. Ministries publish a two-year plan of regulations to be evaluated.

- As part of broader reforms in **Latvia**, *ex post* evaluations are now required for some subordinate regulations and an evaluation of all policy documents conforming to the SDGs was recently conducted.

- **Lithuania** has introduced some general requirements to conduct monitoring and *ex post* reviews of existing primary laws and in 2020, it strengthened the regulatory oversight function and transparency of *ex post* evaluations.

- The **Netherlands** saw an improvement in oversight and quality control for periodic *ex post* evaluation of the effectiveness and efficiency of regulations. The Budget Inspectorate is now responsible for reviewing the quality of *ex post* evaluations and it has developed a toolbox with guidance for officials conducting these evaluations.

- **Portugal**'s main regulatory oversight body was created in 2017 and has taken the role of co-ordinating *ex post* evaluations of subordinate regulations across the public administration and assisting officials in conducting them. Following the COVID-19 pandemic, Portugal introduced sunsetting clauses for some regulations.

- The **European Union**'s *ex post* evaluation system now combines systematic evaluations of individual regulations with comprehensive "fitness checks" of policy sectors, inviting comment on evaluation Calls for evidence. The EU's regulatory oversight body also now provides summary ratings on evaluations that are made publicly available along with compliance statistics.

Ex post evaluation in EU Member States

EU Member States' *ex post* evaluations should be used as a tool of continuous improvement in the regulatory environment. Some examples highlighting the range of benefits that *ex post* evaluations have provided are summarised in Box 4.1. *Ex post* evaluations conducted by EU Member States can potentially improve both their own domestic and the EU regulatory frameworks. The *Outlook* illustrated that although *ex post* evaluations are generally published, little is done in terms of forcing governments to respond to evaluation findings (OECD, 2021[4]).

Box 4.1. Examples of EU Member States' *ex post* evaluations

***Ex post* evaluations provided an opportunity to better understand actual policy impacts...**

An *ex post* evaluation of the regulation of the operation of voluntary fire-fighter organisations was carried out in **Latvia**. The regulation was not effective in achieving previously set policy goals, so the relevant ministry initiated a pilot project in which several voluntary fire-fighter organisations were invited to participate. During the project policy makers had a chance to see real-world problems that arise from the regulation and to identify the main obstacles. The assessment allowed the policy makers to better address the identified problems and to initiate respective improvements in operation model of the voluntary fire-fighter organisations.

have resulted in increased transparency...

In **Denmark**, General Data Protection Regulation (GDPR) rulings from The Danish Protection Agency (DPA) were formerly only published if DPA deemed that the GDPR-rulings were of a "principal character". However, encouraged by an *ex post* evaluation recommendation from the Danish Business Regulation Forum, DPA adopted a new practice of publishing all GDPR-ruling irrespective of their character as long as private or public interests did not outweigh the benefits of allowing businesses to gain more insights over GDPR-rulings in general.

... and led to changes to improve the regulatory framework

A **German** *ex post* evaluation of the Federal Government's Environmental Information Act (*Umweltinformationsgesetz*) was intended to determine whether the legislative objectives of the Act were being met. The assessment concluded that the Act was essentially fulfilling its objective. The evaluation proposed to create the post of Environmental Information Commissioner reporting to the Federal Commissioner for Data Protection, which was taken up in the bill amending the Environmental

---

Damage Act (Umweltschadensgesetz), the Environmental Information Act and other environment-related regulations. The ombudsperson and supervisory functions that the Federal Commissioner for Data Protection and Freedom of Information is to be extended to cover access to environmental information.

As part of an *ex post* evaluation of the Act on Counteracting Excessive Delays in Commercial Transactions in **Poland**, numerous demands appeared, largely related to the new obligation to submit reports on payment practices. The assessment and comments highlighted the need to introduce changes aimed at increasing the effectiveness of proceedings. Amendments to the Act are currently underway.

Source: Supplementary material provided to the indicators of Regulatory Policy and Governance Survey 2021.

For EU Member States with a strong administrative burden focus, *ex post* evaluations could, at a minimum, be used to improve the *ex ante* estimation of those costs in future regulatory proposals. However the extent to which Member States utilise the results of evaluations to feedback into improved *ex ante* assessments of administrative burdens remains unclear.

Where EU Member States undertake fuller reviews that not only look at reducing unnecessary burdens, but also assess whether the regulation remains in the public interest, there is increased scope for learning and improving future *ex ante* assessments. A review, for example, may demonstrate that a particular regulatory approach did not change market participants' behaviours as anticipated, and this information could be used to help guide future policy options. Similarly, a review may note that compliance levels varied widely from what was originally intended when the rule was made. Such information can help to ensure that regulators are armed with a full suite of tools – starting with educational ones – to help achieve sought after compliance levels in the future.

The main type of *ex post* evaluation undertaken by EU Member States is principle-based reviews. The most common guiding principle is on administrative burdens followed by competition. Since 2017, both **Estonia** and **Sweden** undertook in-depth reviews, into the competitiveness of the business environment and environmental assessment system, respectively (Box 4.2).

Figure 4.3. Member States most commonly engage in principle-based reviews and least often conduct reviews that compare regulation

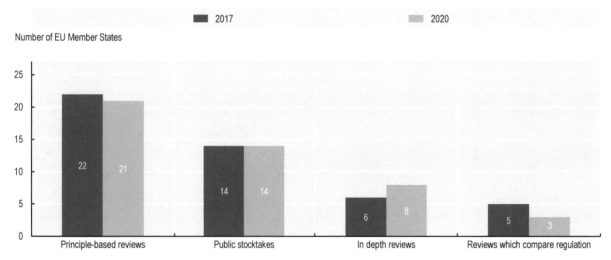

Note: Data is based on 27 EU Member States.
Source: Indicators of Regulatory Policy and Governance (iREG) Surveys 2017 and 2021.

Box 4.2. Recent in-depth reviews conducted in Estonia and Sweden

In 2018, the **Estonian** Ministry of Justice published an in-depth review of its company law. The review was carried out by a working group of legal experts, aimed at assessing the Estonian company law as a whole and to propose possible amendments. In addition to analysing the Estonian law, the working group studied the legal framework in a number of similar countries, the existing case law and the legal literature within the terms of reference given by the Ministry of Justice. The assessment resulted in a large number of regulatory proposals and amendments, which are to be implemented as a part of fundamental changes to the legislative policy framework by 2030.

In January 2018, the Government Offices in **Sweden** authorised an in-depth review of the system for the environmental assessment of hazardous activities. The aim of the review was to assess whether the environmental assessment was designed in a way that promoted investments that drive technology and development towards lower negative environmental impacts, and to propose how the environmental assessment process could become more efficient and effective. The review also assessed whether the review of activities was in line with the Environmental Code and promoted investments contributing to a green transition.

The review highlighted positive aspects of the environmental assessment (e.g. efficiency measures regarding the introduction of change permits), but also areas for improvement (e.g. introduction of e-service for environmental permit application).

Source: Indicators of Regulatory Policy and Governance Survey 2021; Käerdi et al (2018[5]), Ühinguõiguse Revisjon Analüüs-Kontseptsioon, https://www.just.ee/sites/www.just.ee/files/uhinguoiguse_revisjoni_analuus-kontseptsioon.pdf; Regeringskansliet (Swedish Government Office (2018[6]), Anpassad miljöprövning för en grön omställning, https://www.regeringen.se/rattsliga-dokument/departementsserien-och-promemorior/2018/10/ds-201838/.

It is perhaps somewhat surprising that countries with similar values and laws have not taken a more active approach in conducting reviews that compare regulations or regulatory outcomes across jurisdictions. It remains likely that there are opportunities to improve the regulatory environment in various EU Member States based on others' experiences. One explanation could be that training to conduct *ex post* evaluations for officials is limited. Only **Austria**, **France**, **Greece**, and **Italy** report having formal training programs (Box 4.3).

Box 4.3. *Ex post* evaluation training offered by various EU Member States

The training offered by **Austria** is specific to *ex post* evaluation and to the monitoring tools used for this purpose by the Austrian government. It also covers the evaluation principles as well as information and reporting requirements.

Officials in **France** have access to a training on *ex post* evaluation that enables them to get familiarised with the relevant theories and methodologies. In addition, the French government has organised ad hoc training seminars on *ex post* evaluation of public policies, in partnership with French research institutions.

The training programme in **Greece** covers the better regulation framework as a whole, including *ex post* evaluation. The programme runs over several days and *ex post* evaluation is an integral component of the training, along with other core regulatory management tools such as stakeholder engagement and RIA.

In **Italy**, the National School of the Administration organises the training course "How to build RIA and *ex post* evaluation". The course aims to update managers and officials involved in the development of RIA and *ex post* evaluation. It is an operational and practical training course for policy officials, aiming at practicing techniques of consultation, policy option analysis, assessment of impacts. Lessons are rich in interaction on case studies.

Source: Indicators of Regulatory Policy and Governance Survey 2021.

Results from the iREG survey indicate that 16 EU Member States and the European Union require policy makers to identify a process to achieve a regulation's goals at the time when the regulation is first created (Table 4.1). However, when it comes to reviewing regulations via *ex post* evaluations, only 13 EU Member States assess whether the underlying policy goals were in fact achieved or not. Only **Austria**, the **Czech Republic**, **Germany**, **Italy**, and the EU reported doing so systematically. *Ex ante* requirements exist in **Finland**, **Ireland**, **Latvia**, **Lithuania**, **Malta**, **Slovak Republic**, **Slovenia**, and **Spain** without any *ex post* practices, and conversely **Bulgaria**, **Croatia**, **Denmark**, and **Sweden** conduct *ex post* evaluations but have no requirement to identify a process *ex ante*. These results further highlight the current disconnect between regulation making and review.

Table 4.1. Many EU Member States are required to identify how a regulation's goals will be achieved at the development stage, but very few of them conduct *ex post* evaluations that actually assess whether the underlying policy goals were achieved

	When designing laws, policy makers have processes in place to identify the achievement of a regulation's goals.		Do *ex post* evaluations contain by default an assessment of whether the underlying policy goals of regulation have been achieved?	
	Primary laws	Subordinate regulations	Primary laws	Subordinate regulations
Austria				
Belgium				
Bulgaria				
Croatia				
Cyprus				
Czech Republic				
Denmark				
Estonia				
Finland				
France				
Germany				
Greece				
Hungary				
Ireland				
Italy				
Latvia				
Lithuania				
Luxembourg				
Malta				
Netherlands				
Poland				
Portugal				
Romania				
Slovak Republic				
Slovenia				

	When designing laws, policy makers have processes in place to identify the achievement of a regulation's goals.		Do ex post evaluations contain by default an assessment of whether the underlying policy goals of regulation have been achieved?	
	Primary laws	Subordinate regulations	Primary laws	Subordinate regulations
Spain				
Sweden				
European Union				

■ For all primary regulations/ All *ex post* evaluations
▩ For major regulations/ *Ex post* evaluations regarding major regulations
▨ For some regulations/ Some *ex post* evaluations
▤ Never

Note: Data is based on 27 EU Member States and the European Union.
Source: Indicators of Regulatory Policy and Governance (iREG) Survey 2021.

The use of threshold tests in ex post *evaluations across the European Union*

Similar to *ex ante* impact assessments, a threshold with objective criteria to identify when and how to conduct *ex post* evaluation can help to channel resources effectively to the most significant regulations and improve transparency of decision making about which rules get reviewed and why.

Less than a quarter of EU Member States have a threshold in place to determine whether an *ex post* evaluation of primary laws should take place – namely, **Austria**, **Estonia**, **Germany**, **Italy**, **Slovenia** and **Spain**. More information on the **Estonian** threshold test is in Box 4.4. Only Austria, Germany and Spain reported having comprehensive tests that cover both costs and benefits relating to social, economic and environmental impacts (Figure 4.4).

Box 4.4. Requirements and application of the Estonian *ex post* evaluation threshold

In general, *ex post* evaluation of existing regulations is mandatory for some primary laws and subordinate regulations in **Estonia**. A threshold test is used to determine whether *ex post* evaluations of primary laws should be undertaken, but this is not the case for subordinate regulations.

If *ex ante* impact assessment shows the occurrence of significant impacts (as understood in the Estonian legislative system), *ex post* assessment is required by rule and the plan for conducting it must be presented in the explanatory letter of the draft law. *Ex post* evaluations are required to provide qualitative assessment of costs and benefits, but it is not required that they compare the predicted and actual regulatory impacts, although evaluations sometimes reference the initial RIA.

If the line ministry is of the view that *ex post* evaluation is unnecessary, the reasons for such decision have to be shown in the explanatory letter of the draft law. However, the Legislative Quality Division can make suggestions regarding which laws and regulations should be subject to *ex post* assessment.

A new *ex post* evaluation strategy is currently under development in Estonia, under which legislative proposals introduced in response to an emergency must always be subject to *ex post* evaluations, since they may undergo a less detailed RIA.

For example, an *ex post* evaluation of a regulation that aimed to reduce the visibility of alcoholic beverages in retail stores has been carried out recently. The requirement to carry out the evaluation was pre-defined in the draft law. The *ex post* assessment showed that the regulatory amendment changed consumer behaviour and led to fewer impulse purchases of alcohol.

Source: Indicators of Regulatory Policy and Governance Surveys 2021, Kandla et al (2019[7]), Study on partial alcohol point-of-sale display ban, https://www.sm.ee/sites/default/files/summary_study_on_partial_alcohol_point-of-sale_display_ban_estonia_2019.pdf.

Figure 4.4. Few Member States report having a comprehensive threshold test in place to decide whether an *ex post* evaluation should be undertaken

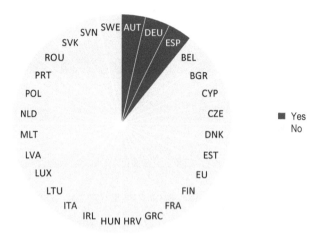

Note: Data is based on 27 EU Member States and the European Union.
Source: Indicators of Regulatory Policy and Governance (iREG) Survey 2021.

Ex post evaluation requirements in **Germany** are determined by threshold tests that include whether the annual compliance costs generated by the regulation are in excess of EUR 1 million for citizens and businesses, as well as political relevance and the level of risk of the regulation. All *ex post* evaluations in Germany are required to contain an assessment of costs (but not benefits) and are required to be quantified. *Ex post* evaluations regarding major primary and subordinate laws also include a comparison of the actual vs predicted impacts of the regulation being reviewed. In November 2019, the German government introduced additional requirements for independent quality control of *ex post* evaluations which the National Regulatory Control Council (NKR) is performing.

In **Denmark** there are no formalised threshold or other factors used to identify regulations that require an *ex post* evaluation. Instead, it is at the discretion of Danish Business Regulation Forum (DBRF) to decide which regulations will be assessed *ex post*. However, the DBRF's decision is based on the regulatory burdens perceived by Danish businesses. Ministerial officials also have the discretion to choose whether to undertake an *ex post* evaluation and this decision is reportedly based on the political significance of a legislation. In practice when conducting evaluations, some contain an assessment of the costs and benefits and some compare the actual vs predicted impacts of the original rule against observed outcomes. The DBRF has an ongoing monitoring role to ensure that regulations are and remain proportionate after their implementation. Where that is no longer the case it is corrected, but it has to be ensured that relief for businesses is not made at the expense of consumers.

Regulatory stock management across the European Union

Left unchecked, the stock of regulations builds up over time creating cumulative burdens on business and citizens. Common forms of regulatory stock management are embedding review clauses and regulatory offset arrangements such as one-in-one-out. The OECD has recently published research on both forms of stock management (OECD, 2020[3]) (Trnka, D. Thuerer, Y, 2019[8]) **Finland**, **France**, **Germany**, **Italy**, **Lithuania** the **Netherlands**, and **Spain** currently have formalised stock management arrangements in place and more recently both the **Slovak Republic** and the European Union introduced one-in-one-out rules.

Embedded review clauses can be ad hoc or systematic. The former are usually reserved for policies with substantive economy-wide impacts that are highly uncertain at the time of implementation and therefore warrant *ex post* evaluation to better understand whether the assumptions at the time the rule was made remain valid. The latter usually take the form of either sunset or automatic evaluation clauses. Sunset clauses provide that a regulation will cease to have effect at a specified future date, unless it is either amended or remade. Automatic evaluation clauses provide a specified date by which either a review of the regulation needs to have commenced or concluded by.

Sunsetting arrangements are more commonplace than automatic evaluation clauses across the European Union (Table 4.2). That said, no EU Member State uses them systematically. **Austria**, **Germany**, **Hungary**, and the European Union itself have systematic automatic review provisions in place. **Bulgaria**, **Croatia**, **Cyprus**, **Latvia**, **Malta**, **Romania**, the **Slovak Republic**, and **Slovenia** do not utilise either sunset or automatic evaluation clauses.

Table 4.2. Around half the EU Member States include sunsetting clauses while automatic evaluation requirements are less common

	Do regulations include 'sunsetting' clauses?		Do regulations include automatic evaluation requirements?	
	Primary laws	Subordinate regulations	Primary laws	Subordinate regulations
Austria				
Belgium				
Bulgaria				
Croatia				
Cyprus				
Czech Republic				
Denmark				
Estonia				
Finland				
France				
Germany				
Greece				
Hungary				
Ireland				
Italy				
Latvia				
Lithuania				
Luxembourg				
Malta				
Netherlands				
Poland				
Portugal				
Romania				
Slovak Republic				
Slovenia				
Spain				
Sweden				
European Union				

■ For all primary laws/ subordinate regulations
■ For major primary laws/ subordinate regulations
■ For some primary laws/ subordinate regulations
■ Never

Note: Data is based on 27 EU Member States and the European Union.

Source: Indicators of Regulatory Policy and Governance (iREG) Survey 2021.

Regulatory oversight of ex post evaluations in the European Union

Regulatory oversight remains underdeveloped across both the European Union and the OECD more generally (see chapter 1 and (OECD, 2021[4])). Despite the fact that 85% of EU Member States reported having conducted *ex post* evaluations in the past five years, oversight remains scarce (Figure 4.5). **Croatia**, **Lithuania**, and **Poland** all reported having instituted an oversight body responsible for quality controlling *ex post* evaluations since 2017. These join **Austria**, **Italy**, and the **Netherlands** as the only EU Member States with an entity responsible for oversight of *ex post* evaluations. *Ex post* evaluations conducted by the European Commission are subject to quality control mechanisms of the Regulatory Scrutiny Board, which publishes its opinions on evaluation quality.

Figure 4.5. It is rare that EU Member States have a body outside the unit conducting the evaluation responsible for reviewing the quality of *ex post* evaluations

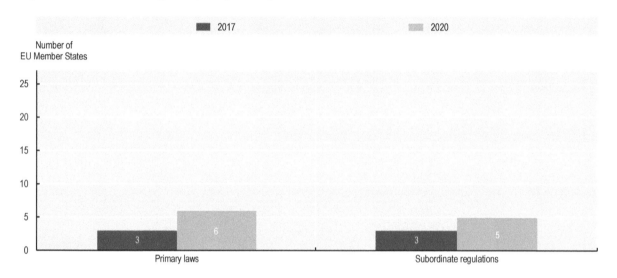

Note: Data is based on 27 EU Member States.
Source: Indicators of Regulatory Policy and Governance (iREG) Surveys 2017 and 2021.

Engaging stakeholders in ex post evaluations

EU Member States involve stakeholders through a variety of mechanisms when reviewing existing rules. Stakeholder engagement can be particularly useful in *ex post* evaluation to provide input into how regulations are actually working and can be a channel for regulators to prompt feedback from those parties affected by a regulation. Stakeholders can be involved both in the actual reviews and in more ongoing processes of identifying areas that may require reform.

Informing stakeholders in advance about forthcoming *ex post* evaluations is rare across EU Member States (Figure 4.6). Providing advanced notice to stakeholders enables them to gather data on actual impacts and experiences to assist policy makers to determine whether rules have worked as originally intended. Only **Lithuania** always informs stakeholders in advance, although it should be noted that this requirement is newly introduced and, in practice, has not been extensively used. **Italy** requires stakeholders to be systematically informed, and **Denmark**, **Latvia**, the **Netherlands** and **Spain** do so for some *ex post* evaluations.

Figure 4.6. It is rare that members of the public are informed in advance about *ex post* evaluations across the EU

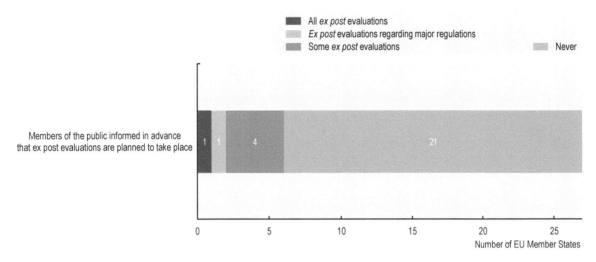

Note: Data is based on 27 EU Member States.
Source: Indicators of Regulatory Policy and Governance (iREG) Survey 2021.

Estonia and **Sweden** and the European Union report to systematically engage stakeholders in *ex post* evaluations. Two-thirds of EU Member States engage stakeholders in some *ex post* evaluations. Since 2017, **Croatia** and **Latvia** now involve stakeholders in evaluations of some regulations.

Most commonly, stakeholders are provided ongoing opportunities to submit comments, participate in interviews and meetings. Their input helps to identify areas for improvement and is often included in the scope of any evaluation. Stakeholder involvement is used in this manner in the following countries, including **Croatia**, **Lithuania**, the **Netherlands**, **Poland**, **Portugal**, and the **Slovak Republic**. For example, in **Italy**, stakeholders are consulted twice: first, early in the planning stage and then during the evaluation process. As for reviews of a large number of regulations, stakeholders are also involved in defining the priorities to simplify administrative and regulatory burdens and monitoring the implementation of the simplification measures. In **Sweden**, experts from business organisations and other interest groups can be appointed as experts in a committee of inquiry established by the responsible ministry to carry out *ex post* evaluation of a regulation. Referral bodies and stakeholders are also invited to provide comments on the final report, which are then dealt with by the responsible ministry in the continuous work within the Government Offices.

Four EU Member States report to systematically reference parts of the initial RIA in the *ex post* evaluations: **Austria**, **Germany**, **Greece** and **Poland**. In addition, seven EU Member States reference the *ex ante* RIA in some evaluations. Compared to 2017, **Estonia** and **Greece** have this requirement in place now. In **Estonia**, objectives and problems identified in the initial RIA are reflected most commonly in *ex post* evaluations. In **Greece**, all parts of the initial RIA should be referenced in *ex post* evaluations. When conducting evaluations, the European Union notes the *ex ante* RIA in all *ex post* evaluations, in particular it refers to the problem definition, policy objectives, regulatory impacts, data collection, enforcement, compliance and monitoring mechanisms in its evaluations.

Only a handful of EU Member States have standing committees to whom the public can provide feedback or make recommendations to modify specific regulations. The four countries with standing committees are: **Denmark**, **Germany**, **Ireland**, and **Malta**. The European Union has its own standing committee. **Germany** has a Committee for petitions which serves as a central point of contact at the Bundestag for citizens, through which they can express concerns and propose regulatory suggestions to the Parliament. The

Parliamentary Committee on Public Petitions in **Ireland** has an online portal through which the public can provide comments on existing regulations.

Use of *ex post* evaluation in the EU legislative process

EU legislative processes can be improved by utilising the results from *ex post* evaluations to improve policy making. Given that the vast majority of EU Member States have undertaken some evaluations, coupled with the evaluations of the European Commission, there is an available evidence base that can be help to improve the rules of both Member States and the European Union more generally.

The opportunity to learn from evaluations is not limited to the policy ministry conducting the review. Results can be widely applicable. Part of the learning process is to integrate results into future policy making and more precisely in any subsequent RIAs. Yet, currently sharing results beyond an individual jurisdiction is rare (Figure 4.7). Despite the fact that around 85% of EU Member States undertook at least one *ex post* evaluation in the past five years, less than 15% shared their results with the European Commission where the evaluation involved areas of EU legislative competencies. As a transparency measure reviews should generally be published and shared with relevant parties.

Figure 4.7. It is rare that EU Member States share the results of their *ex post* evaluations of EU directives/regulations with the European Commission

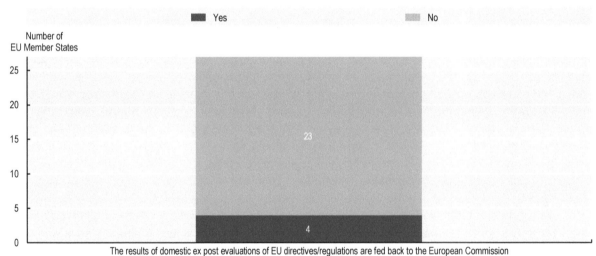

Note: Data is based on 27 EU Member States.
Source: Indicators of Regulatory Policy and Governance (iREG) Survey 2021.

EU Member States that do not feed the results of their *ex post* evaluations of EU directives/regulations with the European Commission, in most cases, do not do so because they do not have EU directive review mechanisms, or because evaluations are rare. However, in **Poland**, despite not having a requirement in place to share the results of domestic *ex post* evaluations with the European Commission, the minister responsible for the field concerned might share the findings of EU-law revisions with the European Commission.

Only **Denmark**, **Finland**, **Germany**, and **Italy** provide the European Commission with the results of their own domestic *ex post* evaluations of EU directives/regulations. **Finland** noted that it is not very common to conduct *ex post* evaluations of EU directives/regulations. However, if an *ex post* evaluation on EU directives is carried out (e.g., for a politically important EU directive for Finland), the results can be delivered to the Commission as part of the efforts to influence any future EU legislation. The Finnish approach is more generally linked to the appropriate insertion of review clauses into national legal acts. Sometimes they reflect the existence of a review clause in the relevant EU act, but do not necessarily have to do so. A more frequent use of national review clauses is often debated as a part of possible measures to improve *ex post* evaluation in Finland. In **Germany**, the analysis and processing of evaluation reports by the European Commission regarding certain dossiers is done by the relevant ministry's desk officers. The desk officers receive the information from their co-ordination units in the ministries and process and distribute the information to all persons and entities concerned. However, there is no special instrument or regime where this is written down. This is naturally part of the ongoing processing of EU dossiers in the federal government.

Use of the results of the European Commission's ex post evaluation by the Member States

The European Commission has an institutionalised approach to conducting *ex post* evaluations (Box 4.5). Under the "evaluate first principle", the European Commission utilises evaluations to improve the existing regulatory environment and inform impact assessments. The European Commission also in some cases utilises evaluations 'back-to-back' with its impact assessment as part of the same process when it proposes legislative changes. Such an approach provides information and evidence about the existing regulatory environment, the extent to which what has occurred was originally expected, and if not (or if the originally envisaged are not currently being attained), allows the Commission to put forward new regulatory directions in the form of a new impact assessment. The feedback loop from evaluation to new proposals should, over time, help to improve the regulatory environment, including aspects of burden reduction and simplification, which the European Commission addresses through its regulatory fitness and performance programme (REFIT). Considering that there are many external factors and developments that may impact on the attainment of regulatory objectives, periodic reviews remain necessary, even if not connected with a policy revision.

Box 4.5. The European Commission's REFIT programme

The regulatory fitness and performance programme (REFIT) is part of the European Commission's better regulation agenda. The REFIT programme aims to ensure that implemented EU laws achieve their intended benefits for European citizens and businesses by cutting red tape and making EU laws more targeted and easier to follow.

The European Commission's proposals for *ex post* evaluation of EU laws should aim to simplify and reduce avoidable regulatory costs while still fulfilling the regulatory objectives. However, where it is not possible to simplify regulations and reduce burdens, it has to be justified in the explanatory memoranda and the evaluation staff working documents. Where simplification and burden reduction is feasible, they should be quantified to the greatest extent possible.

Recently, the new "one in, one out" policy was introduced. It intends to minimise burdens for stakeholders affected by the policy, with emphasis on the regulatory cost burdens for citizens and businesses. The approach involves offsetting new burdens resulting from the European Commission's legislative proposals by equivalently reducing existing burdens in the same policy area. This implies that all compliance costs (i.e. adjustment and administrative costs) are analysed and quantified in impact assessments, where this is feasible and proportionate. Administrative costs are offset and adjustment costs are transparently and systematically presented in impact assessments to the extent this is feasible and proportionate. Other measures are undertaken with a view to compensate those

---

costs to the greatest extent possible. This approach complements the European Commission's efforts through its REFIT programme to reduce burdens and simplify existing EU laws.

The REFIT programme relies on evaluations, impacts assessments as well as citizens' and other stakeholders' input.

Stakeholders can also provide focused input on how to make EU laws more efficient through the Have your say: Simplify! Portal. The relevant input is considered by the Fit for Future Platform, a high level expert group established by the European Commission to provide opinions on how to simplify existing laws, reduce regulatory burdens, and ensure that they are fit for the future. The high-level expert group is composed of representatives from Member States' national, regional and local authorities, the Committee of the Regions, the European Economic and Social Committee and stakeholders representing business, civil society, and non-governmental organisations.

Source: European Commission (2021[9]), Better Regulation Guidelines, https://ec.europa.eu/info/sites/default/files/swd2021_305_en.pdf; European Commission (2021[10]), Better Regulation Toolbox, https://ec.europa.eu/info/sites/default/files/br_toolbox-nov_2021_en_0.pdf.

There are 11 Member States that report using the results of European Commission's *ex post* evaluations to inform their national negotiating position for the development of new or redesigned EU directives/regulations (Figure 4.8). **Slovenia** is the only country that engages in this practice systematically. For example, the **Netherlands** incorporates the results of the Commission's *ex post* evaluations in the BNC-fiches that are sent to the parliament to inform the Dutch starting point for negotiations. **Latvia** uses the information gained from the European Commission's *ex post* evaluations in adopting the national positions to explain the aims and shortcomings of the new/redesigned EU legal acts.

Figure 4.8. EU Member States do not systematically use *ex post* evaluation of the European Commission to inform their national negotiation position

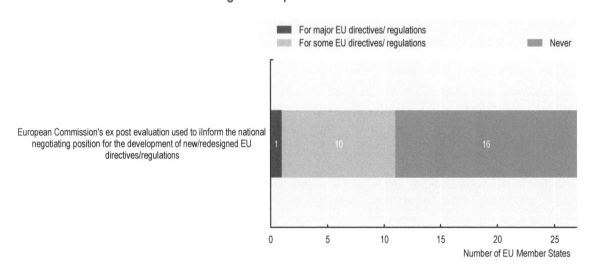

Note: Data is based on 27 EU Member States.
Source: Indicators of Regulatory Policy and Governance (iREG) Survey 2021.

Nine EU Member States reported using the results of the European Commission's evaluations to inform the transposition of new or redesigned EU directives (Figure 4.9). The relatively low uptake may be partially explained in situations where the European Commission undertook a "back-to-back" review and any resultant new European Commission proposals and supporting material were made directly available to

EU Member States through such avenues. **Slovenia** is the only country that systematically utilises the findings of the European Commission's *ex post* evaluations to inform its transposition of major EU directives/regulations. During the transposition of EU directives into national law, **Italy** uses the same requirements and processes described as for other types of regulations originating domestically. Each Administration with prevailing competence is responsible for drafting the legislative text and has continuous contact with the European Commission. The Department for European Policies co-ordinates with the Administrations and verifies the compatibility of the proposed regulations with European law.

Figure 4.9. EU Member States do not systematically use *ex post* evaluation of the European Commission to inform the transposition of new/redesigned EU directives

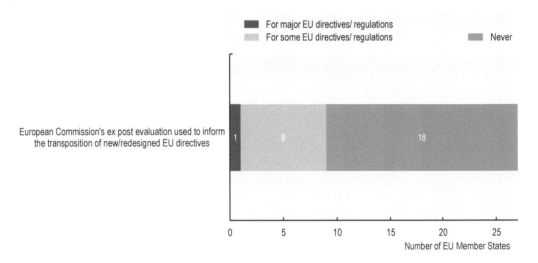

Note: Data is based on 27 EU Member States.
Source: Indicators of Regulatory Policy and Governance (iREG) Survey 2021.

In addition to using the Commission's *ex post* evaluation results to inform the negotiating position and transposition of EU directives/regulations into national law, **Denmark** uses the findings of the Commission's *ex post* evaluations for its own domestic evaluations. For instance, the results of the "Study on the accounting regime of limited liability micro companies" were used for the revision of the Danish Financial Statements Act (*Årsregnskabsloven*).

It stands to reason that EU Member States utilise the European Commission's evaluations more at the negotiation stage than at the transposition stage. During negotiation, with the Commission having identified problems or difficulties with the operation of the law, have then suggested modifications in the form of either an amendment or a new proposed rule. EU Member States may then rely on the European Commission's identified issues and stated future direction to inform their own negotiating position. Since the focus of the transposition stage is more centered on implementation, the original rationale as identified in the evaluation may be of less direct relevance to individual EU Member States. Moreover, Member States are likely to focus on any national additional provisions included as part of the transposition process. The focus on such provisions (to the extent that they are included) helps to ensure that all relevant impacts are included in any ensuing analysis by Member States.

References

European Commission (2021), *Better Regulation Guidelines*, [9]
https://ec.europa.eu/info/sites/default/files/swd2021_305_en.pdf.

European Commission (2021), *Better Regulation Toolbox*, [10]
https://ec.europa.eu/info/sites/default/files/br_toolbox-nov_2021_en_0.pdf.

Käerdi, M. et al. (2018), *Ühinguõiguse Revisjon Analüüs-Kontseptsioon*, [5]
https://www.just.ee/sites/www.just.ee/files/uhinguoiguse_revisjoni_analuus-kontseptsioon.pdf.

Kandla, K. et al. (2019), *Study on partial alcohol point-of-sale display ban*, [7]
https://www.sm.ee/sites/default/files/summary_study_on_partial_alcohol_point-of-sale_display_ban_estonia_2019.pdf.

OECD (2021), *OECD Regulatory Policy Outlook 2021*, OECD Publishing, Paris, [4]
https://doi.org/10.1787/38b0fdb1-en.

OECD (2020), *Reviewing the Stock of Regulation, OECD Best Practice Principles for Regulatory* [3]
Policy, OECD Publishing, Paris, https://doi.org/10.1787/1a8f33bc-en.

OECD (2018), *Key Findings and Conference Proceedings, 9th Conference on Measuring* [2]
Regulatory Performance: Closing the regulatory cycle: effective ex post evaluation for
improved policy outcomes, Lisbon, 20-21 June 2017, https://www.oecd.org/gov/regulatory-policy/Proceedings-9th-Conference-MRP.pdf.

OECD (2012), *Recommendation of the Council on Regulatory Policy and Governance*, OECD [1]
Publishing, Paris, https://doi.org/10.1787/9789264209022-en.

Regeringskansliet (Swedish Government Office) (2018), *Anpassad miljöprövning för en grön* [6]
omställning, https://www.regeringen.se/rattsliga-dokument/departementsserien-och-promemorior/2018/10/ds-201838/.

Trnka, D. Thuerer, Y (2019), *One-In, X-Out: Regulatory offsetting in selected OECD countries,* [8]
OECD Regulatory Policy Working Papers No. 11, OECD Publishing, Paris,
https://doi.org/10.1787/67d71764-en.

5 Country profiles

European Union

Overview and recent developments

The 2016 Interinstitutional Agreement between the European Commission (EC), the European Parliament and the Council recognised stakeholder engagement, regulatory impact assessment (RIA), and *ex post* evaluation as core elements to improve regulatory quality. The EC is the executive of the European Union (EU). It develops and presents regulatory proposals in accordance with its Better Regulation Toolkit to the European Parliament and the Council for adoption. The Commission announced in the 2021 Policy Communication on Better Regulation to further streamline consultations particularly through the call for evidence, integrate foresight, introduce regulatory offsetting and to require policy makers to provide information about the attainment of long-term goals such as climate change and the SDGs.

The Commission's Secretariat General ensures overall coherence of the Commission's work and oversees compliance with its commitment to Better Regulation and develops its policy. It reviews RIAs, stakeholder engagement processes and *ex post* evaluations, oversees burden reduction activities, provides capacity support and draft corporate guidance on better regulation. It also serves as Secretariat to the Regulatory Scrutiny Board (RSB), which consists of three Commission officials and three external experts and is chaired by a Commission's Director General. The RSB checks the quality of all impact assessments and selected evaluations and fitness checks. Its mandate was expanded in 2020 to include outreach activities and oversight regarding the one in-one out rule. The RSB's mandate has been enlarged to reflect the European Commission's decision to embed strategic foresight into its working methods, including to inform the design of new initiatives and the review of existing ones. The European Parliament's Directorate for Impact Assessment and European Added Value also reviews RIAs attached to draft legislation submitted by the Commission, and conducts in-depth analysis and impact assessments of amendments at the request of Parliamentary committees. The Council has also developed its capacity to assess impacts of their substantial amendments, but it has not used it so far.

Ex ante impact assessments continue to be carried out for major primary laws and subordinate legislation. Calls for evidence, including an initial assessment of possible impacts and options to be considered, are prepared and consulted on before a full RIA is conducted. Following or simultaneously with this initial feedback period, the EC conducts public consultations during the development of initiatives with an impact assessment. Legislative proposals and the accompanying full RIA are then published online for feedback following approval of the proposal by the College of Commissioners. Draft subordinate legislation is consulted on publicly. Transparency could be further improved by making RIAs on subordinate legislation available at this stage with the opportunity to comment on the analysis.

The *ex post* evaluation system, combining systematic evaluations of individual regulations with comprehensive "Fitness checks" of policy sectors, invites comment on evaluation Call for evidence and on the main elements of all evaluations. The RSB now provides quality indicators on evaluations which are made publicly available along with compliance statistics. The Fit for Future Platform brings together representatives of Member States and stakeholders (business, civil society, and non-government stakeholders) to make suggestions for simplification and modernisation (including digitalisation) of EU legislation. Indicators below mainly represent practices of the European Commission. The other EU institutions and in particular the Council seems to be lagging behind in terms of the implementation of the 2016 Interinstitutional Agreement.

Indicators of Regulatory Policy and Governance (iREG): European Union, 2021

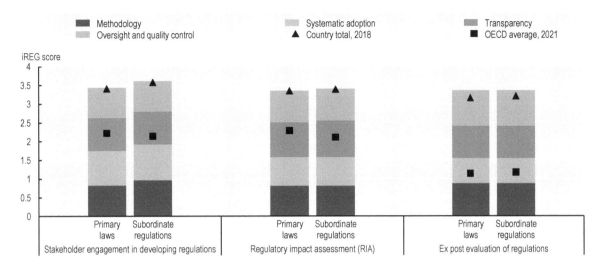

Notes: The more regulatory practices as advocated in the OECD Recommendation on Regulatory Policy and Governance a country has implemented, the higher its iREG score. Results presented apply to all legislation (regulations, directives and implementing and delegated acts) initiated by the European Commission, who is the sole initiator of legislation in the EU system.
Source: Indicators of Regulatory Policy and Governance Surveys 2017 and 2021, http://oe.cd/ireg.

Negotiating and implementing EU legislation

Negotiation stage: Most EU directives and EU regulations are adopted by the Council of the EU and the European Parliament through the ordinary legislative procedure. Throughout this process, the Council and the European Parliament separately review the Commission's legislative proposal. In the Council and its sub-committees, Member States' governments propose amendments and negotiate a common position on the legislative draft. Each Member State may undertake stakeholder engagement and regulatory impact assessment to help inform its negotiation position. The Council's role in conducting impact assessments on amendments made in its committees has so far remained limited. EU legislation is adopted once the Council and the Parliament agree on a joint text.

Transposition stage: Member States are required to transpose EU directives, i.e. to incorporate them into their national laws, by adopting dedicated transposition measures. The transposition of EU directives provides EU countries with considerable latitude on the process and method of implementation. Many directives are designed such that they provide scope for Member States to include additional provisions. Governments usually transpose directives through domestic legislative procedures and may consult stakeholders and conduct regulatory impact assessment throughout this process. Each directive is required to be transposed to a specific deadline set in each directive. The Commission monitors the timely and legally accurate transposition of directives and can initiate infringement procedures where the transposition of directives is delayed.

Austria

Overview and recent developments

In Austria, regulatory impact assessment (RIA) has been mandatory for all primary laws and subordinate regulations since 2013. A comprehensive threshold test introduced in 2015 determines whether a simplified or full RIA has to be conducted for draft regulations. A simplified RIA is carried out for about two thirds of all regulations. The methodology for a full RIA requires the assessment of a range of impacts, including on the environment, social aspects, and gender equality. The aforementioned threshold limits the requirement for *ex post* evaluations introduced in 2013 to regulations passing the threshold. Assessments of whether underlying policy goals have been achieved, the comparison of actual and predicted impacts, and the identification of costs, benefits and unintended consequences of regulations are part of the standard methodology for *ex post* evaluations. In 2019, a principle-based *ex post* review of 200 federal laws has been carried out with a view to reducing administrative burdens stemming from gold-plating.

The Federal Performance Management Office (FPMO) at the Federal Ministry for Arts, Culture, Civil Service and Sport (BMKOES) reviews the quality of all full RIAs and *ex post* evaluations and controls and supports the application of threshold tests for RIA *light*. It publishes its opinions on RIAs for primary laws and can advise civil servants to revise RIAs if not up to standard. The FPMO also issues guidelines, provides training on RIA and *ex post* evaluation and co-ordinates these tools' use across government. In addition, it reports annually to Parliament on RIA and *ex post* evaluation results. The Ministry of Finance supports the FPMO by reviewing assessments of financial impacts and costs in RIAs and *ex post* evaluations, and is also involved in issuing guidelines on the application of these tools.

A resolution by the Austrian Parliament triggered an extension of the scope of public consultations on draft primary laws. Since September 2017, all draft primary laws are available on the website of Parliament together with a short description of the legislative project in accessible language, the RIA and other accompanying documents. The public can submit comments on the draft regulation or support comments made by others online. Since August 2021, the public can also submit comments on all legislative initiatives introduced in Parliament, i.e. government bills, MPs' and popular initiatives during their parliamentary deliberation and support comments made by others online. Furthermore, an interactive crowdsourcing platform has been launched in 2018 to provide the public with an opportunity to express their views ahead of parliamentary initiatives, like the extension of access to open data in 2021. Extending the use of the platform to include consultations on policy issues could be a gateway towards establishing a more systematic approach to involving stakeholders earlier in the development of regulations to inform officials about the policy problem and possible solutions. Austria would benefit from extending the scope of public consultations to subordinate regulations, for which no systematic public consultations are conducted, and from introducing systematic quality control of engagement processes.

Indicators of Regulatory Policy and Governance (iREG): Austria, 2021

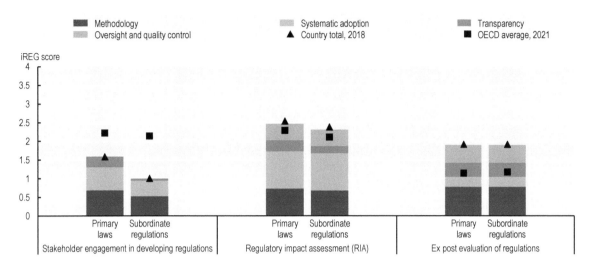

Notes: The more regulatory practices as advocated in the OECD Recommendation on Regulatory Policy and Governance a country has implemented, the higher its iREG score. The indicators on stakeholder engagement and RIA for primary laws only cover those initiated by the executive (57% of all primary laws in Austria).
Source: Indicators of Regulatory Policy and Governance Surveys 2017 and 2021, http://oe.cd/ireg.

Requirements and use of regulatory management tools for EU-made laws: Austria

The government facilitates the engagement of domestic stakeholders in the European Commission's consultation process ▲		
Negotiation stage	Requirement for Member State to conduct stakeholder engagement	
	Use of European Commission's stakeholder engagement results ■	
	Requirement for Member State to conduct RIA	
	Use of European Commission's impact assessment ■	
	Use of European Commission's *ex post* evaluation results	
Transposition stage	Requirement for Member State to conduct stakeholder engagement	
	Use of European Commission's stakeholder engagement results ■	
	Requirement for Member State to conduct RIA	
	Use of European Commission's impact assessment ■	
	Specific assessment of provisions added at national level beyond those in EU directive is conducted ■	
	Use of European Commission's *ex post* evaluation results	
Results of domestic *ex post* evaluations of EU directives/regulations shared with the European Commission ▲		

■ For all EU directives/regulations/ ■ Always/ ▲ Yes
For major EU directives/regulations/ ■ Frequently
For some EU directives/regulations/ ■ Sometimes
Never/ ▲ No
Source: Indicators of Regulatory Policy and Governance (iREG) Survey 2021, http://oe.cd/ireg.

Belgium

Overview and recent developments

Belgium has not improved its institutional and policy framework for regulatory quality at the federal level over the last years. Regulatory impact assessment (RIA) is mandatory for all primary and for some subordinate legislation submitted to the Cabinet of Ministers at the federal level and is usually shared with social partners as a basis for consultation. RIAs for subordinate regulations are however no longer published. Belgium currently does not systematically require an identification and assessment of alternatives to the preferred policy option.

Periodic *ex post* review of legislation is mandatory for some legislation and sunsetting clauses are sometimes used. The Court of Audit is involved in undertaking ad hoc "in-depth" reviews on specific regulatory areas such as agriculture, energy or youth.

The Agency for Administrative Simplification (ASA) within the Prime Minister's Office co-ordinates RIA and steers the implementation of Better Regulation across the federal government. It is also in charge of defining and ensuring the application of cost assessment methods in this context. The ASA is supported by the Impact Assessment Committee (IAC), which provides advice on RIAs upon request by the responsible ministry and reports annually on the quality of RIAs and functioning of the RIA process. The IAC is also part of a project aimed at establishing a government-wide regulatory agenda to co-ordinate and monitor the legislative process. To further enhance quality checks, the Impact Assessment Committee, which currently reviews RIA only at the request of the proposing ministry, could be also earlier and more systematically involved in the review of RIAs.

Consultation and engagement could be further strengthened. For example, consultation with the general public are held on an ad hoc basis by some ministries and are published on their individual ministerial webpage, as there is currently no single central government website listing all ongoing consultations. Systemising the use of consultation for both primary and subordinate regulations across all ministries as well as developing a central platform on which all consultations are published would enhance the transparency and accountability of the regulatory system in Belgium. While RIA can be shared with social partners during consultation, it is not released for consultation with the general public.

Indicators of Regulatory Policy and Governance (iREG): Belgium, 2021

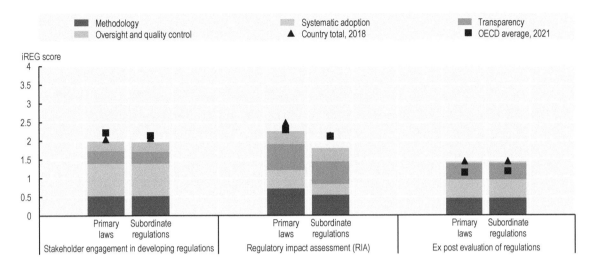

Notes: The more regulatory practices as advocated in the OECD Recommendation on Regulatory Policy and Governance a country has implemented, the higher its iREG score. The indicators on stakeholder engagement and RIA for primary laws only cover those initiated by the executive (61% of all primary laws in Belgium).
Source: Indicators of Regulatory Policy and Governance Surveys 2017 and 2021, http://oe.cd/ireg.

Requirements and use of regulatory management tools for EU-made laws: Belgium

The government facilitates the engagement of domestic stakeholders in the European Commission's consultation process ▲		▨
Negotiation stage	Requirement for Member State to conduct stakeholder engagement	
	Use of European Commission's stakeholder engagement results ■	
	Requirement for Member State to conduct RIA	
	Use of European Commission's impact assessment ■	
	Use of European Commission's ex post evaluation results	
Transposition stage	Requirement for Member State to conduct stakeholder engagement	▨
	Use of European Commission's stakeholder engagement results ■	
	Requirement for Member State to conduct RIA	
	Use of European Commission's impact assessment ■	
	Specific assessment of provisions added at national level beyond those in EU directive is conducted ■	
	Use of European Commission's ex post evaluation results	
Results of domestic ex post evaluations of EU directives/regulations shared with the European Commission ▲		

▨ For all EU directives/regulations/ ■ Always/ ▲ Yes
▨ For major EU directives/regulations/ ■ Frequently
▨ For some EU directives/regulations/ ■ Sometimes
▨ Never/ ▲ No
Source: Indicators of Regulatory Policy and Governance (iREG) Survey 2021, http://oe.cd/ireg.

Bulgaria

Overview and recent developments

Bulgaria has continued to reform its regulatory management system as part of its Strategy for the Development of the State Administration 2014-2020. The strategy has led to important changes in Bulgaria's legal framework for regulatory policy, putting evidence-based regulation-making in the focus. In 2019, the guidelines for regulatory impact assessment were updated to include guidance on cost-benefit-analysis and in 2020, guidelines for *ex post* evaluation were introduced to promote a uniform approach to *ex ante* and *ex post* evaluation within the administration. Previously, amendments to the Law on Normative Acts in 2016 had introduced a requirement to carry out impact assessments for all legislative acts introduced by the Council of Ministers and revised procedures for public consultation of draft regulations, extending the minimum consultation period to 30 days and introducing a requirement to publish draft legislation on the central consultation portal *strategy.bg*. Stakeholder engagement and public consultation is required for all primary laws and subordinate regulations and it is undertaken systematically once a legislative proposal has been drafted.

The Modernisation of the Administration Directorate of the Council of Ministers is responsible for regulatory oversight in Bulgaria. As part of its mandate, it scrutinises the quality of RIA and of stakeholder engagement in case a full RIA is required. It also issues guidance on regulatory management tools. The Directorate also prepares yearly reports on the performance of the RIA and stakeholder engagement systems for draft regulations, including data on the percentage of RIAs and consultations that comply with applicable formal requirements.

Indicators presented on stakeholder engagement and RIA for primary laws only cover processes carried out by the executive, which initiates approximately 47% of primary laws in Bulgaria. There are requirements to conduct RIA to inform the development of primary laws initiated by parliament, although they are relatively less stringent than those for laws made by the executive.

All new primary laws and subordinate regulations introduced by the executive must undergo a full RIA, which requires a comprehensive cost-benefit analysis. While such a commitment to evidence-based policy making can be considered good practice, a more proportionate approach could help target valuable resources to the most impactful laws and regulations.

Since 2016, all new laws, codes and sub-statutory acts of the Council of Ministers are subject to *ex post* evaluation within five years of their respective commencement. Although *ex post* evaluations have been conducted with the support of external experts, they are limited in number and in scope, focussing only on administrative burdens for business. Assessing a wider range of impacts would help to ensure that regulations remain appropriate over time.

Indicators of Regulatory Policy and Governance (iREG): Bulgaria, 2021

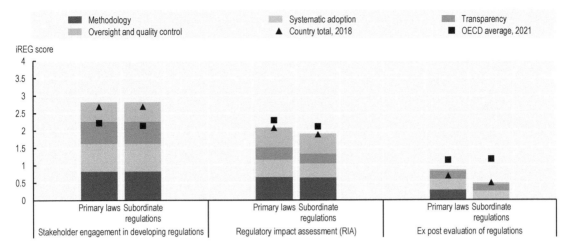

Note: The more regulatory practices as advocated in the OECD Recommendation on Regulatory Policy and Governance a country has implemented, the higher its iREG score. The indicators on stakeholder engagement and RIA for primary laws only cover those initiated by the executive (47% of all primary laws in Bulgaria).

Source: Indicators of Regulatory Policy and Governance Survey 2017 and 2021, http://oe.cd/ireg.

Requirements and use of regulatory management tools for EU-made laws: Bulgaria

The government facilitates the engagement of domestic stakeholders in the European Commission's consultation process ▲		
Negotiation stage	Requirement for Member State to conduct stakeholder engagement	
	Use of European Commission's stakeholder engagement results ■	
	Requirement for Member State to conduct RIA	▓
	Use of European Commission's impact assessment ■	
	Use of European Commission's ex post evaluation results	
Transposition stage	Requirement for Member State to conduct stakeholder engagement	▓
	Use of European Commission's stakeholder engagement results ■	
	Requirement for Member State to conduct RIA	▓
	Use of European Commission's impact assessment ■	
	Specific assessment of provisions added at national level beyond those in EU directive is conducted ■	
	Use of European Commission's ex post evaluation results	
Results of domestic ex post evaluations of EU directives/regulations shared with the European Commission ▲		

▓ For all EU directives/regulations/ ■ Always/ ▲ Yes
▓ For major EU directives/regulations/ ■ Frequently
▓ For some EU directives/regulations/ ■ Sometimes
▓ Never/ ▲ No
Source: Indicators of Regulatory Policy and Governance (iREG) Survey 2021, http://oe.cd/ireg.

Croatia

Overview and recent developments

Croatia continues to improve its regulatory policy. Whilst an *ex post* evaluation framework was recently introduced, Croatia projects to further strengthen it in the coming years. Since 2018, policy makers must evaluate whether primary laws are achieving their objectives two years after their enactment in cases where *ex ante* assessment were required but exempted. These evaluations assess costs and benefits of existing regulations using RIA. Furthermore, stakeholders can provide their feedback to evaluations through Croatia's central interactive consultation portal *e-Savjetovanja*. Policy makers now also have written guidance available on how to conduct the evaluations to ensure consistency. Since 2019, citizens and businesses can report cumbersome administrative procedures on the new online portal *Boljipropisi*. This complements the "Action Plan for Administrative Burden Reduction" that the Ministry of Economy introduced in 2017 to create investment incentives and to provide easier market access.

Croatia systematically engages with stakeholders for the development of major draft primary laws, which continue to be published online for consultation for 30 days. Stakeholders can read, reply or support comments from other users on *e-Savjetovanja*, and can also organise comments from oldest to newest, by popularity, and other criteria. The body drafting the regulation publicly replies on *e-Savjetovanja* to all comments received during the consultation period. Policy makers also engage at early stages before there is a decision to regulate with *ad hoc* working groups including representatives from civil society, businesses and academia, and since 2018 do so with the general public through online consultations.

Since 2017, the RIA law requires an initial RIA to be carried out for all primary laws. A full RIA has to be conducted for laws with a potentially high impact, requiring regulators to assess a broad range of environmental and social impacts. If deemed necessary, a test analysing the impacts on SMEs is undertaken, focusing mostly on administrative costs. In practice, however, RIAs are not of sufficient quality due to a lack of analytical capacity in ministries. Croatia could consider creating analytical centres with "RIA champions" in the most important ministries to strengthen capacities and extend its RIA requirements to subordinate regulations.

The Government Legislation Office (GLO), located at the centre of government, is the central body responsible for a range of regulatory oversight functions. In addition to its existing role as co-ordinator of regulatory policy measures related to RIA, its mandate was extended in 2017 to include the quality control of *ex post* evaluation and in 2019 to include oversight of stakeholder engagement and management of the central consultation portal *e-Savjetovanja*. The GLO reviews all preliminary assessments and full RIA reports, including *ex post* evaluation RIAs, provides advice and can ask administrators to revise RIAs if the quality is deemed insufficient. The Office also publishes yearly reports on the performance of the Croatian RIA system. Furthermore, the Ministry of Economy and Sustainable Development performs a range of oversight functions focusing on impacts of regulations on small- and medium-sized businesses. The Ministry controls the quality of the SME tests included in the RIA and provides guidance and training on the test to civil servants.

Indicators of Regulatory Policy and Governance (iREG): Croatia, 2021

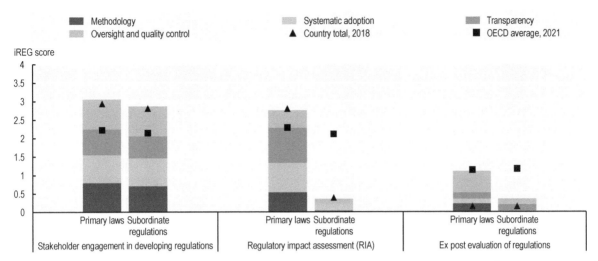

Note: The more regulatory practices as advocated in the OECD Recommendation on Regulatory Policy and Governance a country has implemented, the higher its iREG score. The indicators on stakeholder engagement and RIA for primary laws only cover those initiated by the executive (85% of all primary laws in Croatia).

Source: Indicators of Regulatory Policy and Governance Survey 2017 and 2021, http://oe.cd/ireg.

Requirements and use of regulatory management tools for EU-made laws: Croatia

The government facilitates the engagement of domestic stakeholders in the European Commission's consultation process ▲		
Negotiation stage	Requirement for Member State to conduct stakeholder engagement	
	Use of European Commission's stakeholder engagement results ■	
	Requirement for Member State to conduct RIA	
	Use of European Commission's impact assessment ■	
	Use of European Commission's *ex post* evaluation results	
Transposition stage	Requirement for Member State to conduct stakeholder engagement	
	Use of European Commission's stakeholder engagement results ■	
	Requirement for Member State to conduct RIA	
	Use of European Commission's impact assessment ■	
	Specific assessment of provisions added at national level beyond those in EU directive is conducted ■	
	Use of European Commission's *ex post* evaluation results	
Results of domestic *ex post* evaluations of EU directives/regulations shared with the European Commission ▲		

▰ For all EU directives/regulations/ ■ Always/ ▲ Yes
▰ For major EU directives/regulations/ ■ Frequently
▰ For some EU directives/regulations/ ■ Sometimes
▰ Never/ ▲ No

Source: Indicators of Regulatory Policy and Governance (iREG) Survey 2021, http://oe.cd/ireg.

Cyprus

Overview and recent developments

Cyprus' regulatory policy system has remained stable over the last years with only a few changes mainly related to consultation practices. While public consultations on draft primary laws continues to be mandatory, policy makers now also engage with specific groups such as trade unions, employers' organisations, Cyprus Chamber of Commerce and Industry, NGOs and the business sector on regulatory proposals. Consultations are still not mandatory for subordinate regulations. Further, early stage consultations before a decision to regulate is made are still not yet conducted when developing primary laws nor subordinate regulations, even though it is recommended in the 2015 Action Plan for improving the regulatory framework in Cyprus.

When consulting, regulators are required to take stakeholders feedback into account; they are not however required to respond to participants' comments, which makes it difficult for participants to see how their input has helped shaped regulatory proposals. Participants' views are made public on summaries published once consultations are over. Cyprus is currently developing an eConsultation platform where it plans to undertake all public consultations. This would allow for easier access to ongoing consultations, improving Cyprus' regulatory making process. Cyprus would also benefit from consulting with stakeholders earlier in the process to identify policy options including alternatives to regulation.

Regulatory impact assessment (RIA) is required for all regulatory proposals relating to primary laws. Although Cyprus introduced a new RIA framework in September 2017, a number of gaps remain. The impact assessment system could be improved by considering a broader range of costs and benefits, and establishing an oversight body for RIA quality control. Cyprus would also benefit from a systematic evaluation of the efficiency and effectiveness of its regulatory management system.

Cyprus' SME Envoy is responsible for the quality control of the SME test, which assesses the potential impact of regulations on small and medium-sized enterprises. The SME Envoy is also in charge of ensuring an adequate consultation with the business community. It can issue an opinion on the quality of the SME test and resulting mitigation measures. There is however no institution responsible for regulatory oversight as a whole in Cyprus.

The Law Commissioner, appointed by the President of the Republic, has recently had its functions expanded. It now carries out simplification, consolidation, codification and revision of the national legislation on ad-hoc basis. The Law Commissioner advises the President and the Ministers on any issue concerning the law, its modernization, consolidation, amendment and reform. However, *ex post* evaluation of laws and regulations is not yet systematically undertaken in Cyprus. Having in place a framework for consistent and continuous evaluations could help to ensure that existing regulations remain fit for purpose.

Indicators of Regulatory Policy and Governance (iREG): Cyprus, 2021

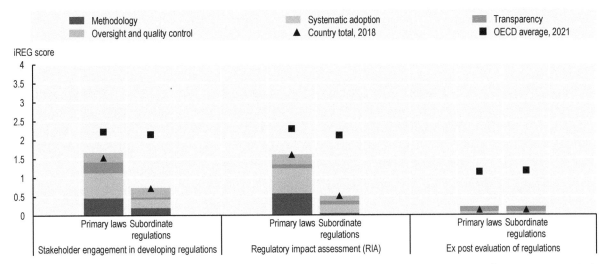

Note: The more regulatory practices as advocated in the OECD Recommendation on Regulatory Policy and Governance a country has implemented, the higher its iREG score. The indicators on stakeholder engagement and RIA for primary laws only cover those initiated by the executive (64% of all primary laws in Cyprus).
Source: Indicators of Regulatory Policy and Governance Survey 2017 and 2021, http://oe.cd/ireg.

Requirements and use of regulatory management tools for EU-made laws: Cyprus

The government facilitates the engagement of domestic stakeholders in the European Commission's consultation process ▲		
Negotiation stage	Requirement for Member State to conduct stakeholder engagement	
	Use of European Commission's stakeholder engagement results ■	
	Requirement for Member State to conduct RIA	
	Use of European Commission's impact assessment ■	
	Use of European Commission's *ex post* evaluation results	
Transposition stage	Requirement for Member State to conduct stakeholder engagement	
	Use of European Commission's stakeholder engagement results ■	
	Requirement for Member State to conduct RIA	
	Use of European Commission's impact assessment ■	
	Specific assessment of provisions added at national level beyond those in EU directive is conducted ■	
	Use of European Commission's *ex post* evaluation results	
Results of domestic *ex post* evaluations of EU directives/regulations shared with the European Commission ▲		

▬ For all EU directives/regulations/ ■ Always/ ▲ Yes
▬ For major EU directives/regulations/ ■ Frequently
▬ For some EU directives/regulations/ ■ Sometimes
▬ Never/ ▲ No
Source: Indicators of Regulatory Policy and Governance (iREG) Survey 2021, http://oe.cd/ireg.

Czech Republic

Overview and recent developments

The Czech Republic has a well-developed regulatory impact assessment (RIA) process including mechanisms for quality control through the RIA Board operating at arm's length from the government. All draft primary and secondary legislation prepared by the executive has to be accompanied by a basic overview of impacts; a full RIA has to be carried out for those drafts with new and significant impacts. The quality of RIA could be improved especially in terms of quantifications of impacts.

The Government Legislative Council is an advisory body to the government overseeing the quality of draft legislation before it is presented to the government. One of its working commissions, the RIA Board, evaluates the quality of RIAs and adherence to the procedures as defined in the mandatory RIA Guidelines, provides assistance to drafting authorities if requested, and issues opinions on whether draft legislation should undergo a full RIA. The RIA Unit of the Government Legislative Council section of the government co-ordinates the RIA process within central government, provides methodological assistance and issues guidance materials for the RIA process.

All legislative drafts submitted to the government are published on a government portal accessible to the general public. It is obligatory to conduct consultations within the RIA process and summarise their outcomes in RIA reports. There are, however, no compulsory rules specifying the length or form of such consultations. The Czech Republic should standardise the public consultation process, stimulate stakeholders including the general public to contribute to consultations and be more proactive in engaging with stakeholders sufficiently early.

The Czech Republic was among the first to launch a programme on reducing administrative burdens. Cutting red tape is still a priority for the government, however, contrary to many other countries, the focus has not yet been widened to other regulatory costs. Evaluation of the effectiveness and efficiency of existing regulations takes place usually on an *ad hoc* basis and is used rather rarely. The Czech Republic has published guidelines on *ex post* evaluation for officials, though they are still considered as voluntary but should be made more systematic in the future.

Indicators presented on RIA and stakeholder engagement for primary laws only cover processes carried out by the executive, which initiates approximately 45% of primary laws in Czech Republic. There is no requirement in the Czech Republic for conducting consultation or RIA to inform the development of primary laws initiated by parliament.

Indicators of Regulatory Policy and Governance (iREG): Czech Republic, 2021

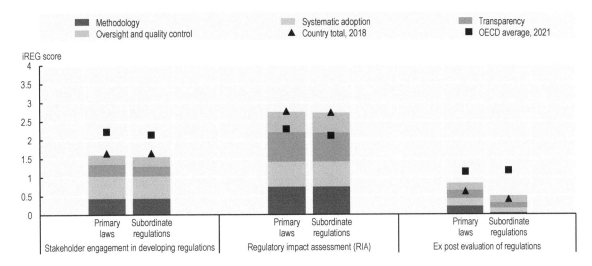

Notes: The more regulatory practices as advocated in the OECD Recommendation on Regulatory Policy and Governance a country has implemented, the higher its iREG score. The indicators on stakeholder engagement and RIA for primary laws only cover those initiated by the executive (45% of all primary laws in the Czech Republic).
Source: Indicators of Regulatory Policy and Governance Surveys 2017 and 2021, http://oe.cd/ireg.

Requirements and use of regulatory management tools for EU-made laws: Czech Republic

The government facilitates the engagement of domestic stakeholders in the European Commission's consultation process ▲		
Negotiation stage	Requirement for Member State to conduct stakeholder engagement	
	Use of European Commission's stakeholder engagement results ■	
	Requirement for Member State to conduct RIA	
	Use of European Commission's impact assessment ■	
	Use of European Commission's *ex post* evaluation results	
Transposition stage	Requirement for Member State to conduct stakeholder engagement	
	Use of European Commission's stakeholder engagement results ■	
	Requirement for Member State to conduct RIA	
	Use of European Commission's impact assessment ■	
	Specific assessment of provisions added at national level beyond those in EU directive is conducted ■	
	Use of European Commission's *ex post* evaluation results	
Results of domestic *ex post* evaluations of EU directives/regulations shared with the European Commission ▲		

▓ For all EU directives/regulations/ ■ Always/ ▲ Yes
▒ For major EU directives/regulations/ ■ Frequently
░ For some EU directives/regulations/ ■ Sometimes
  Never/ ▲ No
Source: Indicators of Regulatory Policy and Governance (iREG) Survey 2021, http://oe.cd/ireg.

Denmark

Overview and recent developments

Regulatory reform has been an important feature of the Danish government agenda since the 1980s. Denmark has recently introduced significant institutional reforms to support the implementation of both the principles on agile (innovation-friendly) business legislation, aiming to support the ability for businesses to test, develop and apply new technologies and business models, as well as the principles on digital-ready legislation, aiming to ensure that legislation can be administered digitally. To ensure optimum results of the new institutional framework, role clarity and effective co-ordination between the distinct bodies will require attention.

The mandate of the Better Regulation Unit (former Team Effective Regulation) at the Danish Business Authority has been expanded. In addition to performing the quality control of RIAs of regulations creating significant burdens for businesses and providing guidance and training in the use of good regulatory management tools, this body is also in charge of overseeing compliance with the country's principles for agile (innovation-friendly) business regulation as well as the principles for implementation of business-oriented EU-regulation.

The Danish Business Regulation Forum (DBRF) was set up in 2019 by merging the Danish Business Forum for Better Regulation and the EU-Implementation Council. Served by a Secretariat in the Ministry of Industry, Business and Financial Affairs, it advises the government on the development and application of the methodology for RIA, and the principles of agile (innovation-friendly) business regulation. It also conducts in-depth reviews of regulations in different policy areas. Finally, the DBRF focuses on identifying simplification options in areas where digitisation and new technological trends will challenge the regulation, as well as business-oriented digital solutions.

The Secretariat for digital-ready legislation was set up within the Ministry of Finance in 2018. It receives draft legislative proposals six weeks before their publication for public consultation and issues recommendations regarding compliance with the seven principles of digital-ready legislation as well as to improve implementation impact assessments. According to Danish authorities, government ministries incorporate at least some of the secretariat's recommendations in the final bills presented before parliament in about 75% of cases.

Denmark systematically engages with stakeholders in the later stage of the regulatory process. Full RIAs are required to be carried out for both primary and subordinate regulations above certain thresholds. The government periodically reviews existing regulation with significant impacts and the DBRF is involved in reviewing existing regulations.

Transparency could be further strengthened by informing the public in advance that a public consultation or a RIA is due to take place. The use of RIA could be further strengthened by the introduction of an oversight function that allows for returning proposed rules for which impact assessments are considered inadequate and which is not limited to regulations affecting business.

Indicators of Regulatory Policy and Governance (iREG): Denmark, 2021

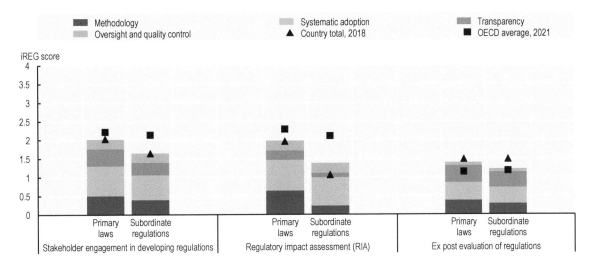

Notes: The more regulatory practices as advocated in the OECD Recommendation on Regulatory Policy and Governance a country has implemented, the higher its iREG score. The indicators on stakeholder engagement and RIA for primary laws only cover those initiated by the executive (99% of all primary laws in Denmark).
Source: Indicators of Regulatory Policy and Governance Surveys 2017 and 2021, http://oe.cd/ireg.

Requirements and use of regulatory management tools for EU-made laws: Denmark

The government facilitates the engagement of domestic stakeholders in the European Commission's consultation process ▲		
Negotiation stage	Requirement for Member State to conduct stakeholder engagement	
	Use of European Commission's stakeholder engagement results ■	
	Requirement for Member State to conduct RIA	
	Use of European Commission's impact assessment ■	
	Use of European Commission's *ex post* evaluation results	
Transposition stage	Requirement for Member State to conduct stakeholder engagement	
	Use of European Commission's stakeholder engagement results ■	
	Requirement for Member State to conduct RIA	
	Use of European Commission's impact assessment ■	
	Specific assessment of provisions added at national level beyond those in EU directive is conducted ■	
	Use of European Commission's *ex post* evaluation results	
Results of domestic *ex post* evaluations of EU directives/regulations shared with the European Commission ▲		

■ For all EU directives/regulations/ ■ Always/ ▲ Yes
■ For major EU directives/regulations/ ■ Frequently
For some EU directives/regulations/ ■ Sometimes
Never/ ▲ No
Source: Indicators of Regulatory Policy and Governance (iREG) Survey 2021, http://oe.cd/ireg.

Estonia

Overview and recent developments

Estonia has not made any major changes to its regulatory framework since 2014. Preliminary regulatory impact assessments (RIAs) are prepared for all primary laws and selected subordinate regulations. Full RIAs tended to be conducted rarely, and while that remains the case, simplified RIAs are included in every explanatory letter of draft laws. The level of analysis contained within them has deepened over time.

The Legislative Quality Division within the Ministry of Justice reviews the quality of RIAs and can return them for revision if quality standards are not met. It is also responsible for the systematic improvement and evaluation of regulatory policy. The Minister of Justice reports annually to parliament on the application of Better Regulation principles, including the compliance of RIA and stakeholder engagement practices with formal requirements. The Division also issues RIA guidelines and scrutinises the legal quality of draft regulations. The Government Office of Estonia complements this work by co-ordinating stakeholder engagement in policy making across government. This includes issuing guidelines on stakeholder engagement, managing the country's e-consultation system and promoting the engagement co-ordinators' programme. The Government Office's EU Secretariat performs a co-ordination function regarding EU law and its transposition, and its Legal Department has a role scrutinising the legislation.

Estonia places a strong focus on accessibility and transparency of regulatory policy by making use of online tools. The online information system EIS tracks all legislative developments and makes RIAs available on a central portal. For public consultations, in addition to EIS, other channels are used to disseminate information such as ministries' websites, social media platforms, and general media. Later-stage consultation is conducted for all regulations. Public online consultations to inform officials about the nature of the policy problem and identify policy options are conducted in some cases.

Ex post evaluation has been mandatory for some regulations since 2012. The first evaluations were undertaken in 2018. In general, *ex post* evaluations take place between 3–5 years after the implementation of the regulation and have covered areas of competition, administrative burden, and regulatory overlap. More recently in-depth reviews have begun to be conducted in some policy areas. The publication of *ex post* evaluations remains at the discretion of the relevant minister. Estonia could support the implementation of its *ex post* evaluation requirements by embedding stronger capacity to scrutinise the quality of *ex post* evaluations into the existing framework. The objective to increase the proportion of *ex post* evaluations is set out in the new strategy document Principles for Legislative Policy until 2030, adopted in November 2020.

Indicators of Regulatory Policy and Governance (iREG): Estonia, 2021

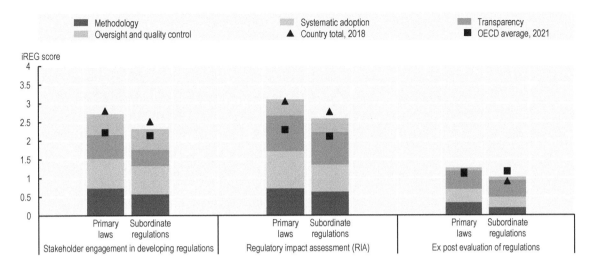

Notes: The more regulatory practices as advocated in the OECD Recommendation on Regulatory Policy and Governance a country has implemented, the higher its iREG score. The indicators on stakeholder engagement and RIA for primary laws only cover those initiated by the executive (85% of all primary laws in Estonia).
Source: Indicators of Regulatory Policy and Governance Surveys 2017 and 2021, http://oe.cd/ireg.

Requirements and use of regulatory management tools for EU-made laws: Estonia

The government facilitates the engagement of domestic stakeholders in the European Commission's consultation process ▲		▓
Negotiation stage	Requirement for Member State to conduct stakeholder engagement	▓
	Use of European Commission's stakeholder engagement results ■	
	Requirement for Member State to conduct RIA	▓
	Use of European Commission's impact assessment ■	
	Use of European Commission's ex post evaluation results	
Transposition stage	Requirement for Member State to conduct stakeholder engagement	▓
	Use of European Commission's stakeholder engagement results ■	
	Requirement for Member State to conduct RIA	▓
	Use of European Commission's impact assessment ■	
	Specific assessment of provisions added at national level beyond those in EU directive is conducted ■	
	Use of European Commission's ex post evaluation results	
Results of domestic ex post evaluations of EU directives/regulations shared with the European Commission ▲		

▓ For all EU directives/regulations/ ■ Always/ ▲ Yes
▓ For major EU directives/regulations/ ■ Frequently
  For some EU directives/regulations/ ■ Sometimes
  Never/ ▲ No
Source: Indicators of Regulatory Policy and Governance (iREG) Survey 2021, http://oe.cd/ireg.

Finland

Overview and recent developments

As part of its broader strategic objective of consolidating a well-functioning democracy, the current Government Programme in place since 2019 pledges to strengthen the role of Finland's regulatory oversight body, introduce government-level system for *ex post* assessments, and draw up a comprehensive action plan for Better Regulation. The government-wide instructions for drafting bills were renewed in 2019 to provide more and clearer information to rule-makers, and reforms on regulatory impact assessment (RIA) and *ex post* evaluations are underway.

RIA is formally required and conducted for all primary laws and for some subordinate regulations. A renewal of the Finnish RIA Guidelines was initiated in 2020, and new guidance is expected to be available in 2021-22. In 2019, a study by the Parliament's Audit Committee on the development of RIA was carried out. It included extensive consultations with stakeholders and parliamentary committees. While e*x post* evaluation of regulations is not mandatory across the government, the government has commissioned a research project on the current use of *ex post* evaluations within the government to gain a better overview on their scope and methods across regulatory authorities.

The Finnish Council of Regulatory Impact Analysis (FCRIA) is Finland's only regulatory oversight body (ROB). It is an arms-length body set up in 2015. The FCRIA reviews selected RIAs based on the criteria of significance and representativeness before approval of the final version of the regulation, and provides advice as well as a formal opinion on the quality of the RIA. The FCRIA has no sanctioning power. The Council also has a mandate to review *ex post* assessments of legislation. In addition to the country's ROB, there is a government-wide co-operative working group for improving law drafting that aims at enhancing co-ordination across ministries and promoting the uptake of best practices. Exceptionally, in the context of COVID-19, oversight functions were partially shared with the Ministry of Justice as far as fundamental and human rights were concerned. The review and use of RIA in Finland could be further strengthened by the introduction of an oversight function that allows for returning proposed rules for which impact assessments are deemed inadequate.

Several stakeholder engagement platforms exist in Finland to inform the public of current draft legislations and to solicit feedback. These include lausuntopalvelu.fi launched in 2015, as well as the Governments Registry for Projects and Initiatives which was revamped in 2017 (http://valtioneuvosto.fi/hankkeet). The COVID-19 pandemic brought an increase in the number of consultations taking place via phone or internet, confirming the importance of these platforms.

Indicators of Regulatory Policy and Governance (iREG): Finland, 2021

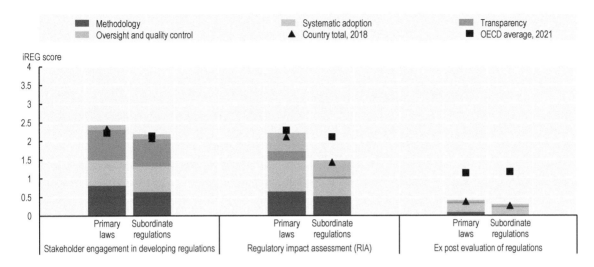

Notes: The more regulatory practices as advocated in the OECD Recommendation on Regulatory Policy and Governance a country has implemented, the higher its iREG score. The indicators on stakeholder engagement and RIA for primary laws only cover those initiated by the executive (100% of all primary laws in Finland).
Source: Indicators of Regulatory Policy and Governance Surveys 2017 and 2021, http://oe.cd/ireg.

Requirements and use of regulatory management tools for EU-made laws: Finland

The government facilitates the engagement of domestic stakeholders in the European Commission's consultation process ▲		
Negotiation stage	Requirement for Member State to conduct stakeholder engagement	
	Use of European Commission's stakeholder engagement results ■	
	Requirement for Member State to conduct RIA	
	Use of European Commission's impact assessment ■	
	Use of European Commission's *ex post* evaluation results	
Transposition stage	Requirement for Member State to conduct stakeholder engagement	
	Use of European Commission's stakeholder engagement results ■	
	Requirement for Member State to conduct RIA	
	Use of European Commission's impact assessment ■	
	Specific assessment of provisions added at national level beyond those in EU directive is conducted ■	
	Use of European Commission's *ex post* evaluation results	
Results of domestic *ex post* evaluations of EU directives/regulations shared with the European Commission ▲		

■ For all EU directives/regulations/ ■ Always/ ▲ Yes
■ For major EU directives/regulations/ ■ Frequently
 For some EU directives/regulations/ ■ Sometimes
 Never/ ▲ No

Source: Indicators of Regulatory Policy and Governance (iREG) Survey 2021, http://oe.cd/ireg.

France

Overview and recent developments

Since 2018, France has taken some steps to improve its regulatory policy system. In June 2019, the Prime Minister of France issued an instruction introducing the requirement for each legislative proposal to be accompanied by five impact indicators that must be included in regulatory impact assessment (RIA). The objective is to enable decision makers to measure the expected impacts of the policy in order to promote *ex post* evaluation. A first assessment of the "one-in, two-out" offsetting approach introduced in 2017 to limit standards imposing new constraints that are not set by law was carried out by the Council of Ministers in July 2019. The government reported net savings from this initiative (EUR 20 million in 2020 and EUR 63 million in July 2021). Since 2020, a communication is usually made after each Council of Ministers to report progress on priority reforms and a barometer of policies results has been made publicly available.

RIAs are required for all primary laws and major subordinate regulations. All RIAs prepared for primary laws or subordinate regulations are available online on a centralised platform, easily accessible by the public. *Ex post* evaluation takes place on an ad hoc basis, mainly for primary regulations, and is fragmented across a range of institutions.

While France still does not require public and stakeholder engagement for the development of new regulations, except for environmental regulations, informal consultations and the consultation of selected groups are frequent. For example, France has led a wide public consultation in 2019-2020 to conceive the Climate and Resilience Bill for which a panel of French citizens was directly involved in the preparation of the law. Public consultations conducted over the internet is used for both early-stage and late-stage stakeholder engagement on non-environmental issues, but not on a systematic basis.

Under the authority of the Prime Minister, the *Secrétariat Général du Gouvernement* (SGG) ensures compliance with procedures (including for RIA and stakeholder engagement), inter-ministerial co-ordination, and liaison with the *Conseil d'État* and the Parliament. It guarantees the minimum quality of RIA, provides guidance, and ensures the appropriate publication of the legal text. The *Conseil d'État* also plays a critical role in regulatory policy, both upstream (through its consultative function for the government including its control of legal quality and stakeholder engagement) and downstream (as the administrative judge of last resort).

France could benefit from broadening its Better Regulation agenda to adapt and improve the quality of its regulatory system. France could for example open consultations more systematically to the general public to fully reap the benefits of stakeholder engagement. France could also improve its *ex post* review system by systemising the practice of evaluation.

Indicators of Regulatory Policy and Governance (iREG): France, 2021

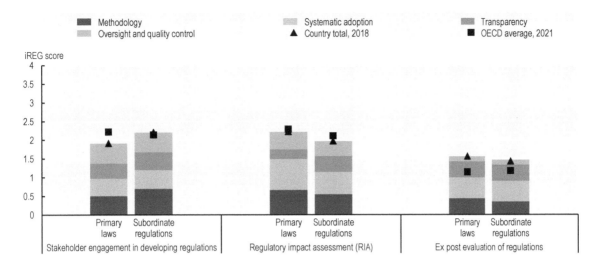

Notes: The more regulatory practices as advocated in the OECD Recommendation on Regulatory Policy and Governance a country has implemented, the higher its iREG score. The indicators on stakeholder engagement and RIA for primary laws only cover those initiated by the executive (72% of all primary laws in France).
Source: Indicators of Regulatory Policy and Governance Surveys 2017 and 2021, http://oe.cd/ireg.

Requirements and use of regulatory management tools for EU-made laws: France

The government facilitates the engagement of domestic stakeholders in the European Commission's consultation process ▲		
Negotiation stage	Requirement for Member State to conduct stakeholder engagement	
	Use of European Commission's stakeholder engagement results ■	
	Requirement for Member State to conduct RIA	
	Use of European Commission's impact assessment ■	
	Use of European Commission's ex post evaluation results	
Transposition stage	Requirement for Member State to conduct stakeholder engagement	
	Use of European Commission's stakeholder engagement results ■	
	Requirement for Member State to conduct RIA	
	Use of European Commission's impact assessment ■	
	Specific assessment of provisions added at national level beyond those in EU directive is conducted ■	
	Use of European Commission's ex post evaluation results	
Results of domestic ex post evaluations of EU directives/regulations shared with the European Commission ▲		

■ For all EU directives/regulations/ ■ Always/ ▲ Yes
■ For major EU directives/regulations/ ■ Frequently
　 For some EU directives/regulations/ ■ Sometimes
　 Never/ ▲ No
Source: Indicators of Regulatory Policy and Governance (iREG) Survey 2021, http://oe.cd/ireg.

Germany

Overview and recent developments

Germany has made some improvements to its regulatory policy system over the past years. Since 2018, Germany makes all ongoing public consultations accessible through one central government website building on the Federal Government's commitment to promote transparency in the legislative process. Regulatory impact assessments, which are mandatory for all laws and regulation, require since 2020 an assessment of the impacts on the equality of living conditions to promote citizen well-being in policy development. The system for assessing impacts of draft legislation *ex ante* is being complemented by recent efforts to improve the *ex post* evaluation of legislation. In 2018, the Bureaucracy Reduction and Better Regulation work programme introduced the requirement to publish all evaluations reports online. In November 2019, the Federal Statistical Office established an evaluation support unit for ministries by decision of the State Secretaries Committee on Bureaucracy Reduction.

The Better Regulation Unit (BRU) in the Federal Chancellery is the central co-ordinating and monitoring body for the implementation of the Federal Government's programme on better regulation and bureaucracy reduction. Its mandate has been broadened to include the evaluation and further strengthening of the *ex ante* procedure used by the Federal Government to assess, at an early stage, the compliance costs for Germany of planned EU legislation. The National Regulatory Control Council (NKR) operates at arm's length from government. It reviews the quality of all RIAs, provides advice during all stages of rulemaking, and has responsibilities in administrative simplification and burden reduction. In November 2019, the German government introduced additional requirements for independent quality control of *ex post* evaluations which the NKR is offering to perform. The Parliamentary Advisory Council on Sustainable Development, in turn, reviews the sustainability checks contained in all RIAs. It examines all legislative proposals and related assessments (for both primary laws and subordinate regulations) of the Federal Government.

Since 2017, all draft regulations are available on ministries' websites. In addition, all ongoing consultations are accessible through one central government website since 2018 due to the Federal Government's commitment to promote transparency in the legislative process. Germany also recently made use of green papers, inviting interested parties to submit comments on the government's draft strategy for moor protection. These initiatives could be a step towards establishing a more systematic approach to involving stakeholders earlier in the development of regulations. While the system to consult with social partners and experts is well established, Germany could open consultations more systematically to the public, release draft impact assessments for public consultation and systematically publish responses to consultation comments online.

Indicators of Regulatory Policy and Governance (iREG): Germany, 2021

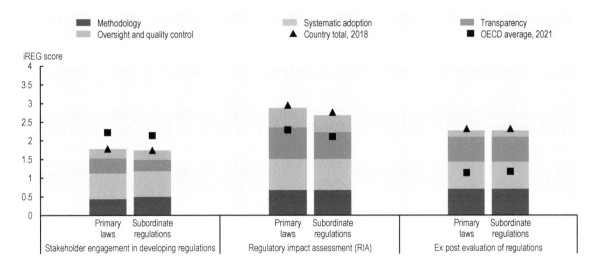

Notes: The more regulatory practices as advocated in the OECD Recommendation on Regulatory Policy and Governance a country has implemented, the higher its iREG score. The indicators on stakeholder engagement and RIA for primary laws only cover those initiated by the executive (87% of all primary laws in Germany).

Source: Indicators of Regulatory Policy and Governance Surveys 2017 and 2021, http://oe.cd/ireg.

Requirements and use of regulatory management tools for EU-made laws: Germany

The government facilitates the engagement of domestic stakeholders in the European Commission's consultation process ▲		
Negotiation stage	Requirement for Member State to conduct stakeholder engagement	
	Use of European Commission's stakeholder engagement results ■	
	Requirement for Member State to conduct RIA	
	Use of European Commission's impact assessment ■	
	Use of European Commission's *ex post* evaluation results	
Transposition stage	Requirement for Member State to conduct stakeholder engagement	
	Use of European Commission's stakeholder engagement results ■	
	Requirement for Member State to conduct RIA	
	Use of European Commission's impact assessment ■	
	Specific assessment of provisions added at national level beyond those in EU directive is conducted ■	
	Use of European Commission's *ex post* evaluation results	
Results of domestic *ex post* evaluations of EU directives/regulations shared with the European Commission ▲		

■ For all EU directives/regulations/ ■ Always/ ▲ Yes
■ For major EU directives/regulations/ ■ Frequently
   For some EU directives/regulations/ ■ Sometimes
   Never/ ▲ No

Source: Indicators of Regulatory Policy and Governance (iREG) Survey 2021, http://oe.cd/ireg.

Greece

Overview and recent developments

Greece has introduced Law 4622 in 2019, which further embeds regulatory management tools into the rule-making process for primary laws. A list of laws to be prepared or modified is now published in advance and the guidance on regulatory impact assessment (RIA) for primary laws has been updated and now includes guidelines on how to conduct stakeholder engagement. A range of mechanisms were introduced to assist officials in the development of *ex post* evaluations which is not yet done systematically in Greece. The relevant guidebook and template is currently being piloted and is planned to be published in 2021. *Ex post* evaluations are planned to be conducted by a new body established by Law 4622, the Special Secretariat for Monitoring and Evaluation of the Government Programme.

RIA is obligatory for all primary laws and for subordinate regulations of major economic or social importance. RIAs for primary laws must now be signed-off by the competent minister before being submitted to the Greek parliament. Based on Law 4622/2019, all analysis shall be proportionate to the significance or expected impacts of the regulation, additional categories of regulatory costs shall be quantified, and regulators shall assess the regulatory impacts on a larger range of factors, including gender equality and the UN's Sustainable Development Goals.

While public consultations are required for all primary laws, there is no requirement for subordinate regulation. In practice, draft primary laws are frequently posted on the consultation portal (www.opengov.gr) and only a few subordinate regulations are subject to public consultation. All consultation on primary laws should be accompanied by a RIA, although this is not always the case in practice.

In December 2020, a presidential decree amended the competences of the Better Regulation Office (BRO) of the Secretariat General of Legal and Parliamentary Affairs (Presidency of the Government). The BRO is no longer in charge of RIA scrutiny or the drafting of an annual report on better regulation but retains a range of responsibilities such as: promoting the "implementation of better regulation principles and tools in the exercise of governmental powers", including appropriate institutional co-operation; initiating and monitoring public consultation procedures in co-operation with the competent law-making committee and the ministry that has the legislative initiative; and preparing an annual report on Regulatory Production and Evaluation (in co-operation with the General Secretariat for Coordination). The presidential decree merged the two Directorates of Legislative Procedure under the Secretariat General of Legal and Parliamentary Affairs. According to the new legal requirements, the resulting directorate plays an important co-ordination role on regulatory policy and is responsible for ensuring the incorporation of any remarks made by the Committee on Evaluation of the Quality of Legislative Procedure, which is an advisory body responsible for scrutinising RIAs and associated draft bills and ensuring the legal quality of government regulations.

Better implementation of the requirements set by the law, especially in the area of impact assessment and stakeholder engagement, are advisable as well as further simplification of the regulatory framework. Applying the existing regulatory management tools to subordinate regulations would also enhance regulatory quality in Greece.

Indicators of Regulatory Policy and Governance (iREG): Greece, 2021

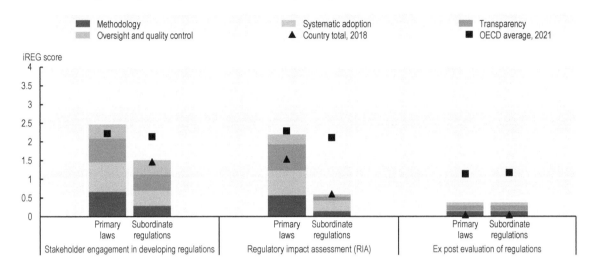

Notes: The more regulatory practices as advocated in the OECD Recommendation on Regulatory Policy and Governance a country has implemented, the higher its iREG score. The indicators on stakeholder engagement and RIA for primary laws only cover those initiated by the executive (100% of all primary laws in Greece).
Source: Indicators of Regulatory Policy and Governance Surveys 2017 and 2021, http://oe.cd/ireg.

Requirements and use of regulatory management tools for EU-made laws: Greece

The government facilitates the engagement of domestic stakeholders in the European Commission's consultation process ▲		
Negotiation stage	Requirement for Member State to conduct stakeholder engagement	
	Use of European Commission's stakeholder engagement results ■	
	Requirement for Member State to conduct RIA	
	Use of European Commission's impact assessment ■	
	Use of European Commission's ex post evaluation results	
Transposition stage	Requirement for Member State to conduct stakeholder engagement	
	Use of European Commission's stakeholder engagement results ■	
	Requirement for Member State to conduct RIA	
	Use of European Commission's impact assessment ■	
	Specific assessment of provisions added at national level beyond those in EU directive is conducted ■	
	Use of European Commission's ex post evaluation results	
Results of domestic ex post evaluations of EU directives/regulations shared with the European Commission ▲		

■ For all EU directives/regulations/ ■ Always/ ▲ Yes
■ For major EU directives/regulations/ ■ Frequently
For some EU directives/regulations/ ■ Sometimes
Never/ ▲ No
Source: Indicators of Regulatory Policy and Governance (iREG) Survey 2021, http://oe.cd/ireg.

Hungary

Overview and recent developments

All primary and subordinate legislations are required to undergo a RIA. However, RIAs are not consulted on nor made publically available. In March 2019, Hungary updated an act from 2010 on law-making to establish new obligations for law-makers. It requires law-makers to consider the results of impact assessments when developing new laws so that they only propose laws that are necessary for achieving regulatory objectives. In addition, it requires that where possible, legislations are drafted in a way that result in simpler, faster and less costly procedures, reduce the number of legal obligations and administrative burdens, and prevent over-regulation and regulatory overlap.

Draft legislation with its statement of purpose is required to be made accessible to the public with the possibility to provide comments by email. However, consultation is not required in the early phases of the design of legislation. The general public can express their recommendations to modify or provide feedback on existing regulations by sending an email to the corresponding ministry. While *ex post* evaluation is required, the OECD has received no evidence that this is done in practice.

The Government Office is responsible for co-ordinating the different phases of preparation of a regulatory proposal, from the consultation with other administrations once a ministry has prepared a regulatory proposal and RIA to the meeting of the State Secretaries to the final government meeting. The Government Office can also propose reforms or modifications related to the RIA and *ex post* evaluation framework. It prepares an annual report on RIA based on feedback from each ministry, which is not publicly available. Within the Prime Minister's Office, the State Secretary in charge of the territorial administration makes proposals for simplifying regulatory burdens on citizens and businesses. There is no oversight body in charge of quality improvements on RIAs or *ex post* reviews. Hungary would benefit from technical quality support for RIAs, *ex post* evaluations and consultations.

Overall Hungary would gain from improving transparency throughout the policy cycle. Stakeholders should be consulted at different stages of the policy cycle and relevant supporting legislative documents and impact assessments should be made available online to a wider public. Furthermore, the public should be informed in advance when consultations, RIA and *ex post* evaluations will take place. This would allow to further improve the efficiency and effectiveness of public policies and promote the accountability of the system.

Indicators of Regulatory Policy and Governance (iREG): Hungary, 2021

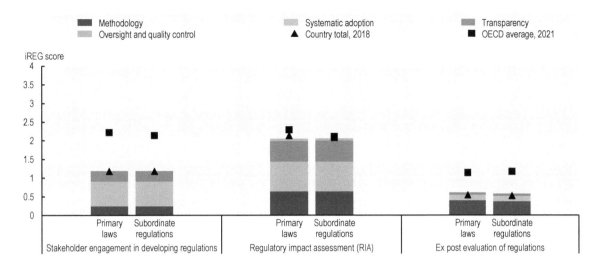

Notes: The more regulatory practices as advocated in the OECD Recommendation on Regulatory Policy and Governance a country has implemented, the higher its iREG score. The indicators on stakeholder engagement and RIA for primary laws only cover those initiated by the executive (74% of all primary laws in Hungary).
Source: Indicators of Regulatory Policy and Governance Surveys 2017 and 2021, http://oe.cd/ireg.

Requirements and use of regulatory management tools for EU-made laws: Hungary

The government facilitates the engagement of domestic stakeholders in the European Commission's consultation process ▲		
Negotiation stage	Requirement for Member State to conduct stakeholder engagement	
	Use of European Commission's stakeholder engagement results ■	
	Requirement for Member State to conduct RIA	▓
	Use of European Commission's impact assessment ■	
	Use of European Commission's *ex post* evaluation results	
Transposition stage	Requirement for Member State to conduct stakeholder engagement	▓
	Use of European Commission's stakeholder engagement results ■	
	Requirement for Member State to conduct RIA	▓
	Use of European Commission's impact assessment ■	
	Specific assessment of provisions added at national level beyond those in EU directive is conducted ■	
	Use of European Commission's *ex post* evaluation results	
Results of domestic *ex post* evaluations of EU directives/regulations shared with the European Commission ▲		

▓ For all EU directives/regulations/ ■ Always/ ▲ Yes
▓ For major EU directives/regulations/ ■ Frequently
  For some EU directives/regulations/ ■ Sometimes
  Never/ ▲ No
Source: Indicators of Regulatory Policy and Governance (iREG) Survey 2021, http://oe.cd/ireg.

Ireland

Overview and recent developments

Ireland is developing, and currently trialling as a prototype, a single central government website on which some of the ongoing consultations are published. Following the Open Government Partnership National Action Plan 2014-2016 and 2016-2018, Ireland had committed to improving consultation by public bodies with citizens, civil society and others. Despite this recent improvement, Ireland's consultation practices do not yet operate on a systematic basis across government departments. As Ireland develops the tools to conduct more transparent and open stakeholder engagement, public consultation could be applied more systematically to a broader range of draft regulations, particularly for subordinate regulations.

The Department of the Taoiseach is responsible for the effectiveness of regulators and, together with the Office of the Attorney General, for ensuring the transparency and quality of legislation. It is also responsible for setting the overall government multi-sectoral policy in Ireland. The Department of the Taoiseach aims to reduce regulatory burdens, promote regulatory quality, encourage a business-friendly regulatory environment, and ensure inter-departmental co-ordination in regulatory development. The Department of Public Expenditure and Reform is responsible for RIA guidance and the provision of training on RIA, *ex post* evaluation, and stakeholder engagement. The implementation of regulatory management tools and oversight of sectoral economic regulators remains the responsibility of the relevant department(s).

Standing orders from Parliament state that the minister responsible for implementing a law must provide an assessment of its functioning within a year. A number of sectoral departments have also started to carry out policy and mandate reviews, which are required at least every seven years according to the Policy Statement on Economic Regulation issued in 2013. Ireland has introduced sunsetting clauses in some of the subordinate regulations relating to the COVID-19 pandemic. Irish policy makers could however be more systematically required to conduct *ex post* evaluations of existing regulations, to assess whether they actually function in practice.

Ireland conducts mandatory RIA for major primary laws and subordinate regulations. In order to more effectively monitor and assess the quality of RIA implementation, Ireland should consider establishing a central oversight body to perform core oversight functions, such as reviewing the quality of RIA and of other regulatory management tools.

Indicators of Regulatory Policy and Governance (iREG): Ireland, 2021

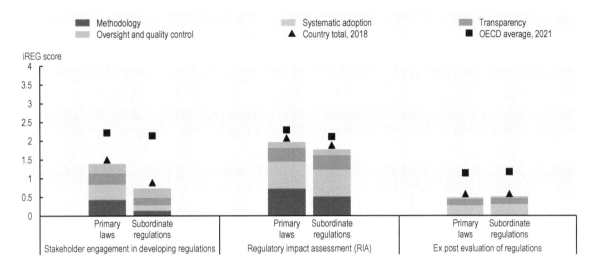

Notes: The more regulatory practices as advocated in the OECD Recommendation on Regulatory Policy and Governance a country has implemented, the higher its iREG score. The indicators on stakeholder engagement and RIA for primary laws only cover those initiated by the executive (93% of all primary laws in Ireland).
Source: Indicators of Regulatory Policy and Governance Surveys 2017 and 2021, http://oe.cd/ireg.

Requirements and use of regulatory management tools for EU-made laws: Ireland

The government facilitates the engagement of domestic stakeholders in the European Commission's consultation process ▲		
Negotiation stage	Requirement for Member State to conduct stakeholder engagement	
	Use of European Commission's stakeholder engagement results ■	
	Requirement for Member State to conduct RIA	
	Use of European Commission's impact assessment ■	
	Use of European Commission's ex post evaluation results	
Transposition stage	Requirement for Member State to conduct stakeholder engagement	
	Use of European Commission's stakeholder engagement results ■	
	Requirement for Member State to conduct RIA	
	Use of European Commission's impact assessment ■	
	Specific assessment of provisions added at national level beyond those in EU directive is conducted ■	
	Use of European Commission's ex post evaluation results	
Results of domestic ex post evaluations of EU directives/regulations shared with the European Commission ▲		

■ For all EU directives/regulations/ ■ Always/ ▲ Yes
■ For major EU directives/regulations/ ■ Frequently
   For some EU directives/regulations/ ■ Sometimes
   Never/ ▲ No
Source: Indicators of Regulatory Policy and Governance (iREG) Survey 2021, http://oe.cd/ireg.

Italy

Overview and recent developments

Ex post evaluations have become more commonplace across a wider range of policy areas, and the public is now informed in advance of e*x post* evaluations that will take place through two-year plans posted on the website of each ministry. Italy also introduced new non-binding guidance on *ex post* evaluation and RIA in 2018.

Ministries have to prepare a simplified RIA, providing a first assessment of expected impacts and a justification for not conducting a full RIA for low impact proposals, which is reviewed by the Department of Legal and Legislative Affairs (DAGL) within the Presidency of the Council of Ministers. Ministries are also required to publish twice a year a 6-month legislative programme, highlighting planned RIAs and consultations. The programmes are to be posted on the central government website and the website of individual ministries.

DAGL reviews the quality of RIAs and *ex post* evaluations. It can issue a negative opinion to the State Secretary to the Presidency if RIA quality is deemed inadequate and before the draft legislation is presented to the Council. The DAGL also validates planned RIAs and consultations included in the 6-month legislative programmes and *ex post* evaluation included in the two-year ministries plans, proposes changes to the regulatory policy framework, promotes training, provides technical guidance and reports annually to Parliament on regulatory quality tools. An Impact Assessment Independent Unit (*Nucleo AIR*) supports the DAGL in reviewing *ex ante* and *ex post* evaluations. This unit is composed of external experts serving a four-year term, selected through an open and competitive process. The Consultative Chamber on draft normative acts of the Council of State checks the quality of RIA and stakeholder engagement practices and evaluates regulatory policy.

In practice, however, several problems persist in implementation. Many RIAs lack sufficient quantification not only in terms of impacts, but also regarding the number of people affected. While RIAs are published, they are difficult to find by the general public. The challenge ahead is therefore to "connect the dots" to develop a culture of evidence-based user-centric policy making: Besides improving their quality, RIAs should be systematically made available when a regulation is proposed on a single webpage. The website could also link to the websites of independent regulators where their RIAs are posted. Most importantly, the planning and preparation of regulations needs to be genuinely informed by RIA, rather than it being an "add-on" for regulations that have fundamentally been already decided upon. While initial steps have been taken to plan *ex post* evaluations when preparing RIAs for major legislation, it is important to ensure that *ex post* evaluations are actually always taking place as planned in practice, and that results are effectively used for improving existing regulations. Consultation processes have been improved by the creation of a single online access point. They could become more systematic and consistent across different ministries and used to understand citizens' preferences, gather evidence on implementation options (early stage) and gaps (evaluation) – and feedback from consultations should be more systematically responded to, and taken into account.

Indicators of Regulatory Policy and Governance (iREG): Italy, 2021

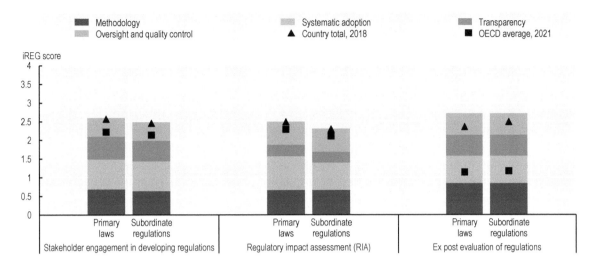

Legend:
- Methodology
- Oversight and quality control
- Systematic adoption
- ▲ Country total, 2018
- Transparency
- ■ OECD average, 2021

Notes: The more regulatory practices as advocated in the OECD Recommendation on Regulatory Policy and Governance a country has implemented, the higher its iREG score. The indicators on stakeholder engagement and RIA for primary laws only cover those initiated by the executive (54% of all primary laws in Italy).
Source: Indicators of Regulatory Policy and Governance Surveys 2017 and 2021, http://oe.cd/ireg.

Requirements and use of regulatory management tools for EU-made laws: Italy

The government facilitates the engagement of domestic stakeholders in the European Commission's consultation process ▲		
Negotiation stage	Requirement for Member State to conduct stakeholder engagement	
	Use of European Commission's stakeholder engagement results ■	
	Requirement for Member State to conduct RIA	
	Use of European Commission's impact assessment ■	
	Use of European Commission's *ex post* evaluation results	
Transposition stage	Requirement for Member State to conduct stakeholder engagement	
	Use of European Commission's stakeholder engagement results ■	
	Requirement for Member State to conduct RIA	
	Use of European Commission's impact assessment ■	
	Specific assessment of provisions added at national level beyond those in EU directive is conducted ■	
	Use of European Commission's *ex post* evaluation results	
Results of domestic *ex post* evaluations of EU directives/regulations shared with the European Commission ▲		

- For all EU directives/regulations/ ■ Always/ ▲ Yes
- For major EU directives/regulations/ ■ Frequently
- For some EU directives/regulations/ ■ Sometimes
- Never/ ▲ No

Source: Indicators of Regulatory Policy and Governance (iREG) Survey 2021, http://oe.cd/ireg.

Latvia

Overview and recent developments

Latvia has recently made several substantive reforms building on its existing regulatory policy framework. The obligation to conduct regulatory impact assessment (RIA) was introduced in 2009. RIA is required for all draft legal acts including subordinate regulations submitted to the Cabinet. RIA should be prepared early in the policy-making process and undergoes public consultation with the draft law. The impacts assessed cover mainly financial, budgetary, and administrative costs, and broader environmental and social costs. Policy makers now have the benefit of guidance material to assist in the preparation of RIAs including in the identification of the baseline, various options, and cost-benefit analysis. Consideration should now be given to improving the quantification of impacts of draft legislation and policy documents, as well as enhancing capacities to conduct cost-benefit analysis.

There is a structured and systematic process for consulting with social and civil partners. Public consultations are now systematically conducted at a late stage of policy development and stakeholders benefit from having a broader range of supporting material to help focus their input in policy proposals. While early stage consultation initiatives exist for planning documents, the next step will be to institutionalise this more broadly. Reviews of regulatory stock are mostly focussed on administrative burdens. While there is no explicit programme on *ex post* evaluations, they are now required for some subordinate regulations and an evaluation of all policy documents conforming to the SDGs was recently conducted.

The main responsibilities for co-ordinating regulatory policy and promoting regulatory quality are divided among the Ministry of Justice and the State Chancellery. The Ministry of Justice issues opinions regarding draft legal acts and draft development planning documents drawn up by other institutions and provides methodological assistance in the development of draft laws and regulations including regular training of state administration personnel at the State Administration School. The Chancellery, through its Legal Department, focuses on compliance of each regulatory draft with the rules for drafting legislation, including the obligation to conduct impact assessment or requirements for stakeholder engagement. The assessment of the Ministry of Justice and the State Chancellery is binding for other ministries, which may be requested to revise their proposals accordingly. The Chancellery also co-ordinates the development and application of uniform rules of regulatory drafting including the impact assessment guidelines. In 2018, its mandate was expanded to include, among other functions, quality control of *ex post* evaluations and systematic evaluation of regulatory policy.

Indicators of Regulatory Policy and Governance (iREG): Latvia, 2021

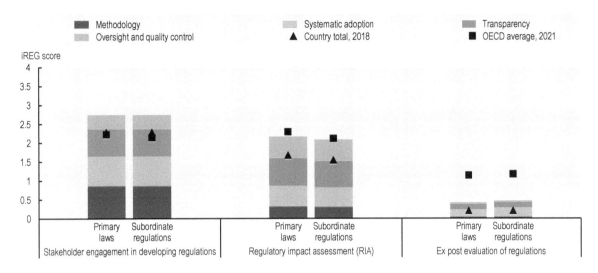

Notes: The more regulatory practices as advocated in the OECD Recommendation on Regulatory Policy and Governance a country has implemented, the higher its iREG score. The indicators on stakeholder engagement and RIA for primary laws only cover those initiated by the executive (69% of all primary laws in Latvia).
Source: Indicators of Regulatory Policy and Governance Survey 2017 and 2021, http://oe.cd/ireg.

Requirements and use of regulatory management tools for EU-made laws: Latvia

The government facilitates the engagement of domestic stakeholders in the European Commission's consultation process ▲		
Negotiation stage	Requirement for Member State to conduct stakeholder engagement	
	Use of European Commission's stakeholder engagement results ■	
	Requirement for Member State to conduct RIA	
	Use of European Commission's impact assessment ■	
	Use of European Commission's ex post evaluation results	
Transposition stage	Requirement for Member State to conduct stakeholder engagement	
	Use of European Commission's stakeholder engagement results ■	
	Requirement for Member State to conduct RIA	
	Use of European Commission's impact assessment ■	
	Specific assessment of provisions added at national level beyond those in EU directive is conducted ■	
	Use of European Commission's ex post evaluation results	
Results of domestic ex post evaluations of EU directives/regulations shared with the European Commission ▲		

For all EU directives/regulations/ ■ Always/ ▲ Yes
For major EU directives/regulations/ ■ Frequently
For some EU directives/regulations/ ■ Sometimes
Never/ ▲ No
Source: Indicators of Regulatory Policy and Governance (iREG) Survey 2021, http://oe.cd/ireg.

Lithuania

Overview and recent developments

There is no single formal government regulatory policy in Lithuania, though some elements are embedded in several strategic documents. A major part of the Lithuanian government's efforts still focuses on administrative burden reduction, mainly for businesses. There are some general requirements to conduct monitoring and *ex post* reviews of existing primary laws, and the government has strengthened the regulatory oversight function and transparency related to *ex post* evaluations in 2020, although efforts remain in order to improve the effectiveness of the *ex post* evaluation framework. For example the Office of Government could be mandated to co-ordinate regulatory evaluations across government, involving all relevant institutions, and allocating appropriate resources.

While impacts are required to be assessed for all primary laws, regulatory impact assessment (RIA) remains a largely formal exercise to justify choices already made, rarely based on data, and is more embedded into regulatory decision-making procedure for primary laws than for subordinate regulations. The RIA processes in Lithuania should be improved, with a special focus on starting early in the policy development in order to inform the choice of policy instruments and on better quantification of regulatory impacts. Lithuania could develop a clear data governance framework for evidence-informed policy making, as well as simplify access to administrative data for analytical purposes by public institutions.

Consultation is systematically required once a regulation is drafted, but it does not frequently take place before a decision to regulate is made. Lithuania has continued developing its stakeholder engagement and consultation methodology, particularly with the development of written guidance on how to conduct stakeholder engagement in 2019.

The institutional responsibility for co-ordinating regulatory policy and promoting regulatory quality lies primarily with the Government Office, which organises and supervises the law-making process when draft laws are initiated by the executive and which is in charge of preparing the annual legislative programme. The two main bodies with this location are the Strategic Competences Group, which is responsible for promoting better regulation, and the Government Strategic Analysis Centre – involved in RIA quality control, consultation and assistance to ministries in conducting RIA. The Better Regulation Policy Division of the Company Law and Business Environment Improvement Department, within the Ministry of Economy and Innovation, co-ordinates initiatives in the field of administrative simplification for business, including licencing and business inspection reforms and administrative burden reduction plans. The Ministry of Justice was mandated for the co-ordination of *ex post* evaluation but there remains scope for strengthening the oversight functions related to *ex post* evaluation.

Concerning regulatory enforcement and inspections reform, Lithuania is ahead of most of OECD countries. Lithuania could consider building on existing efforts for better co-ordination of regulatory policy by bringing the different elements of regulatory policy from a whole-of-government perspective in an integrated strategic plan that includes identified objectives and a clear communication strategy.

Indicators of Regulatory Policy and Governance (iREG): Lithuania, 2021

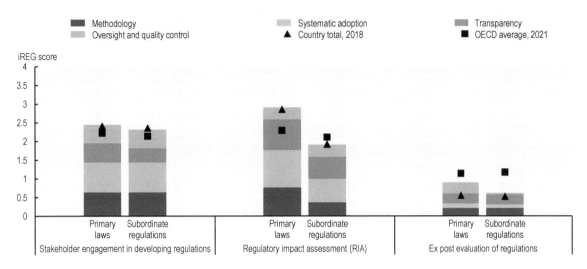

Notes: The more regulatory practices as advocated in the OECD Recommendation on Regulatory Policy and Governance a country has implemented, the higher its iREG score. The indicators on stakeholder engagement and RIA for primary laws only cover those initiated by the executive (70% of all primary laws in Lithuania).
Source: Indicators of Regulatory Policy and Governance Survey 2017 and 2021, http://oe.cd/ireg.

Requirements and use of regulatory management tools for EU-made laws: Lithuania

The government facilitates the engagement of domestic stakeholders in the European Commission's consultation process ▲		
Negotiation stage	Requirement for Member State to conduct stakeholder engagement	
	Use of European Commission's stakeholder engagement results ■	
	Requirement for Member State to conduct RIA	
	Use of European Commission's impact assessment ■	
	Use of European Commission's *ex post* evaluation results	
Transposition stage	Requirement for Member State to conduct stakeholder engagement	
	Use of European Commission's stakeholder engagement results ■	
	Requirement for Member State to conduct RIA	
	Use of European Commission's impact assessment ■	
	Specific assessment of provisions added at national level beyond those in EU directive is conducted ■	
	Use of European Commission's *ex post* evaluation results	
Results of domestic *ex post* evaluations of EU directives/regulations shared with the European Commission ▲		

■ For all EU directives/regulations/ ■ Always/ ▲ Yes
■ For major EU directives/regulations/ ■ Frequently
  For some EU directives/regulations/ ■ Sometimes
  Never/ ▲ No
Source: Indicators of Regulatory Policy and Governance (iREG) Survey 2021, http://oe.cd/ireg.

Luxembourg

Overview and recent developments

While there have been no major reforms since 2018 regarding regulatory management tools, Luxembourg recently made a website available where citizens and business can share their ideas on how to improve public service and how to simplify existing administrative processes (www.vosidees.lu). Luxembourg also recently developed a website where citizens can make public petitions for changes on existing regulations (www.petitiounen.lu). Once a petition reaches 4 500 signatures, there is a live broadcasted public debate with the parliament and the competent minister to which the petitioner is invited. However, stakeholder engagement for developing both primary laws and subordinate regulations is limited to formal consultation with professional groups such as the Chamber of Commerce and the Chamber of civil servants and public employees. An important step for improving Luxembourg's regulatory-making process would be to make stakeholder engagement open to the general public by facilitating avenues for the public to provide feedback on proposed regulatory drafts.

Even though *ex post* evaluations have been undertaken in Luxembourg, they remain an inconsistently applied regulatory management tool. Putting in place an evaluation framework, including a clear methodology, could help to ensure that regulations remain fit for purpose.

In Luxembourg, RIA is undertaken for all regulations in the form of a checklist mainly focussing on administrative burdens and enforcement. In order to enhance the usefulness of RIA, the analysis included in the impact assessments could be extended to other types of costs, impacts and benefits of regulations. While Luxembourg currently refers to the European Commission best practice instead of providing its own guidance material, the limited current focus of RIA in Luxembourg does not reflect EC standards. Luxembourg may consider creating bespoke guidance material to enhance domestic support for regulatory policy.

In 2018, the functions for regulatory oversight – particularly relating to assistance and quality control of stakeholder engagement, RIA, and *ex post* evaluations – were transferred from the Ministry of the Civil Service and Administrative Reform to the Ministry of Digitalisation. However, the Ministry only provides advice and guidance to other ministries and has no gatekeeper role. It is also responsible for a range of other oversight functions including the evaluation of regulatory policy, identifying areas where regulation can be made more effective, and co-ordination on regulatory policy.

Indicators of Regulatory Policy and Governance (iREG): Luxembourg, 2021

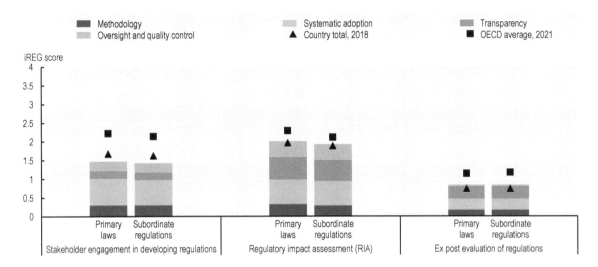

Notes: The more regulatory practices as advocated in the OECD Recommendation on Regulatory Policy and Governance a country has implemented, the higher its iREG score. The indicators on stakeholder engagement and RIA for primary laws only cover those initiated by the executive (99% of all primary laws in Luxembourg).
Source: Indicators of Regulatory Policy and Governance Surveys 2017 and 2021, http://oe.cd/ireg.

Requirements and use of regulatory management tools for EU-made laws: Luxembourg

The government facilitates the engagement of domestic stakeholders in the European Commission's consultation process ▲		
Negotiation stage	Requirement for Member State to conduct stakeholder engagement	
	Use of European Commission's stakeholder engagement results ■	
	Requirement for Member State to conduct RIA	
	Use of European Commission's impact assessment ■	
	Use of European Commission's *ex post* evaluation results	
Transposition stage	Requirement for Member State to conduct stakeholder engagement	█
	Use of European Commission's stakeholder engagement results ■	
	Requirement for Member State to conduct RIA	█
	Use of European Commission's impact assessment ■	
	Specific assessment of provisions added at national level beyond those in EU directive is conducted ■	
	Use of European Commission's *ex post* evaluation results	
Results of domestic *ex post* evaluations of EU directives/regulations shared with the European Commission ▲		

██ For all EU directives/regulations/ ■ Always/ ▲ Yes
▨ For major EU directives/regulations/ ■ Frequently
☐ For some EU directives/regulations/ ■ Sometimes
☐ Never/ ▲ No

Source: Indicators of Regulatory Policy and Governance (iREG) Survey 2021, http://oe.cd/ireg.

Malta

Overview and recent developments

Malta has not made any major changes to its regulatory framework over the last years with the exception of extending their RIA requirements recently to primary laws in May 2021. The "Small Business Act" (SBA), adopted in 2011 and revised in 2017 and 2021, introduced a framework for *ex ante* impact assessment to be applied by ministries when developing subordinate regulations, including an SME-Test, and more recently for developing primary laws. The Maltese government continues to put a strong emphasis on the reduction of regulatory burdens for business and citizens. Whilst *ex post* evaluation of existing regulation is not mandatory, the Maltese government has conducted several *ad hoc* reviews of existing laws and regulations in specific sectors, reflecting limited review resources. However, Malta currently lacks a systematic approach towards reviewing whether laws and regulations achieved the intended policy goals, including a requirement to periodically evaluate existing regulations and a standardised methodology for *ex post* evaluation.

Competences for regulatory policy and regulatory reform are dispersed among various government bodies. The mandate of the Office of the Principal Permanent Secretary and Cabinet Secretary – located within the Maltese Cabinet Office – notably includes oversight on the quality of RIAs, co-ordination on regulatory policy and guidance on regulatory management tools. It is also responsible for administrative simplification and publishes the yearly Simplification Measures Report. Additionally, the Ministry within the Office of the Prime Minister (MSD) was established in 2020 and is responsible for the quality control of stakeholder engagement, particularly online public consultation. Finally, the Policy Development and Programme Implementation Directorate within the Ministry for the Economy, Investment and Small Businesses is responsible for the implementation of the SBA and for improving the regulatory environment for SMEs. It performs a range of core regulatory functions – such as quality control of regulatory management tools, systematic improvement and advocacy, and guidance – insofar as these relate to the SBA and to the SME Test.

Stakeholder engagement and open public consultation are required for all primary laws and subordinate regulations. Online consultations are accompanied by a feedback report, summarizing the views of participants and providing general feedback on the comments received. The transparency of the Maltese regulatory framework could be further strengthened by making RIAs available for consultations with stakeholders. Additionally, Malta could more systematically engage with stakeholders during the early stages of the legislative development process, particularly for primary laws, before a preferred regulatory decision has been identified.

Indicators of Regulatory Policy and Governance (iREG): Malta, 2021

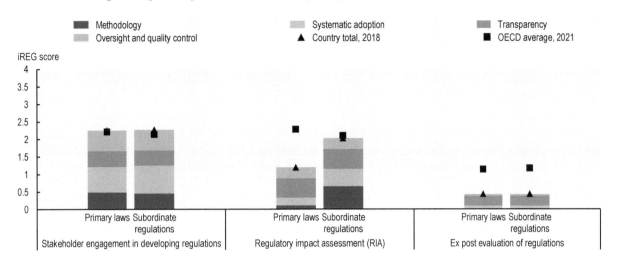

Note: The more regulatory practices as advocated in the OECD Recommendation on Regulatory Policy and Governance a country has implemented, the higher its iREG score. The indicators on stakeholder engagement and RIA for primary laws only cover those initiated by the executive (97% of all primary laws in Malta).
Source: Indicators of Regulatory Policy and Governance Survey 2017 and 2021, http://oe.cd/ireg.

Requirements and use of regulatory management tools for EU-made laws: Malta

The government facilitates the engagement of domestic stakeholders in the European Commission's consultation process ▲		
Negotiation stage	Requirement for Member State to conduct stakeholder engagement	
	Use of European Commission's stakeholder engagement results ■	
	Requirement for Member State to conduct RIA	
	Use of European Commission's impact assessment ■	
	Use of European Commission's *ex post* evaluation results	
Transposition stage	Requirement for Member State to conduct stakeholder engagement	
	Use of European Commission's stakeholder engagement results ■	
	Requirement for Member State to conduct RIA	
	Use of European Commission's impact assessment ■	
	Specific assessment of provisions added at national level beyond those in EU directive is conducted ■	
	Use of European Commission's *ex post* evaluation results	
Results of domestic *ex post* evaluations of EU directives/regulations shared with the European Commission ▲		

▰ For all EU directives/regulations/ ■ Always/ ▲ Yes
▨ For major EU directives/regulations/ ■ Frequently
▢ For some EU directives/regulations/ ■ Sometimes
▨ Never/ ▲ No
Source: Indicators of Regulatory Policy and Governance (iREG) Survey 2021, http://oe.cd/ireg.

Netherlands

Overview and recent developments

The Netherlands has made some progress in its regulatory practices over the past years. Most notably, it saw an improvement in oversight and quality control for periodic *ex post* evaluation of the effectiveness and efficiency of regulations. The country has been an early adopter of regulatory reform policies and exhibits a culture of open stakeholder engagement processes. Under successive governments, the Better Regulation agenda has been largely focused on burden reduction for business and citizens.

The Integraal Afwegingskader (IAK) combines existing requirements and instructions for *ex ante* regulatory impact assessment. Measuring the regulatory burden on companies and citizens is still a key element of the framework, aided by relatively strong regulatory oversight on this component. However, the IAK has seen gradual updates over time to incorporate other impacts e.g. since 2018, the IAK includes new guidelines on the impacts on borders regions, gender equality and developing countries and the Sustainable Development Goals. SMEs are now engaged in the early stages of the development of a regulation as part of an SME Test.

The IAK was updated in 2018 to strengthen requirements on ministries to monitor and evaluate regulations after implementation. This happened in response to Article 3.1 of the Compatibility Act 2016 that came into force in January 2018, which committed government to provide an explanation of the objectives, efficiency and effectiveness pursued when introducing new policy proposals. The Inspectorate of the State Budget within the Ministry of Finance now monitors procedural compliance of ministries with Article 3.1, co-ordinates the government-wide *ex post* evaluation framework, and has developed a toolbox with guidance for officials conducting policy evaluations. As part of its work, the inspectorate is also responsible for training and capacity-building.

The Unit for Judicial Affairs and Better Regulation Policy within the Ministry of Justice and Security is responsible for scrutinising the overall compliance with the RIA framework. The Better Regulation Unit within the Ministry of Economic Affairs and Climate Policy co-ordinates the program for regulatory burden reduction and provides oversight on the quality of assessments of regulatory burden. The main focus of the Unit has shifted from a quantitative reduction target on regulatory burdens for firms towards noticeable reductions in terms of problems, irritations and impediments brought forward by firms. The Dutch Advisory Board on Regulatory Burden (ATR) is an arm's-length body linked to the Ministry of Economic Affairs and Climate. Its core task is to advice on and scrutinise proposals for laws, decrees and regulations during the early stages of the legislative process or before or during the consultation phase.

The Netherlands should strengthen regulatory oversight and supervision capacities beyond the focus on regulatory burdens. It could also consider ways to reform the RIA process, to incentivise ministries to carry it out at an earlier point in the regulatory process and to consider and list alternative policy options. Finally, informing the public systematically in advance that a consultation is planned to take place could help to receive more input for regulations.

Indicators of Regulatory Policy and Governance (iREG): Netherlands, 2021

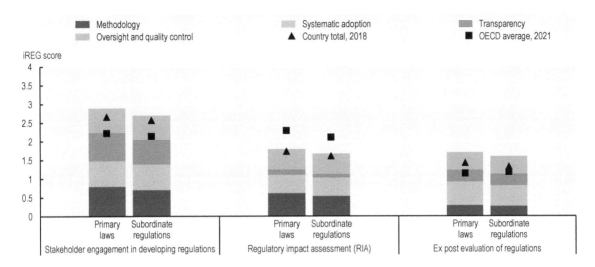

Notes: The more regulatory practices as advocated in the OECD Recommendation on Regulatory Policy and Governance a country has implemented, the higher its iREG score. The indicators on stakeholder engagement and RIA for primary laws only cover those initiated by the executive (97% of all primary laws in the Netherlands).
Source: Indicators of Regulatory Policy and Governance Surveys 2017 and 2021, http://oe.cd/ireg.

Requirements and use of regulatory management tools for EU-made laws: Netherlands

The government facilitates the engagement of domestic stakeholders in the European Commission's consultation process ▲		
Negotiation stage	Requirement for Member State to conduct stakeholder engagement	
	Use of European Commission's stakeholder engagement results ■	
	Requirement for Member State to conduct RIA	
	Use of European Commission's impact assessment ■	
	Use of European Commission's *ex post* evaluation results	
Transposition stage	Requirement for Member State to conduct stakeholder engagement	
	Use of European Commission's stakeholder engagement results ■	
	Requirement for Member State to conduct RIA	
	Use of European Commission's impact assessment ■	
	Specific assessment of provisions added at national level beyond those in EU directive is conducted ■	
	Use of European Commission's *ex post* evaluation results	
Results of domestic *ex post* evaluations of EU directives/regulations shared with the European Commission ▲		

■ For all EU directives/regulations/ ■ Always/ ▲ Yes
■ For major EU directives/regulations/ ■ Frequently
　For some EU directives/regulations/ ■ Sometimes
　Never/ ▲ No
Source: Indicators of Regulatory Policy and Governance (iREG) Survey 2021, http://oe.cd/ireg.

Poland

Overview and recent developments

Poland has made some recent adjustments to its legal framework for regulatory management. Following changes in the Rules of Works of the Council of Ministers in 2019, draft laws can now be returned to ministries if public consultation did not take place or if the consultation process did not comply with the rules, including if the consultation report is absent. In 2018, the requirement for assessing the impact of economic law on SMEs has been strengthened in the Law for Entrepreneurs Act, and the Centre for Strategic Analysis was established as the central government body responsible for assessing regulatory impact assessments (RIAs). RIAs continue to be required for all laws and regulations.

The Department for the Improvement of Business Regulation within the Ministry of Economic Development and Technology is responsible for the systematic improvement of regulation and the better regulation agenda in Poland. The Chancellery of the Prime Minister is responsible for the central oversight of regulatory management tools in Poland. It encompasses several regulatory oversight instances. The Government Programming Board is an auxiliary body to the Council of Ministers that receives administrative support from the Government Programming Department. The Board sets the government work programme, which includes legislation as well as strategic programmes and projects, and is responsible for the quality control of stakeholder engagement, RIA and *ex post* evaluations. The Centre for Strategic Analysis (CAS) was established in April 2018 to act as an advisory body to the Prime Minister. It participates in the legislative process directly as well as indirectly, through the deputy director of the RIA Department, who operates within the CAS and acts as a RIA co-ordinator upon designation by the Prime Minister. It issues opinions on the impact of proposals for the government work programme. Moreover, the CAS is responsible for reviewing all RIAs submitted by government ministries and offices for primary laws and subordinate regulations issued by the Council of Ministers and the Prime Minister, and it also examines RIAs for government acts and bills before their appraisal by the Council of Ministers' Standing Committee.

Ex post evaluations can be required at the request of the Council of Ministers or subsidiary bodies, and since recently at the request of the Chief of Centre for Strategic Analysis, the Ombudsman for SMEs, and the President of the Government Legislative Centre. However, very few evaluations have been conducted according to these recent procedures. Over time, *ex post* evaluations could be conducted more systematically and broadened beyond administrative burdens, focusing more on the total social, economic, and environmental impacts of regulation.

Regulatory policy requirements for the executive including public consultation do not apply to laws initiated by parliament, which constituted 21% of all laws passed on average between 2017 and 2020. The requirements introduced in the Law for Entrepreneurs Act also apply to non-governmental drafts in the field of economic law with the exception of laws initiated by civic initiatives.

Indicators of Regulatory Policy and Governance (iREG): Poland, 2021

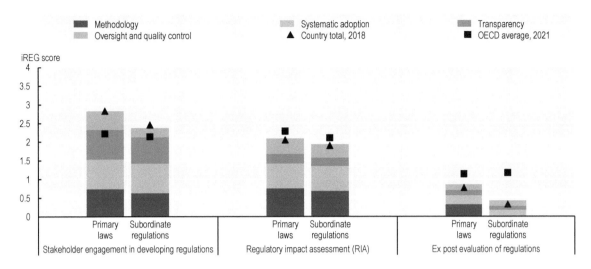

Notes: The more regulatory practices as advocated in the OECD Recommendation on Regulatory Policy and Governance a country has implemented, the higher its iREG score. The indicators on stakeholder engagement and RIA for primary laws only cover those initiated by the executive (75% of all primary laws in Poland).
Source: Indicators of Regulatory Policy and Governance Surveys 2017 and 2021, http://oe.cd/ireg.

Requirements and use of regulatory management tools for EU-made laws: Poland

The government facilitates the engagement of domestic stakeholders in the European Commission's consultation process ▲		
Negotiation stage	Requirement for Member State to conduct stakeholder engagement	
	Use of European Commission's stakeholder engagement results ■	
	Requirement for Member State to conduct RIA	
	Use of European Commission's impact assessment ■	
	Use of European Commission's ex post evaluation results	
Transposition stage	Requirement for Member State to conduct stakeholder engagement	
	Use of European Commission's stakeholder engagement results ■	
	Requirement for Member State to conduct RIA	
	Use of European Commission's impact assessment ■	
	Specific assessment of provisions added at national level beyond those in EU directive is conducted ■	
	Use of European Commission's ex post evaluation results	
Results of domestic ex post evaluations of EU directives/regulations shared with the European Commission ▲		

■ For all EU directives/regulations/ ■ Always/ ▲ Yes
■ For major EU directives/regulations/ ■ Frequently
■ For some EU directives/regulations/ ■ Sometimes
■ Never/ ▲ No
Source: Indicators of Regulatory Policy and Governance (iREG) Survey 2021, http://oe.cd/ireg.

Portugal

Overview and recent developments

The Government of Portugal has recently undertaken a range of key reforms to implement and strengthen regulatory impact assessments (RIA). Since the adoption of Resolution No. 44 to pilot a RIA framework for subordinate regulations in 2017, Portugal has adopted two additional reforms to formally establish the use of RIA and to expand it further in 2018 and 2019 respectively. Regulatory alternatives as well as an increasingly broad range of impacts are now required to be analysed. In addition, the scrutiny of quality of RIA for subordinate regulations has been reinforced.

Portugal's regulatory oversight body is the Technical Unit for Legislative Impact Assessment (UTAIL) within the Legal Centre of the Presidency of the Council of Ministers. It was created in 2017 as a supervising body in support of RIA implementation, with responsibility for the impact assessment framework and methodology. It provides technical support and training to the ministries and other public administrative bodies as well as the review of assessment reports. Upon completion of a pilot phase in 2018, its mandate was made permanent and expanded to encompass a range of additional functions and areas, some of which used to be carried out by the Agency for Administrative Modernisation. New attributions of UTAIL now include quality control of *ex post* evaluations, checking whether stakeholders have been engaged in RIA exercises, and evaluating regulatory policy overall.

Although the role of RIA has expanded, it is not yet used in consultations with stakeholders. A new central consultation platform has been introduced for subordinate regulations, which is only used for late-stage consultation when there is a draft regulation. Portugal could approach stakeholders earlier and before a preferred option is selected. A RIA could also be made available to stakeholders to support discussions.

Portugal has been very involved in administrative simplification programmes for several years and members of the public are still able to submit suggestions about administrative processes. *Ex post* evaluation of existing regulations is not mandatory. Following the COVID-19 pandemic, sunsetting clauses have been introduced for some regulations. UTAIL has taken additional functions regarding *ex post* evaluation, including the role of co-ordinating it across the public administration and assisting officials in conducting *ex post* evaluation. Portugal could consider introducing systematic requirements to undertake *ex post* evaluation as well as introducing "in-depth" reviews in particular sectors or policy areas to identify core reforms to Portugal's regulatory framework.

Indicators presented on RIA and stakeholder engagement for primary laws only cover processes carried out by the executive, which initiates approximately 38% of primary laws in Portugal. There is no mandatory requirement for consultation with the general public or for conducting RIAs for primary laws initiated by the parliament.

Indicators of Regulatory Policy and Governance (iREG): Portugal, 2021

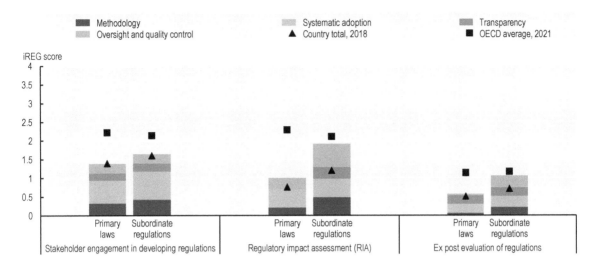

Notes: The more regulatory practices as advocated in the OECD Recommendation on Regulatory Policy and Governance a country has implemented, the higher its iREG score. The indicators on stakeholder engagement and RIA for primary laws only cover those initiated by the executive (38% of all primary laws in Portugal).
Source: Indicators of Regulatory Policy and Governance Surveys 2017 and 2021, http://oe.cd/ireg.

Requirements and use of regulatory management tools for EU-made laws: Portugal

The government facilitates the engagement of domestic stakeholders in the European Commission's consultation process ▲		
Negotiation stage	Requirement for Member State to conduct stakeholder engagement	
	Use of European Commission's stakeholder engagement results ■	
	Requirement for Member State to conduct RIA	
	Use of European Commission's impact assessment ■	
	Use of European Commission's ex post evaluation results	
Transposition stage	Requirement for Member State to conduct stakeholder engagement	
	Use of European Commission's stakeholder engagement results ■	
	Requirement for Member State to conduct RIA	
	Use of European Commission's impact assessment ■	
	Specific assessment of provisions added at national level beyond those in EU directive is conducted ■	
	Use of European Commission's ex post evaluation results	
Results of domestic ex post evaluations of EU directives/regulations shared with the European Commission ▲		

■ For all EU directives/regulations/ ■ Always/ ▲ Yes
■ For major EU directives/regulations/ ■ Frequently
  For some EU directives/regulations/ ■ Sometimes
  Never/ ▲ No
Source: Indicators of Regulatory Policy and Governance (iREG) Survey 2021, http://oe.cd/ireg.

Romania

Overview and recent developments

Romania has gradually developed its regulatory policy since the early 2000s. While Law 24/2000 on drafting legal acts set out an initial obligation to identify the impacts of draft regulations, the requirements for RIA have been further refined in Government Decision no. 1361 issued in 2006. According to these provisions, all regulations are required to be accompanied by an explanatory note, describing the rationale and assessing the impacts of the draft proposal. Additionally, Romania introduced in 2006 a template for assessing the impacts during the development of public policy initiatives, including regulatory initiatives and published guidance on RIA in 2016. Since 2020, Romania has began publishing yearly reports on the performance of the RIA system, which includes data on the percentage of RIAs that comply with formal requirements and guidelines.

Nevertheless, challenges in the implementation of RIA remain. In practice, the quality of explanatory notes varies and the actual assessment of impacts is not always conducted. Romania should strengthen its oversight of RIA to ensure that RIA can effectively inform policy makers on the costs and benefits of different policy options.

Romania does not have central oversight of the quality of RIA in place, but some ministries, such as the Ministry of Finance or the Ministry of Justice, review specific sections of explanatory notes as part the endorsement procedure of regulations. In addition, the Group for Assessing the Economic Impact of Normative Acts on SMEs (GEIEAN) – located within the Ministry of Economy, Energy, and Business Environment – is in charge of ensuring the quality and coherence of regulation affecting SMEs. GEIEAN reviews the application of the SME test in rulemaking as well as the quality of RIA and of stakeholder engagement pertaining to regulatory impacts on SMEs and can issue endorsements as well as recommendations. The Department for Coordinating Policies and Priorities (DCPP) has not performed core oversight functions for the past four years. It has however co-ordinated the review of the RIA performance system as well as the publication of the yearly report and it continues to lead the development of the Romanian RIA system.

Regarding stakeholder engagement, Law no. 52/2003 requires ministries to publish all regulations for comments on their websites. Romania updated its central consultation portal in 2019 which is now more frequently used. However, the minimum period for submitting comments is only ten days. The consultation portal also redirects members of the public to public consultations held by the European Commission. Romania recently began publishing yearly reports on the performance of consultation practices on draft laws and regulations.

Romania lacks a systematic approach for reviewing existing regulations. *Ex post* evaluation is conducted on an *ad hoc* basis by ministries and there is neither methodological guidance nor a requirement for the periodical review of existing regulations. Romania would benefit from systemising *ex post* evaluation to inform the development of new policies and to assess whether existing laws and regulations are meeting their objectives.

Indicators of Regulatory Policy and Governance (iREG): Romania 2021

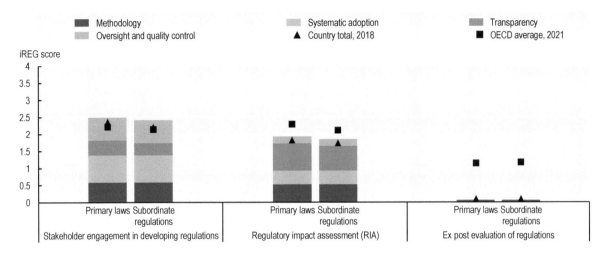

Note: The more regulatory practices as advocated in the OECD Recommendation on Regulatory Policy and Governance a country has implemented, the higher its iREG score. The indicators on stakeholder engagement and RIA for primary laws only cover those initiated by the executive (63% of all primary laws in Romania).
Source: Indicators of Regulatory Policy and Governance Survey 2017 and 2021, http://oe.cd/ireg.

Requirements and use of regulatory management tools for EU-made laws: Romania

The government facilitates the engagement of domestic stakeholders in the European Commission's consultation process ▲		
Negotiation stage	Requirement for Member State to conduct stakeholder engagement	
	Use of European Commission's stakeholder engagement results ■	
	Requirement for Member State to conduct RIA	
	Use of European Commission's impact assessment ■	
	Use of European Commission's *ex post* evaluation results	
Transposition stage	Requirement for Member State to conduct stakeholder engagement	
	Use of European Commission's stakeholder engagement results ■	
	Requirement for Member State to conduct RIA	
	Use of European Commission's impact assessment ■	
	Specific assessment of provisions added at national level beyond those in EU directive is conducted ■	
	Use of European Commission's *ex post* evaluation results	
Results of domestic *ex post* evaluations of EU directives/regulations shared with the European Commission ▲		

▮ For all EU directives/regulations/ ■ Always/ ▲ Yes
▮ For major EU directives/regulations/ ■ Frequently
▮ For some EU directives/regulations/ ■ Sometimes
▮ Never/ ▲ No
Source: Indicators of Regulatory Policy and Governance (iREG) Survey 2021, http://oe.cd/ireg.

Slovak Republic

Overview and recent developments

The Slovak Republic currently works on implementing the RIA 2020 – Better Regulation Strategy adopted in 2018 that represents a comprehensive approach towards a whole-of-government regulatory policy focusing, among other issues, on improving both *ex ante* and *ex post* evaluation of regulations. So far, a draft methodology for *ex post* evaluation was approved in 2019 and underwent pilot testing, whilst a methodology for stakeholder engagement is currently being developed. In 2021, the government introduced a one-in, two-out approach for regulatory offsetting.

The obligation to conduct regulatory impact assessments has been in place since 2008 with reforms introducing a solid methodology for assessing economic, social and environmental impacts, including an SME Test and impacts on innovation in 2015. Despite these improvements and the analytical resources available to decision makers, in many cases Slovak ministries still struggle with the quantification of wider impacts, focusing mainly on budgetary impacts and impacts on businesses.

Procedures for public consultations in the later stage of the regulatory process are well developed, with automatic publication of all legislative documents on the government portal. The 2015 reforms made early-stage consultations more prominent, especially those with business associations. *Ex post* reviews of existing regulations have so far focused mostly on administrative burdens, with three "anti-bureaucratic packages" aimed at reducing administrative burdens for businesses in 2017, 2018 and 2019. In 2020, 115 measures were introduced to reduce administrative burdens, for businesses during the COVID-19 pandemic. The publication of the final methodology for *ex post* evaluation planned for later this year will introduce the requirement for more comprehensive reviews of existing legislation.

The Permanent Working Committee of the Legislative Council of the Slovak Republic at the Ministry of Economy (RIA Committee), established in 2015, is responsible for overseeing the quality of RIAs. Part of its mandate is quality control of stakeholder engagement. Several ministries, including the Ministry of Economy as a co-ordinator, the Ministry of Finance, the Ministry of Labour and Social Affairs, the Ministry of Environment, the Ministry of the Interior and the Deputy Prime Minister's Office for Investments and Informatisation, are represented in the Committee, as are the Government Office and the Slovak Business Agency. They share competencies for checking the quality of RIAs focusing on their respective area of competences.

Slovakia would benefit from further strengthening regulatory oversight by appointing one body close to the centre of government responsible for evaluating integrated impacts, rather than spreading the responsibility across several ministries, as is currently the case with the RIA Committee. This body could also take on the responsibility of evaluating the quality of *ex post* evaluations, once more comprehensive reviews will be mandatory with the introduction of the new methodology for *ex post* evaluation. Finally, the new *ex post* evaluation methodology could serve as a gateway to introducing targeted, in-depth reviews of existing regulations.

Indicators of Regulatory Policy and Governance (iREG): Slovak Republic, 2021

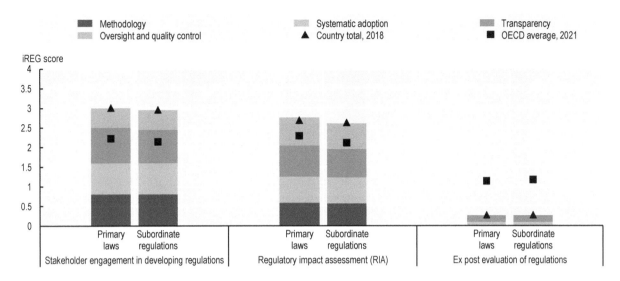

Notes: The more regulatory practices as advocated in the OECD Recommendation on Regulatory Policy and Governance a country has implemented, the higher its iREG score. The indicators on stakeholder engagement and RIA for primary laws only cover those initiated by the executive (68% of all primary laws in the Slovak Republic).
Source: Indicators of Regulatory Policy and Governance Surveys 2017 and 2021, http://oe.cd/ireg.

Requirements and use of regulatory management tools for EU-made laws: Slovak Republic

The government facilitates the engagement of domestic stakeholders in the European Commission's consultation process ▲		
Negotiation stage	Requirement for Member State to conduct stakeholder engagement	
	Use of European Commission's stakeholder engagement results ■	
	Requirement for Member State to conduct RIA	
	Use of European Commission's impact assessment ■	
	Use of European Commission's *ex post* evaluation results	
Transposition stage	Requirement for Member State to conduct stakeholder engagement	
	Use of European Commission's stakeholder engagement results ■	
	Requirement for Member State to conduct RIA	
	Use of European Commission's impact assessment ■	
	Specific assessment of provisions added at national level beyond those in EU directive is conducted ■	
	Use of European Commission's *ex post* evaluation results	
Results of domestic *ex post* evaluations of EU directives/regulations shared with the European Commission ▲		

■ For all EU directives/regulations/ ■ Always/ ▲ Yes
■ For major EU directives/regulations/ ■ Frequently
  For some EU directives/regulations/ ■ Sometimes
  Never/ ▲ No
Source: Indicators of Regulatory Policy and Governance (iREG) Survey 2021, http://oe.cd/ireg.

Slovenia

Overview and recent developments

Slovenia is currently undertaking efforts to strengthen regulatory policy with the Action Plan 2019-2022. The action plan foresees the extension of the RIA guidance document to cover the assessment of non-financial impacts and recommends the introduction of preliminary impact assessments. Currently, regulatory impact assessment (RIA) is carried out for all primary laws and for some subordinate regulations. In 2019, for 96% of the draft primary laws a RIA was conducted during or after the drafting of the legislative text. Impact assessment requirements for subordinate regulations are less stringent than those for primary laws. The development of secondary regulations does not require a quantification of the costs and benefits and assessments of the impacts are done only for some secondary regulations. The RIA process, particularly for subordinate regulations, could be strengthened by introducing a threshold test or proportionality criteria that would help determine which regulations require an in-depth assessment. The Action Plan represents a positive step in this regard as it foresees a deeper analysis of potential social and environmental impacts, among others.

Although the Action Plan introduces changes in the mandate of the General Secretariat of the Government, oversight functions remain spread across different institutions. The General Secretariat of the Government is now responsible for monitoring the implementation of stakeholder consultation. Oversight of RIA is the responsibility of the Ministry of Public Administration (MPA) as well as of the Ministry of Economic Development and Technology. The Government Office of Legislation (GoL) examines legislative proposals from government and those acts for which the National Assembly seeks the opinion of the government and is also involved in the provision of guidance relating to regulatory management tools as well as in the co-ordination on regulatory policy.

Slovenia was an early adopter of the Standard Cost Model (SCM), supported by the application of the SME test, which contributes to the assessments of economic impacts. Slovenia continues to focus the majority of its *ex post* evaluation efforts on reducing administrative burdens. Its webportal Stop Bureaucracy (https://www.stopbirokraciji.gov.si) allows citizens and business representatives to provide suggestions to cut red tape and monitor their implementation through the single document website (www.enotnazbirkaukrepov.gov.si). While *ex post* evaluation is mandatory for primary laws adopted through emergency procedures, Slovenia could expand the use of this tool to other regulations and assess whether the objectives of existing regulations are being met. Stakeholder engagement is mandatory for all primary laws and subordinate regulations. The country could increase further engagement with stakeholders by systematically informing the public in advance of planned consultations, RIAs and *ex post* evaluations.

Indicators of Regulatory Policy and Governance (iREG): Slovenia, 2021

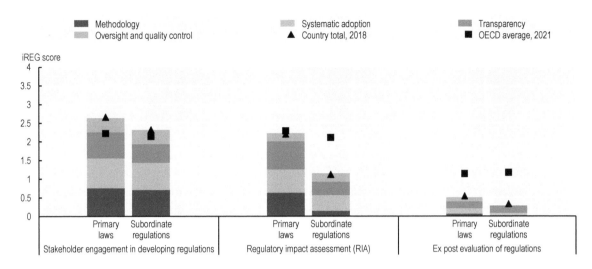

Notes: The more regulatory practices as advocated in the OECD Recommendation on Regulatory Policy and Governance a country has implemented, the higher its iREG score. The indicators on stakeholder engagement and RIA for primary laws only cover those initiated by the executive (90% of all primary laws in Slovenia).

Source: Indicators of Regulatory Policy and Governance Surveys 2017 and 2021, http://oe.cd/ireg.

Requirements and use of regulatory management tools for EU-made laws: Slovenia

The government facilitates the engagement of domestic stakeholders in the European Commission's consultation process ▲		
Negotiation stage	Requirement for Member State to conduct stakeholder engagement	
	Use of European Commission's stakeholder engagement results ■	
	Requirement for Member State to conduct RIA	
	Use of European Commission's impact assessment ■	
	Use of European Commission's *ex post* evaluation results	
Transposition stage	Requirement for Member State to conduct stakeholder engagement	
	Use of European Commission's stakeholder engagement results ■	
	Requirement for Member State to conduct RIA	
	Use of European Commission's impact assessment ■	
	Specific assessment of provisions added at national level beyond those in EU directive is conducted ■	
	Use of European Commission's *ex post* evaluation results	
Results of domestic *ex post* evaluations of EU directives/regulations shared with the European Commission ▲		

▓ For all EU directives/regulations/ ■ Always/ ▲ Yes
▓ For major EU directives/regulations/ ■ Frequently
░ For some EU directives/regulations/ ■ Sometimes
░ Never/ ▲ No

Source: Indicators of Regulatory Policy and Governance (iREG) Survey 2021, http://oe.cd/ireg.

Spain

Overview and recent developments

Spain is gradually stepping up its Better Regulation efforts by expanding its initial focus on administrative simplification through the development of stakeholder engagement and *ex post* evaluation. Moreover, regulatory impact assessment (RIA) has been strengthened through the creation of a dedicated body.

Since 2018, the Regulatory Coordination and Quality Office, within the Ministry of the Presidency, Relations with the Parliament and Democratic Memory is the country's permanent body in charge of promoting the quality, co-ordination and coherence of rulemaking activity undertaken by the executive. To that end, the applicable legal framework foresees the development of an information system enabling direct and secure communication with ministerial departments. The Office oversees the implementation of Better Regulation requirements, chiefly RIA. It also supervises the initial definition of the objectives and methodology for the *ex post* evaluation of regulations covered by RIAs, but does not scrutinise *ex post* evaluations themselves. The Ministry of Territorial Policy and Public Function checks the quality of various RIA components and is responsible for promoting and monitoring administrative burden reduction and public consultation and participation. The Council of State, in turn, assesses the legality of regulations and their development, and watches over the public administration's correct functioning and legal quality of regulations initiated by the executive. It issues statements in response to consultations from ministries, autonomous community presidents and certain state entities.

While stakeholder engagement is not undertaken on a fully systematic basis yet, the country has improved the transparency of its system. The new centralised online platform (http://transparencia.gob.es) lists all ongoing consultations and allows citizens to engage in normative activity at two important points in the policy cycle: before regulatory development starts and at the draft regulation stage. The platform also provides access to the annual regulatory planning agenda for primary laws and subordinate regulations. Moreover, statistics on citizens' use of the platform, which also hosts content related to the broader topic of transparency and good governance in the public administration, are published yearly.

RIA is required for all regulations. Since October 2017, impacts of regulatory proposals on competition and SMEs must be systematically considered, and updated thresholds apply for the conduct of *ex post* evaluations. The legal basis for RIA was updated in October 2017 by means of a Royal Decree aimed at adapting to changes in administrative law and aligning RIA requirements with best practices promoted by the OECD and the EU. Update of the 2009 RIA guidelines is still pending despite the need for clear guidance on data collection methods and assessment methodologies in this area. In the same vein, since *ex post* evaluation of regulations is not systematic, developing targeted guidance and standard evaluation techniques would contribute to a more widespread and consistent evaluation of how regulations actually work in practice.

Indicators of Regulatory Policy and Governance (iREG): Spain, 2021

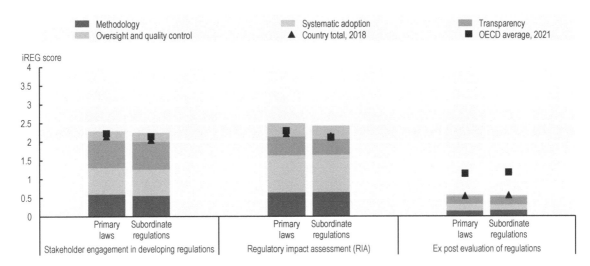

Notes: The more regulatory practices as advocated in the OECD Recommendation on Regulatory Policy and Governance a country has implemented, the higher its iREG score. The indicators on stakeholder engagement and RIA for primary laws only cover those initiated by the executive (90% of all primary laws in Spain).
Source: Indicators of Regulatory Policy and Governance Surveys 2017 and 2021, http://oe.cd/ireg.

Requirements and use of regulatory management tools for EU-made laws: Spain

The government facilitates the engagement of domestic stakeholders in the European Commission's consultation process ▲		
Negotiation stage	Requirement for Member State to conduct stakeholder engagement	
	Use of European Commission's stakeholder engagement results ■	
	Requirement for Member State to conduct RIA	
	Use of European Commission's impact assessment ■	
	Use of European Commission's ex post evaluation results	
Transposition stage	Requirement for Member State to conduct stakeholder engagement	
	Use of European Commission's stakeholder engagement results ■	
	Requirement for Member State to conduct RIA	
	Use of European Commission's impact assessment ■	
	Specific assessment of provisions added at national level beyond those in EU directive is conducted ■	
	Use of European Commission's ex post evaluation results	
Results of domestic ex post evaluations of EU directives/regulations shared with the European Commission ▲		

■ For all EU directives/regulations/ ■ Always/▲ Yes
For major EU directives/regulations/ ■ Frequently
For some EU directives/regulations/ ■ Sometimes
Never/▲ No
Source: Indicators of Regulatory Policy and Governance (iREG) Survey 2021, http://oe.cd/ireg.

Sweden

Overview and recent developments

Stakeholder engagement continues to be engrained into the law-making process in Sweden. Sweden now makes more systematic use of their central government portal where consultations and their relevant documentation are posted to receive feedback from authorities, organisations, municipalities, relevant stakeholders and the general public. Stakeholders can provide their feedback by email to the corresponding policy maker, which are then made publicly available on the same website. Sweden could benefit from moving towards a more interactive consultation website, where the public at large can publicly provide their feedback and react to the suggestions of other stakeholders.

When a committee of inquiry is appointed to investigate a policy issue, it normally includes a mix of policy makers, experts, and politicians, enabling consultation early in the process. The committee analyses and evaluates the proposal. The final report is sent to relevant stakeholders for consideration, before the joint draft procedure continues within the government offices.

Simplification remains a cornerstone of Sweden's regulatory policy. In 2020, the Committee for Technological Innovation and Ethics (Komet) created a forum to receive feedback from citizens and businesses on regulatory barriers for technological development. This was followed by feasibility studies on 11 of the received proposals regarding health, science and transport. In September 2021, the Government published new goals for simplifying policy and the regulatory environment for businesses.

Ex ante evaluation is required for all primary laws and subordinate regulations by the 2007 Ordinance on Impact Analysis of Regulation. In 2018, the guidelines for conducting impact assessment were updated to provide more detailed guidance on assessing economic, social and environmental impacts, as well as on how consultations with relevant actors can be conducted. *Ex post* evaluation is normally conducted *ad hoc* by a ministry, government agency, or by a committee of inquiry, as there is no requirement to carry out *ex post* evaluations systematically. Individuals or interest groups can also make suggestions to conduct *ex post* evaluations by sending proposals directly to the responsible ministry or government agency. Sweden could consider expanding *ex post* evaluation through carrying out comprehensive in-depth reviews in particular sectors or policy areas.

The Swedish Better Regulation Council is a is a decision-making body responsible for reviewing the quality of impact assessments to legislative proposals with effects on businesses. Its secretariat is located within the Swedish Agency for Economic and Regional Growth. The Agency, in turn, is responsible for methodological development, guidance and training in regulatory management tools. It also develops and proposes simplification measures, participates in international activities aimed at simplifying regulation for businesses, and promotes awareness among other government agencies of how businesses are affected by the enforcement of regulations.

Indicators of Regulatory Policy and Governance (iREG): Sweden, 2021

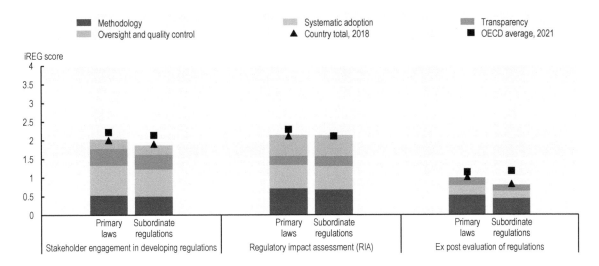

Notes: The more regulatory practices as advocated in the OECD Recommendation on Regulatory Policy and Governance a country has implemented, the higher its iREG score.
Source: Indicators of Regulatory Policy and Governance Surveys 2017 and 2021, http://oe.cd/ireg.

Requirements and use of regulatory management tools for EU-made laws: Sweden

The government facilitates the engagement of domestic stakeholders in the European Commission's consultation process ▲		
Negotiation stage	Requirement for Member State to conduct stakeholder engagement	
	Use of European Commission's stakeholder engagement results ■	
	Requirement for Member State to conduct RIA	
	Use of European Commission's impact assessment ■	
	Use of European Commission's ex post evaluation results	
Transposition stage	Requirement for Member State to conduct stakeholder engagement	
	Use of European Commission's stakeholder engagement results ■	
	Requirement for Member State to conduct RIA	
	Use of European Commission's impact assessment ■	
	Specific assessment of provisions added at national level beyond those in EU directive is conducted ■	
	Use of European Commission's ex post evaluation results	
Results of domestic ex post evaluations of EU directives/regulations shared with the European Commission ▲		

■ For all EU directives/regulations/ ■ Always/ ▲ Yes
For major EU directives/regulations/ ■ Frequently
For some EU directives/regulations/ ■ Sometimes
Never/ ▲ No
Source: Indicators of Regulatory Policy and Governance (iREG) Survey 2021, http://oe.cd/ireg.

Lightning Source UK Ltd.
Milton Keynes UK
UKHW050606150722
405894UK00001B/10